A Textbook of Data Structures and Algorithms 2

One of the greatest lessons I have learnt in my life is
to pay as much attention to the means of work as to its end...
I have been always learning great lessons from that one principle,
and it appears to me that all the secret of success is there;
to pay as much attention to the means as to the end....
Let us perfect the means; the end will take care of itself.

– Swami Vivekananda
(Lecture Delivered at Los Angeles, California, January 4, 1900)

A Textbook of Data Structures and Algorithms 2

Mastering Nonlinear Data Structures

G A Vijayalakshmi Pai

WILEY

First published 2022 in Great Britain and the United States by ISTE Ltd and John Wiley & Sons, Inc.

Previous edition published in 2008 as "Data Structures and Algorithms: Concepts, Techniques and Applications" by McGraw Hill Education (India) Pvt Ltd. © McGraw Hill Education (India) Pvt Ltd. 2008

ISTE Ltd
27-37 St George's Road
London SW19 4EU
UK

www.iste.co.uk

John Wiley & Sons, Inc.
111 River Street
Hoboken, NJ 07030
USA

www.wiley.com

Any opinions, findings, and conclusions or recommendations expressed in this material are those of the author(s), contributor(s) or editor(s) and do not necessarily reflect the views of ISTE Group.

Library of Congress Control Number: 2022947241

British Library Cataloguing-in-Publication Data
A CIP record for this book is available from the British Library
ISBN 978-1-78630-891-7

Contents

Preface

Efficient problem solving using computers, irrespective of the discipline or application, calls for the design of efficient algorithms. The inclusion of appropriate data structures is of critical importance to the design of efficient algorithms. In other words, *good algorithm design must go hand in hand with appropriate data structures for an efficient program design to solve a problem.*

Data structures and algorithms is a fundamental course in computer science, which most undergraduate and graduate programs in computer science and other allied disciplines in science and engineering offer during the early stages of the respective programs, either as a core or as an elective course. The course enables students to have a much-needed foundation for efficient programming, leading to better problem solving in their respective disciplines.

Most of the well-known text books/monographs on this subject have discussed the concepts in relation to a programming language – beginning with Pascal and spanning a spectrum of them such as C, C++, C#, Java, Python and so on, essentially calling for ample knowledge of the language, before one proceeds to try and understand the data structure. There does remain a justification in this. The implementation of data structures in the specific programming language need to be demonstrated or the algorithms pertaining to the data structures concerned need a convenient medium of presentation and when this is the case, why not a programming language?

Again, while some authors have insisted on using their books for an advanced level course, there are some who insist on a working knowledge of the specific programming language as a prerequisite to using the book. However, in the case of a core course, as it is in most academic programs, it is not uncommon for a novice or a sophomore to be bewildered by the "miles of code" that demonstrate or explain a data structure, rendering the subject difficult to comprehend. In fact, the efforts that one needs to put in to comprehend the data structure and its applications are distracted by the necessity to garner sufficient programming knowledge to follow the code. It is indeed ironic that while a novice is taught data structures to appreciate programming, in reality it turns out that one learns programming to appreciate data structures!

In my decades-old experience of offering the course to graduate programs, which admits students from diverse undergraduate disciplines, with little to no strong knowledge of programming, I had several occasions to observe this malady. In fact, it is not uncommon in some academic programs, especially graduate programs which, due to their shorter duration, have a course in programming and data structures running in parallel in the same semester, much to the chagrin of the novice learner! That a novice is forced to learn data structures through their implementation (in a specific programming language), when in reality it ought to be learning augmented with the implementation of the data structures, has been the reason behind the fallout.

A solution to this problem would be to

i) Frame the course such that the theory deals with the concepts, techniques and applications of data structures and algorithms, not taking recourse to any specific programming language, but instead settling for a pseudo-language, which clearly expounds the data structure. Additionally, supplementing the course material with illustrative problems, review questions and exercises to reinforce the students' grasp of the concepts would help them gain useful insights while learning.

ii) Augment the theory with laboratory sessions to enable the student to implement the data structure in itself or as embedded in an application, in the language of his/her own choice or as insisted upon in the curriculum. This would enable the student who has acquired sufficient knowledge and insight into the data structures to appreciate the beauty and merits of employing the data structure by programming it themself, rather than "look" for the data structure in a prewritten code.

This means that text books catering to the fundamental understanding of the data structure concepts for use as course material in the classroom are as much needed as the books that cater to the implementation of data structures in a programming language for use in the laboratory sessions. While most books in the market conform to the latter, bringing out a book to be classroom course material and used by instructors handling a course on data structures and algorithms, comprehensive enough for the novice students to benefit from, has been the main motivation in writing this book.

As such, the book details concepts, techniques and applications pertaining to data structures and algorithms, independent of any programming language, discusses several examples and illustrative problems, poses review questions to reinforce the understanding of the theory, and presents a suggestive list of programming assignments to aid implementation of the data structures and algorithms learned.

In fact, the book may either be independently used as a textbook since it is self-contained or serve as a companion for books discussing data structures and algorithms implemented in specific programming languages such as C, C++, Java, Python, and so on.

At this juncture, it needs to be pointed out that a plethora of programming resources and freely downloadable implementations of the majority of the data structures in almost all popular languages are available on the Internet, which can undoubtedly serve as good guides for the learner. However, it has to be emphasized that an earnest student of data structures and algorithms must invest a lot of time and self-effort in trying to implement the data structures and algorithms learned, in a language of one's choice, all by oneself, in order to attain a thorough grasp of the concepts.

About this edition

This edition is a largely revised and enlarged version of its predecessor, published by McGraw Hill, USA. The earlier edition published in 2008 saw 15 reprints in its life span of 13 years (ending January 2022) and was recommended as a text book for the course in several universities and colleges. It comprised 17 chapters categorized into five parts and reinforced learning through 133 illustrative problems, 215 review questions and 74 programming assignments.

The features of this new edition are as follows:

– There are 22 chapters spread across three volumes that detail sequential linear data structures, linked linear data structures, nonlinear data structures, advanced data structures, searching and sorting algorithms, algorithm design techniques and NP-completeness.

– The data structures of k-d trees and treaps have been elaborated in a newly included chapter (Chapter 15) in Volume 3.

– The data structures of strings, bit rays, unrolled linked lists, self-organizing linked lists, segment trees and k-ary trees have been introduced in the appropriate sections of the existing chapters in Volumes 1 and 2.

– The concepts of counting binary search trees and Kruskal's algorithm have been detailed in the appropriate sections of the existing chapters in Volume 2.

– Skip list search, counting sort and bucket sort have been included in the chapters on searching and sorting algorithms in Volume 3.

– The algorithm design techniques of divide and conquer, the greedy method and dynamic programming have been elaborately discussed in Chapters 19–21 in Volume 3.

– The concept of NP-completeness has been detailed in a newly included chapter, Chapter 22 in Volume 3.

– Several illustrative problems, review questions and programming assignments have been added to enrich the content and aid in understanding the concepts. The new edition thus includes 181 illustrative problems, 276 review questions and 108 programming assignments.

Organization of the book

The book comprises three volumes, namely, Volume 1: Chapters 1–7, Volume 2: Chapters 8–12 and Volume 3: Chapters 13–22.

Volume 1 opens with an *introduction to data structures* and concepts pertaining to the *analysis of algorithms*, detailed in Chapters 1 and 2, which is essential to appreciate the theories and algorithms related to data structures and their applications.

Chapters 3–5 detail sequential linear data structures, namely, *arrays*, *strings*, *bit arrays*, *stacks*, *queues*, *priority queues* and *dequeues*, and their applications. Chapters 6 and 7 elucidate linked linear data structures, namely *linked lists*, *linked stacks* and *linked queues*, and their applications.

Volume 2 details nonlinear data structures. Chapters 8 and 9 elaborate on the nonlinear data structures of *trees*, *binary trees* and *graphs*, and their applications. Chapters 10–12 highlight the advanced data structures of *binary search trees*, *AVL trees*, *B trees*, *tries*, *red-black trees* and *splay trees*, and their applications.

Volume 3 details an assortment of data structures, algorithm design strategies and their applications.

Chapters 13–15 discuss *hash tables*, *files*, *k-d trees* and *treaps*. Chapter 16 discusses the search algorithms of *linear search*, *transpose sequential search*, *interpolation search*, *binary search*, *Fibonacci search*, *skip list search* and other search techniques.

Chapter 17 elaborates on the internal sorting algorithms of *bubble sort, insertion sort, selection sort, merge sort, shell sort, quick sort, heap sort, radix sort, counting sort* and *bucket sort,* and Chapter 18 discusses the external sorting techniques of *sorting with tapes, sorting with disks, polyphase merge sort* and *cascade merge sort.*

Chapters 19–21 detail the algorithm design strategies of *divide and conquer,* the *greedy method* and *dynamic programming* and their applications.

Chapter 22 introduces the theories and concepts of *NP-completeness.*

For a full list of the contents of Volumes 1 and 3, see the summary at the end of this book.

Salient features of the book

The features of the book are as follows:

– all-around emphasis on theory, problems, applications and programming assignments;

– simple and lucid explanation of the theory;

– inclusion of several applications to illustrate the use of data structures and algorithms;

– several worked-out examples as illustrative problems in each chapter;

– list of programming assignments at the end of each chapter;

– review questions to strengthen understanding;

– self-contained text for use as a text book for either an introductory or advanced level course.

Target audience

The book could be used both as an introductory or an advanced-level textbook for undergraduate, graduate and research programs, which offer data structures and algorithms as a core course or an elective course. While the book is primarily meant to serve as a course material for use in the classroom, it could be used as a companion guide during the laboratory sessions to nurture better understanding of the theoretical concepts.

An introductory level course for a duration of one semester or 60 lecture hours, targeting an undergraduate program or first-year graduate program or a diploma program or a certificate program, could include Chapters 1–7 of Volume 1, Chapter 8 of Volume 2, Chapters 13, 16 (sections 16.1, 16.2, 16.5) and 17 (sections 17.1–17.3, 17.5, 17.7) of Volume 3 in its curriculum.

A middle-level course for a duration of one semester or 60 lecture hours targeting senior graduate-level programs and research programs such as MS/PhD could include Chapters 1–7 of Volume 1, Chapters 8–11 of Volume 2, Chapter 13 and selective sections of Chapters 16–17 of Volume 3.

An advanced level course that focuses on advanced data structures and algorithm design could begin with a review of Chapter 8 and include Chapters 9–12 of Volume 2, Chapters 14 and 15 and selective sections of Chapters 16–18, and Chapters 19–22 of Volume 3 in its curriculum based on the level of prerequisite courses satisfied.

Chapters 8–10 and Chapter 11 (sections 11.1–11.3) of Volume 2 and Chapters 13, 14 and 18 of Volume 3 could be useful to include in a curriculum that serves as a prerequisite for a course on database management systems.

To re-emphasize, all theory sessions must be supplemented with laboratory sessions to encourage learners to implement the concepts learned in an appropriate language that adheres to the curricular requirements of the programs concerned.

Acknowledgments

The author is grateful to ISTE Ltd., London, UK, for accepting to publish the book, in collaboration with John Wiley & Sons Inc., USA. She expresses her appreciation to the publishing team, for their professionalism and excellent production practices, while bringing out this book in three volumes.

The author expresses her sincere thanks to the Management and Principal, PSG College of Technology, Coimbatore, India for the support extended while writing the book.

The author would like to place on record her immense admiration and affection for her father, Late Professor G. A. Krishna Pai and her mother Rohini Krishna Pai for their unbounded encouragement and support to help her follow her life lessons and her sisters Dr. Rekha Pai and Udaya Pai, for their unstinted, anywhere-anytime-anything kind of help and support, all of which were instrumental and inspirational in helping this author create this work.

G. A. Vijayalakshmi Pai
August 2022

8

Trees and Binary Trees

8.1. Introduction

In Chapters 3–5 (Volume 1), we discussed the sequential data structures of arrays, stacks and queues. These are termed as *linear data structures* since they are inherently unidimensional in structure. In other words, the items form a sequence or a linear list. In contrast, the data structures of trees and graphs are termed *nonlinear data structures* since they are inherently two dimensional in structure. *Trees* and their variants, *binary trees* and *graphs*, have emerged as truly powerful data structures registering an immense contribution to the development of efficient algorithms or efficient solutions to various problems in science and engineering.

In this chapter, we first discuss the tree data structure, the basic terminologies and representation schemes. An important variant of the tree, viz., binary tree, its basic concepts, representation schemes and traversals are elaborately discussed next. A useful modification to the binary tree, viz., *threaded binary tree,* is introduced. Finally, *expression trees*, *segment trees* and their related concepts are discussed as applications of binary trees.

8.2. Trees: definition and basic terminologies

8.2.1. *Definition of trees*

A *tree* is defined as a finite set of one or more nodes such that

i) there is a specially designated *node* called the *root*;

ii) the rest of the nodes could be partitioned into t disjoint sets ($t \geq 0$) each set representing a tree T_i, $i = 1,2, \ldots t$ known as *subtree* of the tree.

A **node** in the definition of the tree represents an item of information, and the links between the nodes termed as **branches** represent an association between the items of information. Figure 8.1 illustrates a tree.

The definition of the tree emphasizes on the aspect of (i) **connectedness** and (ii) absence of closed loops or what are termed **cycles**. Beginning from the root node, the structure of the tree permits connectedness of the root to every other node in the tree. In general, any node is reachable from anywhere in the tree. Also, with branches providing the links between the nodes, the structure ensures that no set of nodes link together to form a closed loop or a cycle.

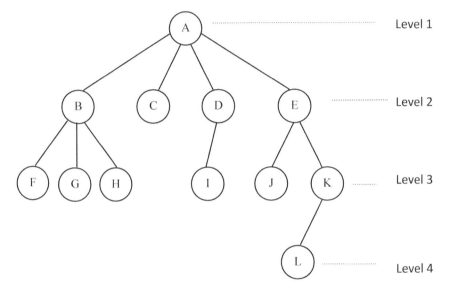

Figure 8.1. *An example tree*

8.2.2. *Basic terminologies of trees*

There are several basic terminologies associated with the tree. The specially designated node called root has already been introduced in the definition.

The number of subtrees of a node is known as the **degree of the node**. Nodes that have zero degree are called **leaf nodes** or **terminal nodes**. The rest of them are called **non-terminal nodes**.

The nodes which hang from branches emanating from a node are known as *children* and the node from which the branches emanate is known as the ***parent node***. Children of the same parent node are referred to as ***siblings***. The ***ancestors*** of a given node are those nodes that occur on the path from the root to the given node.

The ***degree of a tree*** is the maximum degree of the node in the tree. The level of a node is defined by letting the root to occupy level 1 (some authors let the root occupy level 0). The rest of the nodes occupy various levels depending on their association. Thus, if a parent node occupies level *i*, its children should occupy level *i + 1*. This renders the tree to have a ***hierarchical structure*** with root occupying the top most level of 1. The ***height*** or ***depth*** of a tree is defined to be the maximum level of any node in the tree. Some authors define depth of a node to be the length of the longest path from the root node to that node, which yields the relation,

depth of the tree = height of the tree – 1

A *forest* is a set of zero or more disjoint trees. The removal of the root node from a tree results in a forest (of its subtrees!).

In Figure 8.1, A is the root node. The degree of node E is 2 and L is 0. F, G, H, C, I, J and L are leaf or terminal nodes and all the remaining nodes are non-leaf or non-terminal nodes. Nodes F, G and H are children of B, hence B is a parent node. Nodes J, K and nodes F, G, H are sibling nodes with E and B as their respective parents. For the node L, nodes A, E and K are ancestors. The degree of the tree is 4 which is the maximum degree and this is reported by node A. While node A which is the root node that occupies level 1, its children B, C, D and E occupy level 2 and so on. The height of the tree is its maximum level which is 4. Removal of A yields a forest of four disjoint (sub) trees viz., {B F G H}, {C}, {D, I} and {E, J, K, L}.

8.3. Representation of trees

Though trees are better understood in their pictorial forms, a common representation of a tree to suit its storage in the memory of a computer, is a *list*. The tree of Figure 8.1 could be represented in its list form as (A (B(F,G,H), C, D(I), E(J,K(L)))). The root node comes first followed by the list of subtrees of the node. This is repeated for each subtree in the tree. This list form of a tree, paves way for a naïve representation of the tree as a linked list. The node structure of the linked list is shown in Figure 8.2(a).

The DATA field of the node stores the information content of the tree node. A fixed set of LINK fields accommodate the pointers to the child nodes of the given node. In fact the *maximum number of links the node would require is equal to the degree of the tree*. The linked representation of the tree shown in Figure 8.1 is illustrated in Figure 8.2(b). Observe the colossal wastage of space by way of null pointers!

An alternative representation would be to use a node structure as shown in Figure 8.3(a). Here TAG = 1 indicates that the next field (DATA/DOWNLINK) is occupied by data (DATA) and TAG = 0 indicates that the same is used to hold a link (DOWNLINK). The node structure of the linked list holds a DOWNLINK whenever it encounters a child node which gives rise to a subtree. Thus, the root node A has four child nodes, three of which, viz., B, D and E, give rise to subtrees. Note the DOWNLINK active fields of the nodes in these cases with TAG set to 0. In contrast, observe the linked list node corresponding to C which has no subtree. The DATA field records C with TAG set to 1.

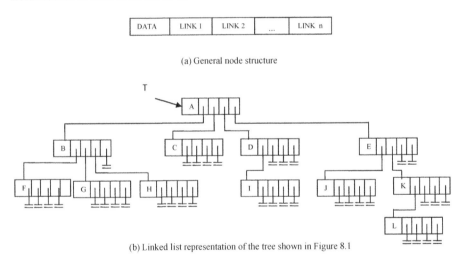

(a) General node structure

(b) Linked list representation of the tree shown in Figure 8.1

Figure 8.2. *Linked list representation of a tree*

EXAMPLE 8.1.–

We illustrate a tree structure in the organic evolution which deals with the derivation of new species of plants and animals from the first formed life by descent with modification. Figure 8.4(a) illustrates the tree, and Figure 8.4(b) shows its linked representation.

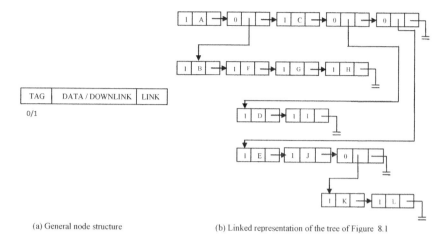

(a) General node structure

(b) Linked representation of the tree of Figure 8.1

Figure 8.3. *An alternative elegant linked representation of a tree*

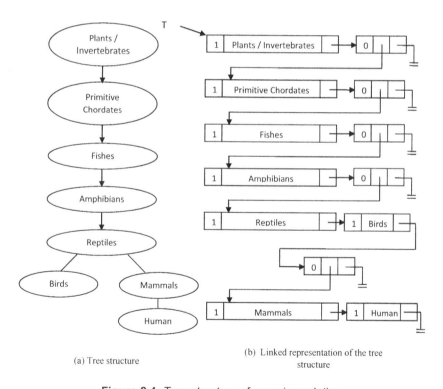

(a) Tree structure

(b) Linked representation of the tree structure

Figure 8.4. *Tree structure of organic evolution*

8.4. Binary trees: basic terminologies and types

8.4.1. *Basic terminologies*

A *binary tree* has the characteristic of all nodes having at most two branches, that is, all nodes have a *degree of at most 2*. A binary tree can therefore be *empty* or consist of a root node and two disjoint binary trees termed *left subtree* and *right subtree*.

Figure 8.5 illustrates a binary tree.

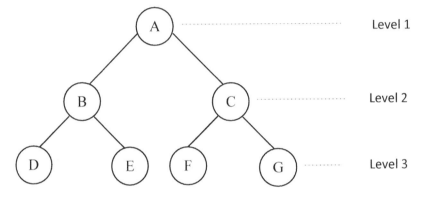

Figure 8.5. *An example binary tree*

It is essential that the distinction between trees and binary trees are brought out clearly. While a binary tree can be empty with zero nodes, a tree can never be empty. Again while the ordering of the subtrees in a tree is immaterial, in a binary tree the distinction of left and right subtrees are very clearly maintained. All other terminologies applicable to trees such as levels, degree, height, leaf nodes, parent, child, siblings etc. are also applicable to binary trees. However, there are some important observations regarding binary trees.

i) The maximum number of nodes on level i of a binary tree is 2^{i-1}, $i \geq 1$.

ii) The maximum number of nodes in a binary tree of height h is $2^h - 1$, $h \geq 1$ (for proof refer to illustrative problem 8.6).

iii) For any non-empty binary trees, if t_o is the number of terminal nodes and t_2 is the number of nodes of degree 2, then $t_o = t_2 + 1$ (for proof refer to illustrative problem 8.7).

These observations could be easily verified on the binary tree shown in Figure 8.5. The maximum number of nodes on level 3 is $2^{3-2} = 2^2 = 4$. Also, with the height of the binary tree being 3, the maximum number of nodes $= 2^3 - 1 = 7$. Again $t_0 = 4$ and $t_2 = 3$ which yields $t_0 = t_2 + 1$.

The *diameter of a binary tree* also known as the *width of a binary tree*, is the number of nodes in the longest path between any two leaf nodes of the binary tree. Thus, for the binary tree shown in Figure 8.5 the diameter or width is 5 and as can be observed, there is more than one path with the same diameter for the binary tree. The longest path between leaf node pairs (D, G), (E, F), (D, F) and (E, G) all result in a diameter of 5. It is also possible to have the longest paths traversing through the root node of the binary tree or merely confining themselves to the subtrees, thereby excluding the root node. Thus, the width of the binary tree shown in Figure 8.7(a) has a width of 4 and the longest path between the leaf node pair (c, e) or (c, f) excludes the root node.

8.4.2. *Types of binary trees*

A binary tree of height h which has all its permissible maximum number of nodes, viz., $2^h - 1$ intact is known as a *full binary tree of height h*. Figure 8.6(a) illustrates a full binary tree of height 4. Note the specific method of numbering the nodes.

A binary tree with n' nodes and height h is **complete** if its nodes correspond to the nodes which are numbered *1* to n ($n' \leq n$) in a full binary tree of height h. In other words, a *complete binary tree* is one in which its nodes follow a sequential numbering that increments from a left-to-right and top-to-bottom fashion. A full binary tree is therefore a special case of a complete binary tree. Also, the height of a complete binary tree with n elements has a height h given by $h = \lceil log_2(n+1) \rceil$. A complete binary tree obeys the following properties with regard to its node numbering:

i) If a parent node has a number i then its left child has the number *2i (2i $\leq$ n)*. If *2i>n* then i has no left child.

ii) If a parent node has a number i, then its right child has the number *2i + 1 (2i + 1 $\leq$ n)*. If *2i + 1 > n* then i has no right child.

iii) If a child node (left or right) has a number i then the parent node has the number $\lfloor i / 2 \rfloor$ if $i \neq 1$. If $i = 1$ then i is the root and hence has no parent.

In the full binary tree of height 4 illustrated in Figure 8.6(a), observe how the parent-child numbering is satisfied. For example, consider node s (number 4): its left child w has the number $2*4 = 8$ and its right child has the number $2*4+1 = 9$. Again, the parent of node v (number 7) is the node with number $\lfloor 7\ /2 \rfloor = 3$ (i.e.) node 3 which is r.

Figure 8.6(b) illustrates an example of a complete binary tree. A binary tree which is dominated solely by left child nodes or right child nodes is called a *skewed binary tree* or more specifically *left skewed binary tree* or *right skewed binary tree* respectively. Figure 8.6(c) illustrates examples of skewed binary trees.

A *k-ary tree* is one where every node has either 0 or k child nodes. Figure 8.6(d) illustrates a k-ary tree for $k = 4$. In a k-ary tree where every node has either 0 or k children, the following result holds true.

$$L = (k-1).I + 1,$$

where L is the number of leaf nodes, I the number of internal nodes and k is the arity of the tree. This result is derived using **Handshaking Lemma** discussed in Chapter 9 and proved in illustrative problem 9.13.

Thus, for the example of the k-ary tree shown in Figure 8.6(d), $L = 7 = (4-1).2 + 1$, since $I = 2$ and $k = 4$.

8.5. Representation of binary trees

A binary tree could be represented using a sequential data structure (arrays) as well as a linked data structure.

8.5.1. *Array representation of binary trees*

To represent the binary tree as an array, the sequential numbering system emphasized by a complete binary tree comes in handy. Consider the binary tree shown in Figure 8.7(a). The array representation is as shown in Figure 8.7(b). The association of numbers pertaining to parent and left/right child nodes makes it convenient to access the appropriate cells of the array. However, the missing nodes in the binary tree and hence the corresponding array locations, are left empty in the array. This obviously leads to a lot of wastage of space. However, the array representation ideally suits a full binary tree due to its non-wastage of space.

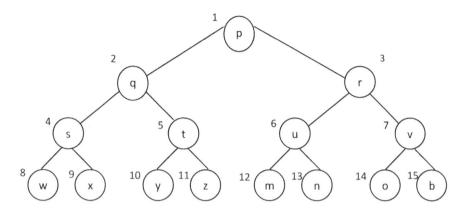

(a) Full binary tree of height 4

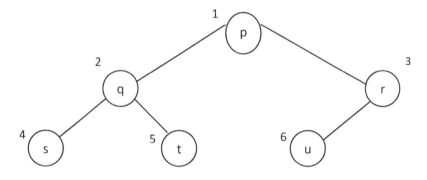

(b) A complete binary tree of height 3

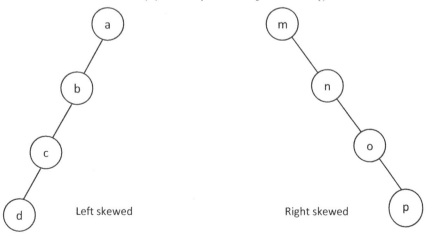

(c) Skewed binary trees

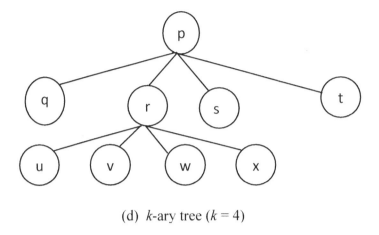

(d) *k*-ary tree (*k* = 4)

Figure 8.6. *Examples of full binary tree, complete binary tree, skewed binary trees and k-ary tree*

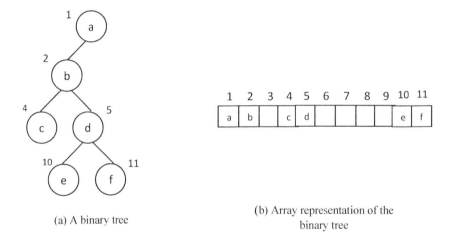

(a) A binary tree

(b) Array representation of the binary tree

Figure 8.7. *Array representation of a binary tree*

8.5.2. *Linked representation of binary trees*

The linked representation of a binary tree has the node structure shown in Figure 8.8(a). Here, the node besides the DATA field needs two pointers LCHILD and RCHILD to point to the left and right child nodes, respectively. The tree is accessed by remembering the pointer to the root node of the tree.

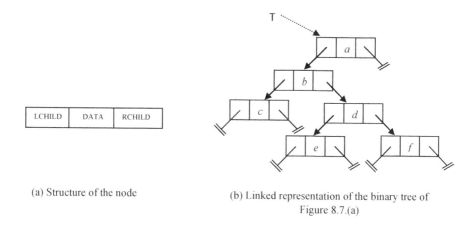

(a) Structure of the node
(b) Linked representation of the binary tree of
Figure 8.7.(a)

Figure 8.8. *Linked representation of a binary tree*

In the binary tree T shown in Figure 8.8(b), LCHILD (T) refers to the node storing *b*, RCHILD (LCHILD (T)) refers to the node storing *d* and so on. The following are some of the important observations regarding the linked representation of a binary tree:

i) If a binary tree has *n* nodes, then the number of pointers used in its linked representation is *2 * n*.

ii) The number of null pointers used in the linked representation of a binary tree with *n* nodes is *n* + 1.

However, in a linked representation, it is difficult to determine a parent given a child node. If an application requires knowing the parent as well, then a fourth field PARENT may be included in the node structure.

8.6. Binary tree traversals

An important operation that is performed on a binary tree is its ***traversal***. A traversal of a binary tree is where its nodes are visited in a particular but repetitive order, rendering a linear order of the nodes or information represented by them.

A traversal is governed by three actions, viz., ***move left*** (**L**), ***move right*** (**R**) and ***process node*** (**P**). In all, it yields six different combinations of LPR, LRP, PLR,

PRL and RLP. Of these, three have emerged as significant in computer science. They are as follows:

– LPR: inorder traversal;

– LRP: postorder traversal;

– PLR: preorder traversal.

The algorithms for each of the traversals are elaborated here.

8.6.1. *Inorder traversal*

The traversal keeps moving left in the binary tree until one can move no further, processes the node and moves to the right to continue its traversal again. In the absence of any node to the right, it retracts backwards by a node and continues the traversal.

Algorithm 8.1 illustrates a recursive procedure to perform inorder traversal of a binary tree. For clarity of application, the action *process node* (P) is interpreted as *print node*. Observe how the recursive procedure reflects the maxim LPR repetitively. Example 8.2 illustrates the inorder traversal of the binary tree shown in Figure 8.9.

EXAMPLE 8.2.–

An easy method to obtain the traversal would be to run one's fingers on the binary tree with the maxim: *move left until no more nodes, process node, then move right* and *continue the traversal.*

An alternative method is to trace the recursive steps of the algorithm using the following scheme:

Execute the traversal of the binary tree as **traverse left subtree, process root node** and **traverse right subtree**. Repeat the same for each of the left and right subtrees encountered. Table 8.1 illustrates the traversal of the binary tree shown in Figure 8.9 using this scheme. Each open box in the inorder traversal output (see column 2 of Table 8.1) represents the output of the call to the procedure INORDER_TRAVERSAL with the root of the appropriate subtree as its input. The final output of the inorder traversal is S T Q P W U R V.

Binary Tree	Inorder Traversal Output	Remarks
Step 1 Inorder Traverse Binary Tree Node → P Q R S U V T W Left subtree 1 Right subtree 1	Process Root ? P ? Inorder traverse Left subtree 1 Inorder traverse Right subtree 1	Inorder traversals of the Left and Right subtrees of the root node are yet to yield their output.
Step 2 Inorder Traverse Left subtree 1 Q S Right subtree empty T Left subtree 2	Process Root NIL ? Q ? P ? Inorder traverse Left subtree 2 Inorder traverse Right subtree 1	Inorder traversal of the Left subtree 1 yields Inorder traversal of Left subtree 2, process root Q, and Inorder traverse Right subtree. However, since the Right subtree is empty, its traversal yields NIL output.
Step 3 Inorder Traverse Left subtree 2 S Left subtree empty Right subtree 2	Process Root NIL NIL S ? Q P ? Inorder traverse Right subtree 2 Inorder traverse Right subtree 1	

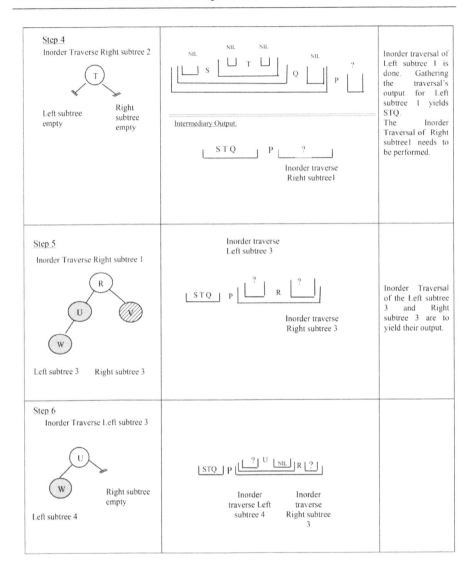

Step 4 Inorder Traverse Right subtree 2		Inorder traversal of Left subtree 1 is done. Gathering the traversal's output for Left subtree 1 yields STQ. The Inorder Traversal of Right subtree1 needs to be performed.
Step 5 Inorder Traverse Right subtree 1		Inorder Traversal of the Left subtree 3 and Right subtree 3 are to yield their output.
Step 6 Inorder Traverse Left subtree 3		

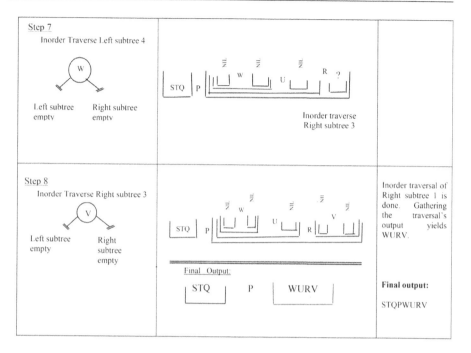

Table 8.1. *Inorder traversal of binary tree shown in Figure 8.9*

```
procedure INORDER_TRAVERSAL (NODE)
/*  NODE refers to the Root node of the binary tree in
its first call to the procedure. Root node is the
starting point of the traversal */

  If NODE ≠ NIL then
  { call INORDER_TRAVERSAL (LCHILD(NODE));
    / * Inorder traverse the left subtree (L) */
    print (DATA (NODE)) ;
                       /* Process node  (P) */
    call INORDER_TRAVERSAL (RCHILD(NODE));
     /* Inorder traverse the right subtree  (R)*/
  }
end INORDER_TRAVERSAL.
```

Algorithm 8.1. *Recursive procedure to*
perform inorder traversal of a binary tree

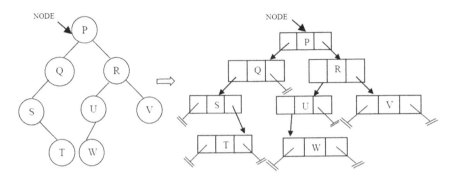

Figure 8.9. *Binary tree to demonstrate inorder, postorder and preorder traversals*

8.6.2. *Postorder traversal*

The traversal proceeds by keeping to the left until it is not possible to proceed further, turning right to begin again or if there is no node to the right, processing the node and retracing its direction by one node to continue its traversal.

Algorithm 8.2 illustrates a recursive procedure to perform the postorder traversal of a binary tree. The recursive procedure reflects the maxim LRP invoked repetitively. Example 8.3 illustrates the postorder traversal of the binary tree shown in Figure 8.9. The traversal output is TSQWUVRP.

```
procedure POSTORDER_TRAVERSAL (NODE)
/*  NODE refers to the Root node of the binary tree in
its first call to the procedure. Root node is the
starting point of the traversal */

    If NODE ≠ NIL then
        { call POSTORDER_TRAVERSAL (LCHILD(NODE));
        / * Postorder traverse the left subtree (L) */

        call POSTORDER_TRAVERSAL (RCHILD(NODE));
        /* Postorder traverse the right subtree  (R)*/
        print (DATA (NODE)) ;
                            /* Process node  (P) */

        }
end POSTORDER_TRAVERSAL.
```

Algorithm 8.2. *Recursive procedure to perform postorder traversal of a binary tree*

EXAMPLE 8.3.–

As pointed out in example 8.2, an easy method would be to run one's fingers on the binary tree with the maxim: *move left until there are no more nodes* and *turn right to continue traversal. If there is no right node, process node, retract by one node and continue traversal.*

An alternative method would be to trace the recursive steps of the algorithm using the scheme: *traverse left subtree, traverse right subtree* and *process root node.* Table 8.2 illustrates the traversal of the binary tree shown in Figure 8.9 using this scheme.

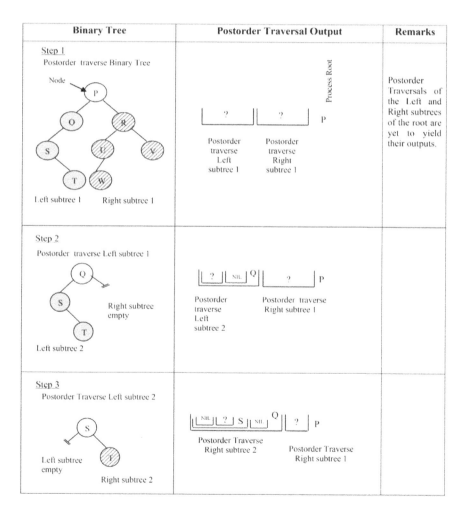

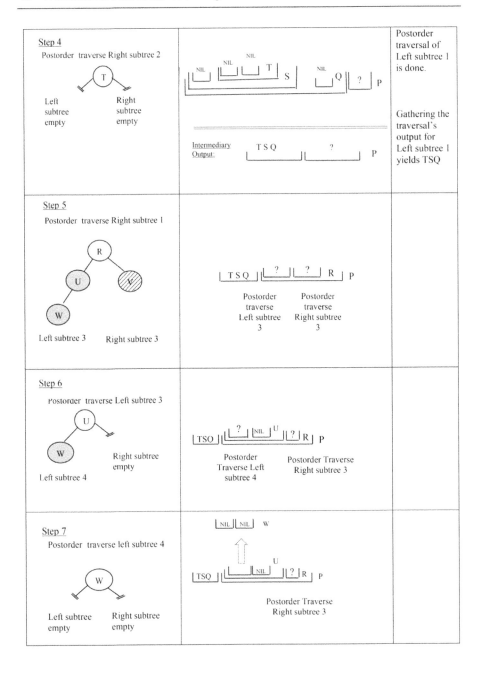

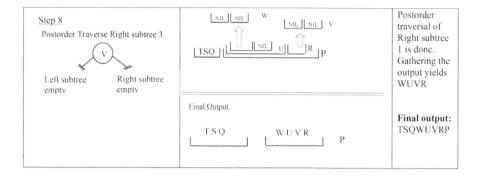

Table 8.2. *Postorder traversal of binary tree shown in Figure 8.9*

8.6.3. Preorder traversal

The traversal processes every node as it moves left until it can move no further. Now it turns right to begin again or if there is no node to the right, retracts back until it can move right to continue its traversal.

The recursive procedure for the preorder traversal is illustrated in Algorithm 8.3. The recursive procedure reflects the maxim PLR invoked repetitively. Example 8.4 illustrates the preorder traversal of the binary tree shown in Figure 8.9. The traversal output is PQSTRUWV.

EXAMPLE 8.4.–

An easy method as discussed before would be to trace the traversal on the binary tree using the maxim: *process nodes while moving left until no more nodes, turn right*, and otherwise *retract to continue the traversal.*

An alternative method is to trace the recursive steps of the algorithm using the following scheme:

Execute the traversal of the binary tree as *process root node, traverse left subtree* and *traverse right subtree*, repeating the same for each of the left and right subtrees encountered.

Table 8.3 illustrates the preorder traversal of the binary tree shown in Figure 8.9 using this scheme.

Binary Tree	Preorder Traversal Output	Remarks
Step 1 Preorder traversal of Binary Tree Node ───► P O, R S, U, V T, W Left subtree 1 Right subtree 1	Process Root P ⌐___?___⌐ ⌐___?___⌐ Preorder Preorder traverse traverse Left Right subtree 1 subtree 1	Preorder traversals of the Left subtree 1 and Right subtree 1 are yet to yield their outputs.
Step 2 Preorder traverse Left subtree 1 O S Right subtree empty T Left subtree 2	P ⌐Q ? ⌐ ⌐NIL⌐ ⌐___?___⌐ Preorder Preorder traverse traverse Left Right subtree 2 subtree 1	

Step 3
Preorder traverse Left subtree 2
 	
S
Left subtree   T
empty
        Right subtree 2
	Preorder Traverse
	Right subtree 2
	
	P ⌐Q S NIL ? ⌐ ⌐NIL⌐ ⌐?⌐
	                    Preorder Traverse
	                    Right subtree 1	

Step 4 Preorder traverse Right subtree 2 T Left subtree Right subtree empty empty	T ⌐NIL⌐ ⌐NIL⌐ P ⌐Q S NIL ⌐↑⌐ NIL⌐ ⌐?⌐ _____ Intermediary Output: P ⌐ Q S T ⌐ ⌐?⌐	Preorder traversal of Left subtree 1 is done. Gathering the traversal's output yields QST

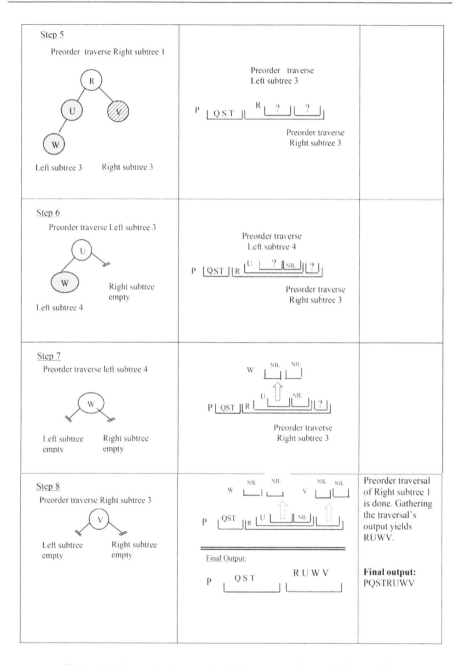

Table 8.3. *Preorder traversal of binary tree shown in Figure 8.9*

```
procedure PREORDER_TRAVERSAL (NODE)
/*  NODE refers to the Root node of the binary tree in
its first call to the procedure. Root node is the
starting point of the traversal */

  If NODE ≠ NIL then
  { print (DATA (NODE)) ;
                    /* Process node  (P) */

    call PREORDER_TRAVERSAL (LCHILD(NODE));
       / * Preorder traverse the left subtree (L) */

    call PREORDER_TRAVERSAL (RCHILD(NODE));
      /* Preorder traverse the right subtree (R)*/

  }

end PREORDER_TRAVERSAL.
```

Algorithm 8.3. *Recursive procedure to perform preorder traversal of a binary tree*

Some significant observations pertaining to the traversals of a binary tree are as follows:

i) Given a preorder traversal of a binary tree, the root node is the first occurring item in the list.

ii) Given a postorder traversal of a binary tree, the root node is the last occurring item in the list.

iii) Inorder traversal does not directly reveal the root node of the binary tree.

iv) An inorder traversal coupled with any one of preorder or postorder traversal helps to trace back the structure of the binary tree (refer to illustrative problems 8.3 and 8.4).

8.7. Threaded binary trees

The linked representation of the binary tree discussed in section 8.5 showed that for a binary tree with n nodes, $2n$ pointers are required of which $(n + 1)$ are null pointers. A.J. Perlis and C. Thornton (Perlis 1960) devised a prudent method to utilize these $(n + 1)$ empty pointers, introducing what are called ***threads***. Threads are also links or pointers but replace null pointers by pointing to some useful information in the binary tree. Thus, for a node NODE if RCHILD(NODE) is NIL, then the null pointer is replaced by a thread which points to the node which would occur after NODE when the binary tree is traversed in inorder. Again, if LCHILD (NODE) is NIL, then the null pointer is replaced by a thread to the node which would immediately precede NODE when the binary tree is traversed in inorder.

Figure 8.10 illustrates a ***threaded binary tree***. The threads are indicated using broken lines to distinguish them from the normal links indicated with solid lines. The inorder traversal of the binary tree is also shown in the figure.

Note that the left child of G and the right child of E have threads, which are left dangling due to the absence of an inorder predecessor and successor, respectively.

There are many ways to thread a binary tree T, corresponding to the specific traversal chosen. In this work, we have the threading correspond to an inorder traversal. Also, the threading can be of two representations, viz., ***one-way threading*** and ***two-way threading***.

One-way threading is where a thread appears only on the RCHILD field of a node, when the said field is null and it points only to the inorder successor of the node (refer illustrative problem 8.10).

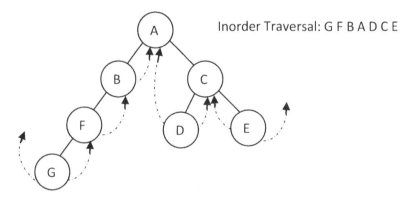

Inorder Traversal: G F B A D C E

Figure 8.10. *A threaded binary tree*

On the other hand, in two-way threading, which had already been introduced above, a thread appears in the LCHILD field also, if the said field is null and it points only to the inorder predecessor of the node. Needless to say, the first and the last of the nodes in the inorder traversal will carry dangling threads.

8.7.1. *Linked representation of a threaded binary tree*

A linked representation of the threaded binary tree (two-way threading) has a node structure as shown in Figure 8.11.

LEFT THREAD TAG	LCHILD	DATA	RCHILD	RIGHT THREAD TAG

(True or False)   (True or False)

Figure 8.11. *Node structure of a linked representation of a threaded binary tree*

Since the LCHILD and RCHILD fields are utilized to represent both links and threads, it becomes essential for the node structure to clearly distinguish between them to avoid confusion while processing the threaded binary tree. Hence, it is necessary that the node structure includes two more fields, which act as flags to indicate if the LCHILD and RCHILD fields represent a thread or a link.

If the LEFT THREAD TAG or RIGHT THREAD TAG is marked *true*, then LCHILD and RCHILD fields represent tags, otherwise they represent links. Also, to tuck in the dangling threads which are bound to arise, the linked representation of a threaded binary tree includes a *head node*. The dangling threads point to the head node. The head node by convention has its LCHILD pointing to the root node of the threaded binary tree and therefore has its LEFT THREAD TAG set to *false*. THE RIGHT THREAD TAG field is also set to *false* but the RCHILD link points to the head node itself. Figure 8.12(a) shows the linked representation of an empty threaded binary tree, and Figure 8.12(b) shows the linked representation of a non-empty threaded binary tree.

8.7.2. *Growing threaded binary trees*

Here, we discuss the insertion of nodes contributing to the growth of threaded binary trees. The insertion of a node calls not only for the realignment of links but also of the threads involved.

Consider the case of inserting a node NEW to the right of a node NODE in the threaded binary tree. If the node NODE had no right subtree, then the case is trivial. Attach NEW as right child of NODE and appropriately reset the threads of NEW to point to its inorder predecessor and successor, respectively. Figure 8.13(a) illustrates this insertion.

In the next case, if NODE already had a right subtree, then attach NEW as the right child of the node NODE and link the previous right subtree of NODE to the right of node NEW. When this is done, the threads of the appropriate nodes are reset as shown in Figure 8.13(b).

A similar procedure is followed to insert a node in the left subtree of a threaded binary tree.

8.8. Applications

In this section, we discuss applications of binary trees in expression trees, which have a significant role to play in the principles of compiler design and segment trees that can efficiently handle repeated queries and updates on an array of elements.

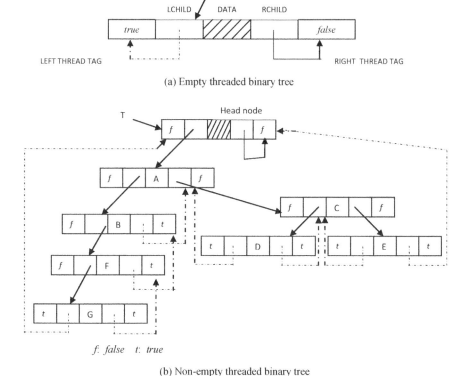

(a) Empty threaded binary tree

f: false   t: true

(b) Non-empty threaded binary tree

Figure 8.12. *Linked representation of threaded binary trees*

8.8.1. *Expression trees*

Expressions – *arithmetic* and *logical* – are an inherent component of programming languages. The following are examples of arithmetic and logical expressions:

((A + B) * C-D) ↑ *G* (arithmetic expression);

(¬ A ∧B) ∨ *(B∧E)* ∧ ¬ *F* (logical expression);

(T < W) ∨*(A ≤ B)* ∧ *(C ≠E)* (logical expression).

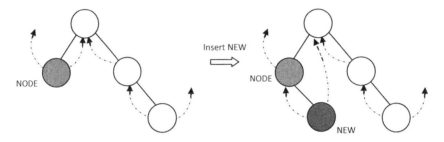

(a) Insertion of node NEW to the right of NODE: Right subtree of NODE is empty

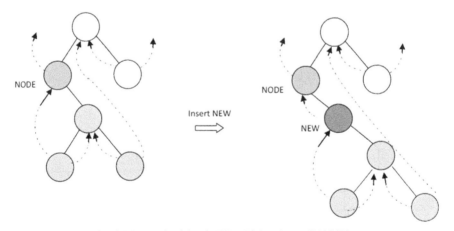

(b) Insertion of node NEW to the right of NODE: Right subtree of NODE is non empty

Figure 8.13. *Insertion of a node in the right subtree of a threaded binary tree*

Expressions are represented in three forms, viz., infix, postfix and prefix, as detailed in section 4.3.2 (see Chapter 4, Volume 1). To quickly review, an infix expression which is the commonly used representation of an expression follows the scheme:

< *operand* > < *operator*> < *operand* >.

Examples are *A* + *B*, *A* * *B*.

Postfix expressions follow the scheme: < *operand* > < *operand* > < *operator* >.

Examples are *AB+*, *AB**.

Prefix expressions follow the scheme: < *operator* > < *operand* > < *operand* >.

Examples are +*AB*, **AB*.

Binary trees have found an application in the representation of expressions. An **expression tree** has the operands of the expression as its terminal or leaf nodes and the operators as its non-terminal nodes. The arity of the operator is therefore restricted to be 1 or 2 (unary or binary) and this is what is commonly encountered in arithmetic and logical expressions. Figure 8.14 illustrates examples of expression trees.

The **hierarchical precedence** and **associativity rules** of the operators in terms of the expressions are reflected in the orientation of the subtrees or the sibling nodes. Table 8.4 illustrates some examples showing the orientation of the binary tree in accordance with the precedence and associatively rules of the operators in the expression terms.

8.8.2. *Traversals of an expression tree*

Section 8.6 detailed the traversals of a binary tree. With an expression tree essentially being a binary tree, the traversal of an expression tree also yields significant results. Thus, the inorder traversal of an expression tree yields an infix expression, the postorder traversal, a postfix expression and preorder traversal, a prefix expression. The output of the algorithms INORDER_TRAVERSAL(), PREORDER_TRAVERSAL() and POSTORDER_TRAVERSAL () on any given expression tree can be verified against the hand computed infix, prefix and postfix expressions (discussed in section 4.3.2 of Chapter 4, Volume 1).

8.8.3. *Conversion of infix expression to postfix expression*

We utilize this opportunity to introduce a significant concept of infix to postfix expression conversion, which finds a useful place in the theory of compiler design.

Given an infix expression, for example A+B*C, the objective is to obtain its postfix equivalent ABC*+. In section 4.3.2 (see Chapter 4, Volume 1), a hand coded method of conversion was illustrated. In this section, we introduce an algorithm to perform the same.

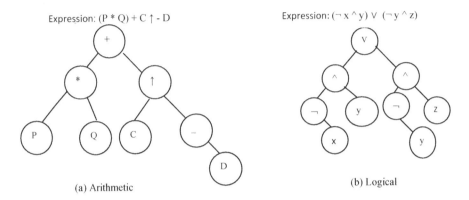

Figure 8.14. *Example expression trees*

The algorithm makes use of a stack as its work space and is governed by two priority factors, viz., *in stack priority* (ISP) and *incoming priority* (ICP) of the operators participating in the conversion. Thus, those operators, already pushed into the stack during the process of conversion, command an ISP in relation to those which are just about to be pushed into the stack (ICP). Table 8.5 illustrates the ISP and ICP of a common list of arithmetic operators.

The rule which operates during conversion of infix to postfix expression is as follows: *pop operators out of the work stack so long as the ICP of the incoming operator is less than or equal to the operators already available in the stack.*

The input infix expression is padded with a "$" to signal end of input. The bottom of the work stack is also signaled with a "$" symbol with ISP($) = −1. Algorithm 8.4 illustrates the pseudo-code procedure to convert an infix expression into postfix expression.

Expression	Expression tree	Remarks
A+B		Observe the orientation of the sibling nodes. The left operand A and the right operand B become the left and right child nodes of the operator +, respectively.

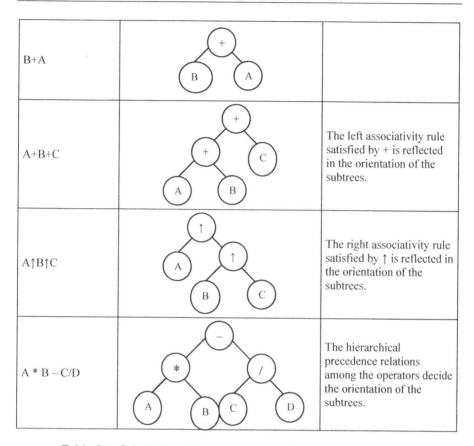

Table 8.4. *Orientation of the binary trees with regard to expressions*

Operator	ISP	ICP
)	–	–
↑	3	4
*, /	2	2
+, –	1	1
(	0	4

Table 8.5. *ISP and ICP of a common list of arithmetic operators*

```
procedure INFIX_POSTFIX_CONV(E)
/* to convert an infix expression E padded with a    "$ "
as its end-of-input symbol into its equivalent postfix
expression */

  x:= getnextchar(E);
                /* obtain the next character from E */
  while x ≠ "$ " do
        case x of
          : x is an operand: print x;
          : x = ' )'           : while (top element of
                                        stack ≠'(') do
                                   print top element of
                                   stack and pop stack;
                                 end while
                                 pop '( ' from stack;

          : else  :            while ICP(x) ≤ ISP(top
                                   element of stack) do
                                   print top element of
                                   stack and pop stack;
                                 end while
                                 push x  into stack;

        end case
        x: = getnextchar(E);
  end while
  while stack is non empty do
    print top element of stack and pop stack;
  end while
end INFIX_POSTFIX_CONV.
```

Algorithm 8.4. *Procedure to convert infix expression to postfix expression*

Example 8.5 illustrates the conversion of an infix expression into its equivalent postfix expression using Algorithm INFIX_POSTFIX_CONV( ).

EXAMPLE 8.5.–

Consider an infix expression A * (B + C) – G. Table 8.6 illustrates the conversion into its postfix equivalent, which is A B C + * G - .

Input character fetched by `getnextchar( )`	Work stack	Postfix expression	Remarks
A	$	A	Print A
*	$*	A	Since ISP (*) > ISP ($) push * into stack.
(	$*(	A	Since ICP (" (") > ISP (*) push (into stack.
B	$*(	AB	Print B.
+	$*(+	AB	Since ICP (+) > ISP(" (")) push + into stack.
C	$*(+	ABC	Print C
)	$*	ABC+	Pop elements from stack until "(is reached. Also, pop "(from stack.
–	$ –	ABC+*	Since ICP (–) < ISP (*) pop * from the stack. Push ' – ' into stack
G	$ –	ABC+*G	Print G
$	$	ABC+*G–	End of input ($) reached. Empty contents of stack.

Table 8.6. *Conversion of A* (B + C) – G$ into its postfix form*

8.8.4. Segment trees

Segment tree invented by Jon Louis Bentley in 1977 is a data structure built on binary trees that can efficiently store information about an interval or segment or list of elements. It is a **static** data structure in that once the information is stored as a binary tree, the structure cannot be modified.

Given an array of elements, there are instances when queries such as finding the minimum or maximum or sum or product of a range of elements belonging to the array, or even updates to the elements of the array, are frequently undertaken. The worst case complexity of a query operation over an array is $O(n)$, where n is the size of the array and in the case of m such operations on the array, the worst case time complexity is $O(m.n)$. The time complexity becomes significant when m and n are very large. In such cases, it is effective to represent the array of elements as a segment tree, which supports handling the queries and updates elegantly. Thus, segment tree being a binary tree reports a worst case time complexity of $O(\log_2 n)$ for a query operation and in the event of m such operations, the worst case time complexity would be $O(m.\log_2 n)$.

8.8.4.1. *Definition*

A *segment tree* is a binary tree that stores details about the intervals or segments of the array of elements, upon which it is structured. Each node in the segment tree represents an interval. Given an array $A[1:n]$ of n elements, the segment tree T for a query Q is defined as follows:

i) The root node of T represents the result of the query Q over the whole array $A[1:n]$.

ii) Each leaf node of T represents the array element $A[i]$, $1 \leq i \leq n$.

iii) The internal nodes of T represent the result of the query Q over the interval $A[i:j]$, $0 \leq i, j \leq n$, that they represent.

Figure 8.15(a) represents the structure of a segment tree for $A[1:7]$.

8.8.4.2. *Construction*

Given the array $A[1: n]$, the root node of the segment tree T represents the result of query Q over the whole array $A[1:n]$. To get the result, the range $[1: n]$ is broken into two halves:

$$\left[1 : \left\lfloor \frac{(n+1)}{2} \right\rfloor\right] \text{ and } \left[\left\lfloor \frac{(n+1)}{2} \right\rfloor + 1 : n\right].$$

Two child nodes for the root node are created: the left child node representing the result of query Q over subarray $A\left[1 : \left\lfloor \frac{(n+1)}{2} \right\rfloor\right]$ and the right child node representing the result of the query Q over subarray $A\left[\left\lfloor \frac{(n+1)}{2} \right\rfloor + 1 : n\right]$. Proceeding in a similar way, each node branches out into two child nodes with each child node representing the lower half or the upper half of the interval represented by its parent node. This progresses level after level until the leaf nodes represent single elements $A[i:i]$ (that is $A[i]$) of the array. Thus, the total number of nodes in the segment tree T would be $n+ (n-1) = 2.n - 1$.

It is to be noted that for an array $A[1 : n]$ for a query Q, the structure of the segment tree is fixed and cannot be altered. However, updates to the elements in the array can be undertaken by altering the contents of the nodes $A[i]$ and propagating the change upwards ending with the root node. A segment tree could be conveniently represented using a linear array.

EXAMPLE 8.6.–

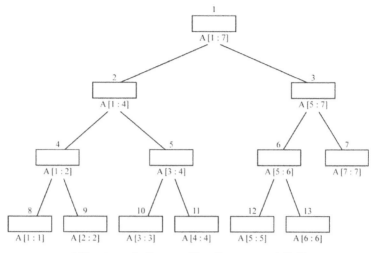

a) Structure of a Segment Tree for an array A [1:7]

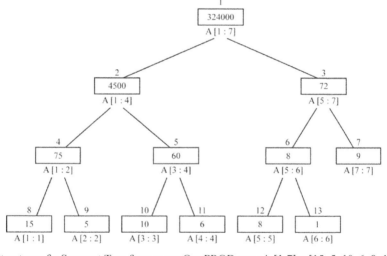

b) Structure of a Segment Tree for a query Q = PROD over A [1:7] = [15, 5, 10, 6, 8, 1, 9]

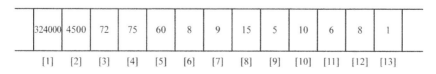

324000	4500	72	75	60	8	9	15	5	10	6	8	1
[1]	[2]	[3]	[4]	[5]	[6]	[7]	[8]	[9]	[10]	[11]	[12]	[13]

c) Array representation of the Segment tree shown in (b)

Figure 8.15. *Structure and representation of a segment tree*

Consider an array $A[1:7] = [15, 5, 10, 6, 8, 1, 9]$ over which a query Q = PROD, which finds the product of a range of elements belonging to A, is frequently undertaken. The segment tree over Q = PROD for $A[1:7]$ is as shown in Figure 8.15(b). It can be deciphered that each node represents the product of the array elements in the interval they represent. Thus, node 1, the root node, represents the product of the array $A[1:7]$ and node 5 represents product of the array $A[3:4]$. Observe how the *leaf nodes of the segment tree are represented by the individual array elements A[i]*. Figure 8.15(c) represents an array representation of the segment tree shown in Figure 8.15(b).

8.8.4.3. Operations

The segment tree supports two operations, namely,

i) *query Q* over a range $A[l : r]$ of the array $A[1:n]$;

ii) *update A[i]* such that $A[i] = x$, where x is the updated value for the array element concerned.

8.8.4.4. Querying a segment tree

While trying to obtain the output of the query Q over an interval $A[l : r]$ using the segment tree, the following cases may present themselves.

Let *[start, end]* represent the interval of the current node in the segment tree and *[l, r]* the interval specified by query Q:

i) If the interval *[start, end]* of the node is completely outside the given interval *[l,r]*, then the result returned by the node is a constant α, where α can be 0 or 1 or a very large number or a very small number, depending on the query Q. The objective behind returning an appropriate constant is to circumvent the exception that this case throws during the querying of the tree. This case acts as a base case in a recursive implementation of the query Q over the segment tree.

ii) If the interval *[start, end]* of the node is completely inside the given interval *[l,r]*, then return the result of the query Q over the node, which is the value of query Q worked over the elements in the interval *[start, end]* of the array A represented by the node. This case also works as another base case in a recursive implementation of the query Q over the segment tree.

iii) If the interval *[start, end]* is partially inside and partially outside interval *[l, r]*, then return the value of the query Q executed over the left child and the right child of the node. This case triggers double recursion in a recursive implementation of the query Q over the segment tree, when both the left subtree and the right subtree are traversed.

EXAMPLE 8.7.–

Figure 8.16 illustrates a recursive pseudo-code procedure QUERYPROD_TREE that undertakes querying product operations over a segment tree. Here, node is the current node, [start, end] are the intervals of the current node and [l, r] is the interval over which query Q = PROD (product operation) has to work. SEGMENTTREE is an array that stores the values of the query Q over the elements of the array A, as well as the individual elements of the array themselves, which occupy the leaf nodes of the segment tree (see Figure 8.15(c)). As can be observed, 2*node and 2*node+1 indicate the left child node and the right child node of the current node in the segment tree.

```
procedure QUERYPROD_TREE (node, start, end, l, r)

    /*[start, end]  is completely outside the given
       range[l, r]*/
    if  (r < start or end < l)then return 1;

    /*[start, end]  is completely inside the given
       range[l, r]*/
    if  (l <= start and end <= r) then return
                              SEGMENTTREE [node];

    /*[start, end]  is partially inside and
        partially outside the given range[l, r]*/

    mid = (start + end) / 2;
    leftQ = call QUERYPROD_TREE (2*node, start,
                                 mid, l, r);
    rightQ = call QUERYPROD_TREE (2*node+1, mid+1,
                                  end, l, r);
    return(leftQ * rightQ);

end QUERYPROD_TREE
```

Figure 8.16. *Recursive pseudo-code to undertake querying of a segment tree for query Q = PROD over array segment A[l:r]*

EXAMPLE 8.8.–

For the segment tree shown in Figures 8.15(b) and (c) for the query Q = PROD (product) over array $A[1:7]$ = $[15, 5, 10, 6, 8, 1, 9]$, the tree of recursive calls when the product of elements in $A[2:5]$ is queried using the procedure QUERYPROD_TREE, is shown in Figure 8.17.

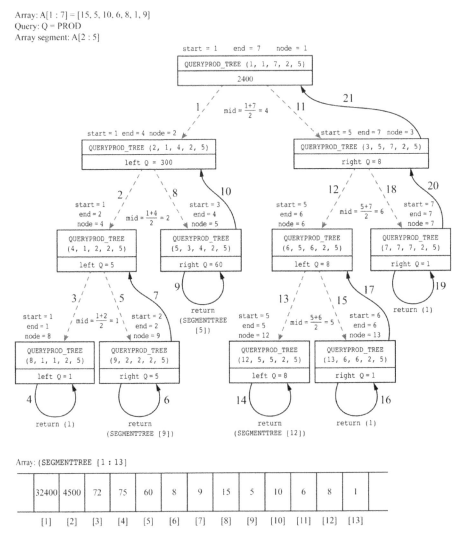

Array: $A[1 : 7]$ = $[15, 5, 10, 6, 8, 1, 9]$
Query: Q = PROD
Array segment: $A[2 : 5]$

Figure 8.17. *Tree of recursive calls during execution of QUERYPROD_TREE to obtain product of the array segment discussed in Example 8.8*

The opening call is QUERYPROD_TREE(1, 1, 7, 2, 5) and the result returned by the recursive procedure is 2400. Each box in the figure represents a call to the recursive procedure QUERYPROD_TREE(node, start, end, l, r). The upper compartment of the box denotes the call to the recursive function, and the lower compartment denotes the value returned to the function. While the parameters l, r are constant for all the recursive calls, the input parameters node, start, end that vary with each recursive call have been displayed on top of each box in the figure. The broken lines show the forward calls to the recursive function, and the solid lines denote the stage when the recursive calls terminate and return values to the calling function. mid, which bifurcates the array and therefore results in building the recursive calls to the left child and right child of a parent node in the segment tree, is displayed beneath the boxes.

It can be observed that the solid edges labeled 4, 16 and 19 represent the base case in the recursive procedure when a 1 is returned, because [start, end] is completely outside the given range [l, r] for the specific nodes. On the other hand, solid edges labeled 6, 9 and 14 represent the base case in the recursive procedure when SEGMENTTREE [node] is returned, because [start, end] is completely inside the given range [l, r] for the specific nodes. The array which stores the segment tree is also shown in the figure. The calls and returns can be easily understood by following the edges of the tree of recursive calls in the order of their serial number labels. When the first recursive call ends (solid edge labeled 21), the result of the query Q = PROD for the array segment $A[2:5]$, which is 2400, is output.

8.8.4.5. *Updating a segment tree*

A segment tree cannot be modified in structure and supports only updates to the array elements which build it. Let us suppose an array element $A[k]$ needs to be updated with a new value. Though updating an array element is an $O(1)$ time complexity operation, since the nodes of the segment tree represent values of query Q over different intervals of the array A, the updated value of $A[k]$ beginning with the leaf node has to be propagated until the root node of the segment tree is reached, while updating the values stored in the nodes along the path.

The procedure is simple in that we start with the root node whose interval is [start, end], split the interval at its midpoint, mid = (start + end)/2 and check if the index k lies within the subinterval [start, mid] or [mid+1, end]. In the case of the former, traverse down the left subtree and in the case of the latter traverse down the right subtree. The procedure repeats until the leaf node storing the value of A[k] is reached. The value is updated and the path retraced, only to update all the values in the intermediate nodes until the root node. The segment tree now represents the updated array elements for the query Q.

Figure 8.18 shows a recursive pseudo-code procedure to undertake the update operation on a segment tree that queries product operations over an array of elements.

```
procedure UPDATEPROD_TREE (node, start, end, index, value)

    if (start == end) then SEGMENTTREE [node] = value;
                    /* Update leaf node representing A[k] */
    else

        mid = (start + end) / 2;
        if index ∈ [ start, mid] then
        call UPDATEPROD_TREE (2*node, start, mid, index, value);
            /* recursively traverse through the left subtree */
        else
        call UPDATEPROD_TREE (2*node+1, mid+1, end, index, value);
            /* recursively traverse through the right subtree */
        end
        SEGMENTTREE[node]  = SEGMENTTREE[2*node]  *
                                        SEGMENTTREE [2*node+1];
    end
end UPDATEPROD_TREE
```

Figure 8.18. *Recursive pseudo-code procedure to undertake updates on a segment tree for query Q = PROD*

EXAMPLE 8.9.–

For the segment tree shown in Figures 8.15(b) and (c) over the query Q = PROD and array *A[1:7] = [15, 5, 10, 6, 8, 1, 9]*, the tree of recursive calls when the array element *A[6]* is updated to 12, using the procedure UPDATEPROD_TREE is shown in Figure 8.19. The opening call is UPDATEPROD_TREE(1, 1, 7, 6, 12). The broken lines show the forward calls to the recursive function and the solid lines when the recursive calls terminate and return values to the calling function. The recursive function ensures updating the value of the array element, as well as those of all the intermediate nodes of the segment tree on the path from the leaf node to the root node, as it propagates the updated value of *A*[6] upwards. The calls and returns of the recursive procedure can be easily understood by following the edges of the tree of recursive calls in the order of their serial number labels. The shaded cells of the array SEGMENTTREE in Figure 8.18 shows the updates made to node 13 (SEGMENTTREE [13]) representing *A*[6], as well as the intermediate nodes labeled node 6 (SEGMENTTREE [6]), node 3 (SEGMENTTREE [3]) and the root, node 1 (SEGMENTTREE [1]).

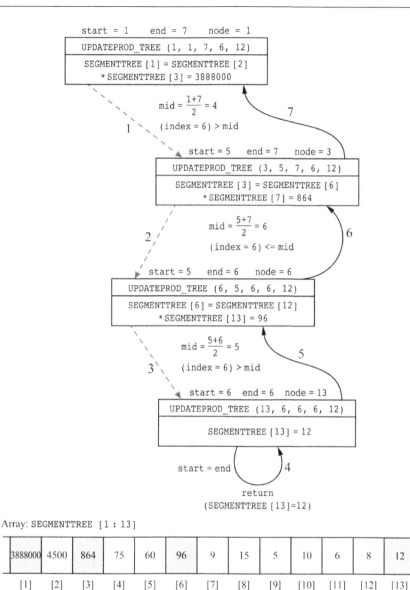

Figure 8.19. *Tree of recursive calls during execution of UPDATEPROD_TREE for the array update discussed in Example 8.9*

ADT for binary trees

Data objects:
A   binary tree of nodes each holding one (or more)
data field(s) DATA and   two link fields, LCHILD and
RCHILD.   T points to the root node of the binary tree.

Operations:
Check if binary tree T is empty
CHECK_BINTREE_EMPTY(T)   (Boolean function)

Make a binary tree T empty by setting T to NIL
MAKE_BINTREE_EMPTY (T)

Move to the left subtree of a node X by moving
down its LCHILD pointer
MOVE_LEFT_SUBTREE(X)

Move to the right subtree of a node X by moving
down its RCHILD pointer
MOVE_RIGHT_SUBTREE(X)

Insert node containing element ITEM as the root of the
binary tree T; Ensure that T does not point to any node
before execution
INSERT_ROOT (T, ITEM)

Insert node containing ITEM as the left child of
node X; Ensure that X does not have a left child
node before execution
INSERT_LEFT (X, ITEM)

Insert node containing ITEM as the right child of node
X; Ensure that X does not have a right child node
before execution
INSERT_RIGHT (X, ITEM)

Delete root node of binary tree T; Ensure that the root
does not have child nodes
DELETE_ROOT (T)

Delete   node pointed to by X from the binary tree
and set X to point to the left child of the node;
Ensure that the node pointed to by X does not have a
right child

DELETE_POINT_LEFTCHILD(X)

Delete node pointed to by X from the binary tree
and set X to point to the right child of the node;
Ensure that the node pointed to by X does not have a
left child

DELETE_POINT_RIGHTCHILD(X)

Store ITEM into a node whose address is X

STORE_DATA(X, ITEM)

Retrieve data of a node whose address is X and return
it in ITEM

RETRIEVE_DATA(X, ITEM)

Perform Inorder traversal of binary tree T

INORDER_TRAVERSAL(T)

Perform Preorder traversal of binary tree T

PREORDER_TRAVERSAL(T)

Perform Postorder traversal of binary tree T

POSTORDER_TRAVERSAL(T)

Summary

– Trees and binary trees are nonlinear data structures, which are inherently two dimensional in structure.

– While trees are non-empty and may have nodes of any degree, a binary tree may be empty or hold nodes of degree of two, at most.

– The terminologies of root node, height, level, parent, children, sibling, ancestors, leaf or terminal nodes and non-terminal nodes are applicable to both trees and binary trees.

– While trees are efficiently represented using linked representations, binary trees are represented using both array and linked representations.

– The traversals of a binary tree are inorder, postorder and preorder.

– A prudent use of null pointers in the linked representation of a binary tree yields a threaded binary tree.

– The application of binary trees has been demonstrated on expression trees, segment trees and their related concepts.

– The ADT of the binary tree is presented.

8.9. Illustrative problems

PROBLEM 8.1.–

For the binary tree shown in Figure P8.1:

a) Identify.

(i) Root, (ii) Children of G, (iii) Parent of D, (iv) Siblings of Z, (v) Level of C, (vi) Ancestors of Y, (vii) Leaf nodes, (viii) Height of the binary tree.

b) Obtain the inorder, postorder and preorder traversals of the binary tree.

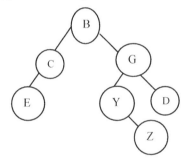

Figure P8.1. *An example binary tree*

Solution:

a) (i) Root: B, (ii) Children of G: Y,D, (iii) Parent of D: G, (iv) Siblings of Z: None, (v) Level of C: 2, (vi) Ancestors of Y: G, B, (vii) Leaf nodes: E, Z, D, (viii) Height of the binary tree: 4.

b) Inorder traversal: ECBYZGD.

The output of the traversal which follows the scheme of Algorithm 8.1 can be dissected as

E   C
|_____|
traverse left subtree of root

B
process root

Y   Z   G   D
|_____|
traverse right subtree of root

Postorder traversal: ECZYDGB.

The output of the traversal following the scheme of Algorithm 8.2 can be dissected as

E   C
|_____|
traverse left subtree of root

Z   Y   D   G
|_____|
traverse right subtree of root

B
process root

Preorder traversal: BCEGYZD

The output of the traversal following the scheme of Algorithm 8.3 can be dissected as

B
Process root

C   E
|_____|
traverse left subtree of root

G   Y   Z   D
|_____|
traverse right subtree of root

PROBLEM 8.2.–

Obtain an array representation and a linked representation of the binary tree shown in Figure P8.1.

Solution:

To obtain the array representation we first number the nodes of the binary tree akin to that of a complete binary tree, as shown below:

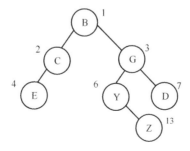

The array representation is given as:

B	C	G	E		Y	D					Z
[1]	[2]	[3]	[4]	[5]	[6]	[7]	[8]	[9]	[10]	[11]	[12] [13]

The linked representation where T is the pointer to the root node, is given as:

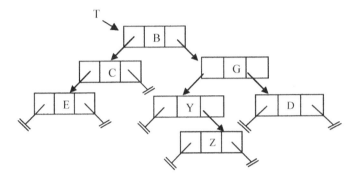

PROBLEM 8.3.–

A binary tree T has nine nodes. The inorder and preorder traversals of T yield the following:

– Inorder traversal (I): E A C K F H D B G

– Preorder traversal (P): F A E K C D H G B

Draw the binary tree T.

Solution:

The key to the solution of this problem is the observation that the first occurring node in a preorder traversal is the root of the binary tree and that once the root is known, the nodes forming the left and the right subtrees can be extracted from the Inorder traversal list. Application of this key to each of the left and right subtree by obtaining their respective roots from the preorder traversal and moving on to inorder traversal to obtain the nodes forming the respective subtrees can eventually lead to the tracing of the binary tree.

From P: Root of the binary tree is F.

From I: The nodes forming the left and right subtrees of F are

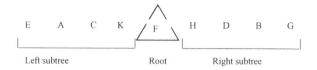

Left subtree   Root   Right subtree

The binary tree can be roughly traced as shown below:

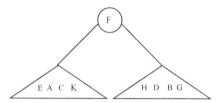

In the next step, we proceed to obtain the structure of the left and right subtrees.

From P: Root of the left subtree is A and root of the right subtree is D.

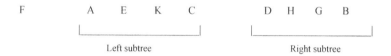

Left subtree   Right subtree

From I: The nodes forming the left and right sub-subtrees are

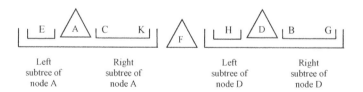

Left   Right   Left   Right
subtree of   subtree of   subtree of   subtree of
node A   node A   node D   node D

Tracing the binary tree yields,

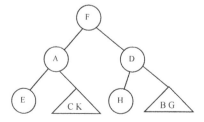

Proceeding in a similar fashion, we obtain the roots of the subtrees {C,K} and {B,G} to be K and G, respectively. The final trace yields the binary tree:

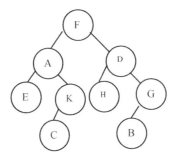

PROBLEM 8.4.–

Make use of the infix and postfix expressions given below to trace the corresponding expression tree:

Infix: A + B * C / F ↑ H

Postfix: A B C * F H ↑ / +

Solution:

The key to the problem is similar to the one discussed in illustrative problem 8.3 but for the difference that the root node to be picked from the postfix expression is the last occurring node.

Thus, the expression tree traced in the first step is:

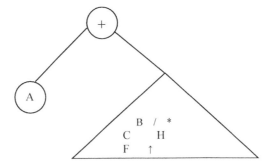

In the next step, the expression tree traced would be

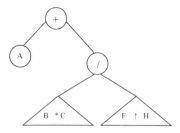

Progressing in this way, the final expression tree is obtained as

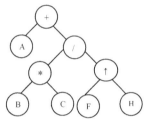

NOTE.– Though the expression tree could be easily traced from infix expression alone, the objective of the problem is to emphasize the fact that a binary tree can be traced from its inorder and postorder traversals as well.

PROBLEM 8.5.–

What does the following pseudo-code procedure do to the binary tree given in Figure P8.5, when invoked as WHAT_DO_I_DO (THIS) ?

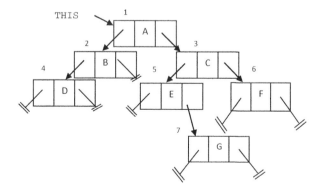

Figure P8.5. *A binary tree* THIS

```
procedure WHAT_DO_I_DO(HERE)
  if HERE ≠ NIL then
    {call WHAT_DO_I_DO(LEFT CHILD(HERE));
     if (LEFT CHILD(HERE) = NIL)and
        (RIGHT  CHILD(HERE) =  NIL)
     then print DATA (HERE);
     call WHAT_DO_I_DO (RCHILD(HERE));
    }
  end WHAT_DO_I_DO.
```

Solution:

We trace the recursive procedure using a stack and for convenience of representing the nodes in the stack, the nodes are numbered from 1 to 7. For every call of WHAT_DO_I_DO(), we keep track of HERE, LCHILD(HERE) and RCHILD (HERE).

The first call of WHAT_DO_I_DO(THIS) results in the following snapshot of the stack:

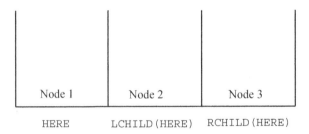

Node 1	Node 2	Node 3
HERE	LCHILD(HERE)	RCHILD(HERE)

In the subsequent calls, the snapshot of the stack is given by

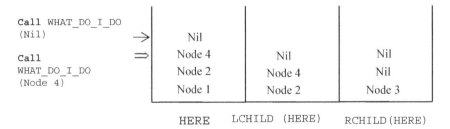

Call WHAT_DO_I_DO (Nil) → Call WHAT_DO_I_DO (Node 4) ⇒	Nil		
	Node 4	Nil	Nil
	Node 2	Node 4	Nil
	Node 1	Node 2	Node 3
	HERE	LCHILD (HERE)	RCHILD(HERE)

When HERE = NIL, that call of WHAT_DO_I_DO (HERE) (marked $\rightarrow$) terminates and the control returns to the previous call, viz., WHAT_DO_I_DO (Node 4) (marked $\Rightarrow$). Here, LCHILD (HERE) = RCHILD (HERE) = NIL. Hence, DATA (Node 4), viz., D is printed. Now the control moves further to invoke the call WHAT_DO_I_DO(RCHILD(Node 4)) that is WHAT_DO_I_DO (NIL), which again terminates. Now the control returns to the call WHAT_DO_I_DO (Node 2) and so on. It is easy to see that WHAT_DO_I_DO (THIS) prints the data fields of all leaf nodes of the binary tree. Hence, the output is D, G and F.

PROBLEM 8.6.–

Show that the maximum number of nodes in a binary tree of height h is $2^h - 1$, $h \geq 1$.

Solution:

It is known that the maximum number of nodes in level i of a binary tree is 2^{i-1}. Given the height of the binary tree to be h which is the maximum level, the maximum number of nodes is given by:

$$\sum_{i=1}^{h} 2^{i-1} = 1 + 2 + 2^2 + \dots + 2^{h-1}$$

$$= 2^h - 1$$

PROBLEM 8.7.–

Show that for a non-empty binary tree T if n_o is the number of leaf nodes and n_2 is the number of nodes of degree 2, then $n_o = n_2 + 1$.

Solution:

Let n be the number of nodes in a non-empty binary tree and let n_1 be the number of nodes of degree 1.

Now, $n = n_o + n_1 + n_2$ .... (i)

Again if b is the number of links or branches in the binary tree, all nodes except the root node hang from a branch yielding the relation

$$b = n - 1 \ldots\ldots \tag{ii}$$

Also, each branch emanates from a node whose degree is either 1 or 2. Hence,

$$b = n_1 + 2.n_2 \ldots\ldots \tag{iii}$$

Subtracting (iii) from (ii) yields

$$n = n_1 + 2n_2 + 1 \ldots\ldots \tag{iv}$$

From (iv) and (i), we obtain

$$n_o = n_2 + 1$$

PROBLEM 8.8.–

A binary tree is stored in the memory of a computer as shown below. Trace the structure of the binary tree.

	LCHILD	DATA	RCHILD
1	2	844	6
2	0	796	0
3	0	110	0
4	0	565	9
5	12	444	0
6	10	116	0
7	4	123	1
8	0	444	0
9	8	767	3
10	0	344	0

Root : 7

Solution:

Given the root node's address is 7, we begin tracing the binary tree from the root onwards. The binary tree is given by:

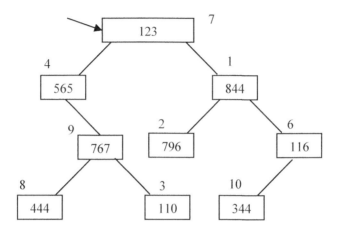

PROBLEM 8.9.–

Outline a linked representation for the tree and threaded binary tree representation for the binary tree shown in Figure P8.9(a) and (b), respectively.

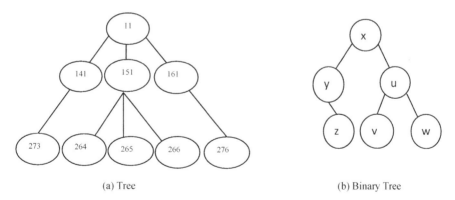

(a) Tree

(b) Binary Tree

Figure P8.9. *A tree and a binary tree*

Solution:

Following the node structure of TAG, DATA/ DOWNLINK, LINK illustrated in section 8.3, the linked representation of the (TREE) is given by:

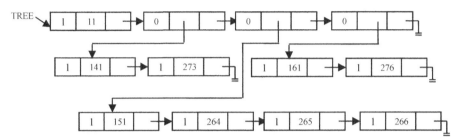

The threaded binary representation (T) of Figure P8.9(b) is illustrated below and is obtained by following the node structure detailed in section 8.7.1.

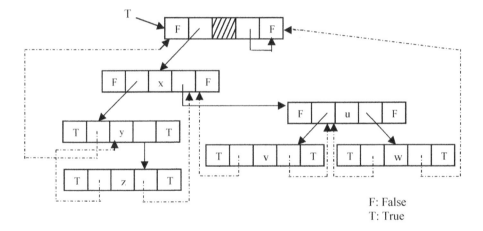

F: False
T: True

The inorder traversal sequence to be tracked by the threads is: y z x v u w. The threads are linked to the appropriate inorder successors and predecessors.

PROBLEM 8.10.–

For the binary tree T given in Figure P8.10, obtain (i) a one-way inorder threading of T and (ii) one-way preorder threading of T.

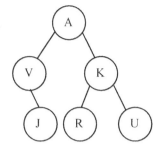

Figure P8.10. *A binary tree T*

Solution:

(i) The inorder traversal of the binary tree T yields: V J A R K U.

A one-way threading of T is obtained by replacing the RCHILD links of the nodes, which are null by threads pointing to the inorder successor of the node. Thus, the RCHILD link of J points to A, that of R points to K and that of U is either kept dangling (or if there is a head node, it points to the same). The threaded binary tree is shown below:

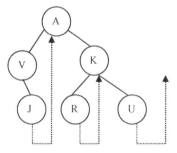

(ii) The preorder traversal of binary T yields: A V J K R U.

For the one-way preorder threading, the RCHILD links of the nodes, which are null, are set to point to the preorder successors of the node. Thus, the RCHILD link of J points to K, that of R points to U and the same of U is a dangling thread or may be connected to the head node if available. The threaded tree for the same is shown below:

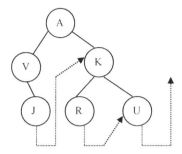

PROBLEM 8.11.–

The *range minimum query* (**RMQ**) problem in computer science involves finding the index of the minimum element of a segment or interval in an array of elements that are comparable. Thus, given an array $A[1:n]$ and an interval $[l:r]$, RMQ finds k such that $A[k]$ = min, where min is the minimum element of $A[l:r]$. The worst case complexity to execute RMQ over array $A[1:n]$ is $O(n)$.

Build a segment tree for query Q = RMQ over $A[1:6]$ = [16, 7, 3, 5, 1, 3] and find RMQ over $A[3:5]$ using the segment tree.

Solution:

Figure P8.11 illustrates the segment tree constructed for Q = RMQ over $A[1:6]$ = [16, 7, 3, 5, 1, 3]. RMQ over $A[3:5]$ yields the minimum element as $A[5]$ = 1. Recursive procedures similar to QUERYPROD_TREE and UPDATEPROD_TREE discussed in Figures 8.16 and 8.18 can be constructed for the query Q = RMQ.

Array: A[1 : 6] = [16, 7, 3, 5, 1, 3]
Query: Q = RMQ

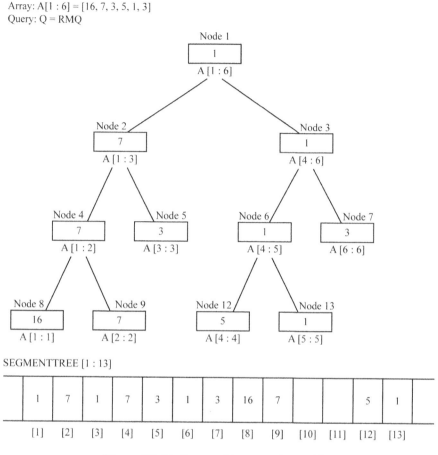

SEGMENTTREE [1 : 13]

1	7	1	7	3	1	3	16	7			5	1
[1]	[2]	[3]	[4]	[5]	[6]	[7]	[8]	[9]	[10]	[11]	[12]	[13]

Figure P8.11. *Segment tree constructed for
QUERY Q = RMQ over array A[1:6]=[16, 7, 3, 5, 1, 3]*

Review questions

1) Which among the following is not a property of a tree?

i) There is a specially designated node called the root.

ii) The rest of the nodes could be partitioned into t disjoint sets

(t > 0) each set representing a tree T_i, i = 1,2, . . . t known as subtree of the tree.

iii) Any node should be reachable from anywhere in the tree.

iv) At most one cycle could be present in the tree.

a) (i)   b) (ii)   c) (iii)   d) (iv)

2) The maximum number of nodes in a binary tree of depth k is:

a) 2^{k-1},   b) $2^{(k+1)} - 1$ c) $2^k - 1$ d) $2^{(k+1)-1}$

3) For a binary tree of $2.k$ nodes, $k > 1$, the number of pointers and the number of null pointers that the tree would use for its representation is, respectively, given by:

a) k and $k + 1$ b) $2.k$ and $2.k + 1$ c) $4.k$ and $4.k + 1$

d) $4.k$ and $2.k + 1$

4) An inorder and postorder traversal of a binary tree was "claimed" to yield the following sequence:

Inorder traversal: HAT GLOVE SOCKS SCARF GLASSES

Post order traversal: GLOVE SCARF HAT GLASSES SOCKS

What are your observations?

i) HAT is the root of the binary tree.

ii) SOCKS is the root of the binary tree.

iii) The binary tree is a skewed binary tree.

iv) The traversals are incorrect.

a) (i)   b) (ii)   c) (iii)   d) (iv)

5) Which of the following observations with regard to binary tree traversals is incorrect?

i) Given a preorder traversal of a binary tree, the root node is the first occurring item in the list.

ii) Given a postorder traversal of a binary tree, the root node is the last occurring item in the list.

iii) Inorder traversal does not directly reveal the root node of the binary tree.

iv) To trace back the structure of the binary tree, inorder, postorder and preorder traversal sequences are needed.

6) Sketch (i) an array representation and (ii) a linked list representation for the following binary tree:

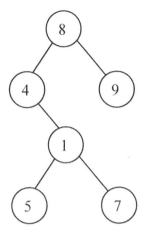

7) Sketch a linked representation for a threaded binary tree equivalent to the binary tree shown in review question 6.

8) Obtain inorder and postorder traversals for the binary tree shown in review question 6.

9) Draw an expression tree for the following logical expression:

p **and** (q **or not** k) **and** (s **or** b **or** h).

10) Undertake postorder traversal of the expression tree obtained in review question 9 and compare it with the hand-computed postfix form of the logical expression.

11) Given the following inorder and preorder traversals, trace the binary tree:

Inorder traversal: B F G H R S T W Y Z

Postorder traversal: F B H G S R Y T W Z

12) Making use of Algorithm 8.4, convert the following infix expression to its equivalent postfix form and evaluate the postfix expression for the specified values:

$(x + y + z) \uparrow (a + b) - g * n * m + r$

$x = 1, y = 2, z = -1, a = 1, b = 2, g = 5, n = 2, m = 1, r = 7$

13) What are the advantages of representing a list of elements over which a query Q is repeatedly executed, as a segment tree rather than a linear array?

14) Construct a segment tree for a query Q = SUM over an array $A[1:n]$ of elements.

Programming assignments

1) Write a program to input a binary tree implemented as a linked representation. Execute Algorithms 8.1-8.3 to perform inorder, postorder and preorder traversals of the binary tree.

2) Implement Algorithm 8.4 to convert an infix expression into its postfix form.

3) Write a recursive procedure to count the number of nodes in a binary tree.

4) Implement a threaded binary tree. Write procedures to insert a node NEW to the left of node NODE when:

i) the left subtree of NODE is empty;

ii) the left subtree of NODE is non-empty.

5) Write non-recursive procedures to perform the inorder, postorder and preorder traversals of a binary tree.

6) **Level order traversal**: It is a kind of binary tree traversal where elements in the binary tree are traversed by levels, top to bottom and within levels, left to right. Write a procedure to execute the level order traversal of a binary tree. (Hint: Use a queue data structure.)

Example: Level order traversal of the following binary tree is: 8 4 7 5 3 9.

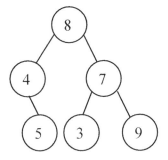

7) Implement the ADT of a binary tree in a language of your choice. Include operations to (i) obtain the height of a binary tree and (ii) the list of leaf nodes.

8) Write a recursive function BUILDRMQ_TREE which will construct a segment tree for a query Q = RMQ over an array A[1:n], as discussed in illustrative problem 8.11.

9) Write recursive functions QUERYRMQ_TREE and UPDATERMQ_TREE, on the lines of the recursive procedures QUERYPROD_TREE and UPDATEPROD_ TREE discussed in Figures 8.16 and 8.18, for query Q = RMQ over the segment tree obtained by BUILDRMQ_TREE in programming assignment 8. Tie the recursive functions together under a menu-driven program, which will help perform repeated queries and updates on the segment tree.

9

Graphs

In Chapter 8, we introduced trees and graphs as examples of nonlinear data structures. To recall, nonlinear data structures, unlike linear data structures which are unidimensional in structure (e.g. arrays), are inherently two dimensional in structure.

In the field of computer science, trees have been recognized as efficient nonlinear data structures with their own set of terminologies and concepts to suit the needs of the digital computer. **Graph theory**, which has emerged as an independent field, encompasses studies on trees as well. In other words, in the field of graph theory, a tree is a special kind of graph holding a definition which in principle agrees with that of a tree data structure, but is devoid of most of the terminologies and concepts tagged to it from the view point of data structures. This distinction needs to be borne in mind when one defines a tree – rather "redefines" a tree as a special kind of graph in this chapter.

Graph theory has turned out to be a vast area with innumerable applications. However, in this book, we restrict the scope of this chapter to introducing graphs as effective data structures only. Hence, only those concepts and terminologies needed to promote this aspect of graphs and specific applications, which are relevant to computer science, are dealt with.

9.1. Introduction

The history of graphs dates back to 1736 in what is now referred to as the classical **Koenigsberg bridge problem**. In the town of Koenigsberg in Eastern Prussia, the island of Kneiphof existed in the middle of the river Pregal. The river bifurcated itself bordering the land areas as shown in Figure 9.1. There were seven bridges connecting the land areas as we can see from the figure. The problem was to find whether the people of the town could **walk** on the seven bridges once only, starting from any land area, and returning to the starting land area after traversing all the bridges.

An example walk is listed as follows:

Start from land area P – traverse bridge 1; land area R – traverse bridge 3; land area Q – traverse bridge 4; land area R – traverse bridge 5; land area S – traverse bridge 7; land area Q – traverse bridge 7; land area S – traverse bridge 6; land area P – traverse bridge 2; land area R.

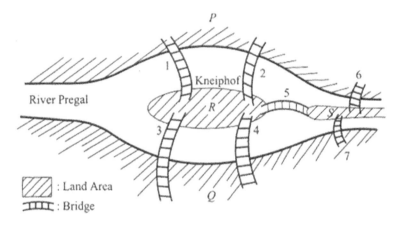

Figure 9.1. *The Koenigsberg bridge problem*

This walk, neither traverses all bridges once only nor reaches its starting point which is land area P.

It was left to Euler to solve the puzzle of Koenigsberg bridge problem by stating that there is no way that people could walk across the bridges once only and return to the starting point. The solution to the problem was arrived at by representing the land areas as circles called **vertices** and bridges as arcs called **links** or **edges** connecting the circles. Defining the **degree of a vertex** to be the number of arcs converging on it, or in other words, the number of bridges which descend on a land area, Euler showed that *a walk is possible only when all the vertices have even degree*. That is, every land area needs to have only even number of bridges descending on it. In the case of the Koenigsberg bridge problem, all the vertices turned out to have an **odd degree**. Figure 9.2 illustrates the graph representation of the Koenigsberg bridge problem. This vertex-edge representation is what came to be known as a **graph** (here it is a **multigraph**). The walk which, beginning from a vertex and returning to it after traversing all edges in the graph exactly once, is known as an **Eulerian walk**.

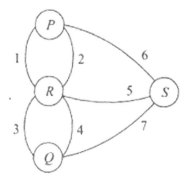

Figure 9.2. *Graph representation of the Koenigsberg bridge problem*

Since this first application, graph theory has grown *in leaps and bounds* to encompass a wide range of applications in the fields of cybernetics, electrical sciences, genetics and linguistics, to quote a few.

9.2. Definitions and basic terminologies

Graph

A *graph* G = (*V, E*) consists of a finite non-empty set of *vertices* *V* also called *points* or *nodes* and a finite set *E* of unordered pairs of distinct vertices called *edges* or *arcs* or *links*.

Example

Figure 9.3 illustrates a graph. Here, V = {*a, b, c ,d*} and E = {(*a, b*), (*a, c*), (*b, c*), (*c, d*)}. However, it is convenient to represent edges using labels as shown in the figure.

V. Vertices. {*a, b, c, d*}

E. Edges. {*e₁, e₂, e₃, e₄*}

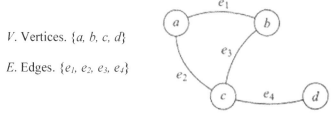

Figure 9.3. *A graph*

A graph $G = (V, E)$, where $E = \phi$, is called as a **null** or **empty graph**. A graph with one vertex and no edges is called a **trivial graph**.

Multigraph

A **multigraph** $G = (V, E)$ also consists of a set of vertices and edges except that E may contain **multiple edges**, that is, edges connecting the same pair of vertices, or may contain **loops** or **self edges**, that is, an edge whose end points are the same vertex.

Example

Figure 9.4 illustrates a multigraph.

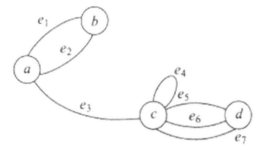

Figure 9.4. *A multigraph*

Observe the multiple edges e_1, e_2 connecting vertices a, b and e_5, e_6, e_7 connecting vertices c, d, respectively. Also note the self edge e_4.

However, it has to be made clear that graphs do not contain multiple edges or loops and hence are different from multigraphs. The definitions and terminologies to be discussed in this section are applicable only to graphs.

Directed and undirected graphs

A graph whose definition makes reference to *unordered pairs of vertices* as edges is known as an **undirected graph**. The edge e_{ij} of such an undirected graph is represented as (v_i, v_j), where v_i, v_j are distinct vertices. Thus, an undirected edge (v_i, v_j) is equivalent to (v_j, v_i).

On the other hand, ***directed graphs*** or ***digraphs*** make reference to edges which are directed, that is, edges which are ***ordered pairs of vertices***. The edge e_{ij} is referred to as $<v_i, v_j>$ which is distinct from $<v_j, v_i>$, where v_i, v_j are distinct vertices. In $<v_i, v_j>$, v_i is known as ***tail*** of the edge and v_j as the ***head***.

Example

Figures 9.5(a) and (b) illustrate a digraph and an undirected graph.

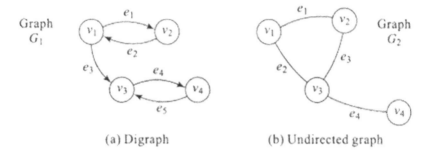

(a) Digraph   (b) Undirected graph

Figure 9.5. *A digraph and an undirected graph*

In Figure 9.5(a), e_1 is a directed edge between v_1 and v_2, that is, $e_1 = <v_1, v_2>$, whereas in Figure 9.5(b), e_1 is an undirected edge between v_1 and v_2, that is, $e_1 = (v_1, v_2)$.

The list of vertices and edges of graphs G_1 and G_2 are as follows:

– vertices (G_1). $\{v_1, v_2, v_3, v_4\}$

– vertices (G_2). $\{v_1, v_2, v_3, v_4\}$

– edges (G_1). $\{<v_1,v_2> <v_2,v_1> <v_1,v_3> <v_3,v_4> <v_4,v_3>\}$ or $\{e_1, e_2, e_3, e_4, e_5\}$

– edges (G_2). $\{(v_1,v_2) (v_1,v_3) (v_2,v_3) (v_3,v_4)\}$ or $\{e_1, e_2, e_3, e_4\}$

In the case of an undirected edge (v_i, v_j) in a graph, the vertices v_i, v_j are said to be ***adjacent*** or the edge (v_i,v_j) is said to be ***incident on vertices*** v_i, v_j. Thus, in Figure 9.5(b) vertices v_1,v_3 are adjacent to vertex v_2 and edges e_1: (v_1,v_2), e_3: (v_2,v_3) are incident on vertex v_2.

On the other hand, if $<v_i, v_j>$ is a directed edge, then v_i is said to be ***adjacent to*** v_j and v_j is said to be ***adjacent from*** v_i. The edge $<v_i, v_j>$ is ***incident*** to both v_i and v_j.

Thus, in Figure 9.5(a) vertices v_2 and v_3 are adjacent from v_1, and v_1 is adjacent to vertices v_2 and v_3. The edges incident to vertex v_3 are $<v_1, v_3>$, $<v_3, v_4>$ and $<v_4, v_3>$.

Complete graphs

The number of distinct unordered pairs (v_i, v_j), $v_i \neq v_j$ in a graph with n vertices is

$$n_{C_2} = \frac{n.(n-1)}{2}$$

An n vertex undirected graph with exactly $\frac{n.(n-1)}{2}$ edges is said to be **complete.**

A complete graph with n vertices is indicated by the symbol K_N.

Example

Figure 9.6 illustrates a complete graph K_4. The undirected graph with four vertices has all its $^4C_2 = 6$ edges intact.

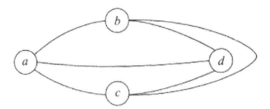

Figure 9.6. A complete graph K_4

In the case of a digraph with n vertices, the maximum number of edges is given by $n_{P_2} = n.(n-1)$. Such a graph with exactly $n.(n-1)$ edges is said to be a **complete digraph**.

Example

Figure 9.7(a) illustrates a digraph, which is complete, and Figure 9.7(b) illustrates a digraph, which is not complete.

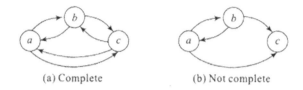

(a) Complete   (b) Not complete

Figure 9.7. *Digraphs which are complete and not complete*

Subgraph

A *subgraph* $G' = (V',E')$ of a graph $G = (V, E)$ is such that $V' \subseteq V$ and $E' \subseteq E$.

Example

Figure 9.8 illustrates some subgraphs of the directed and undirected graphs shown in Figure 9.5 (see Graphs G_1 and G_2).

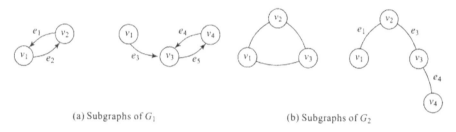

(a) Subgraphs of G_1 (b) Subgraphs of G_2

Figure 9.8. *Subgraphs of graphs G_1 and G_2 (see Figure 9.5)*

Path

A *path* from a vertex v_i to vertex v_j in an undirected graph G is a sequence of vertices $v_i, v_{l_1}, v_{l_2}, \ldots v_{l_k}, v_j$ such that (v_i,v_{l_1}) $(v_{l_1},v_{l_2}), \ldots (v_{l_k}, v_j)$ are edges in G. If G is directed, then the path from v_i to v_j more specially known as a *directed path* consists of edges $<v_i,v_{l_1}> < v_{l_1},v_{l_2}> \ldots <v_{l_k}, v_j>$ in G.

Example

Figure 9.9(a) illustrates a path P_1 from vertex v_1 to v_4 in graph G_1 of Figure 9.5(a), and Figure 9.9(b) illustrates a path P_2 from vertex v_1 to v_4 in graph G_2 of Figure 9.5(b).

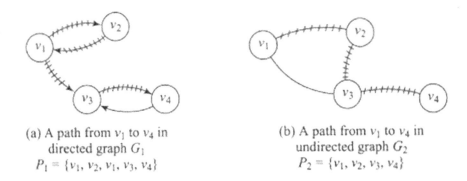

(a) A path from v_1 to v_4 in
directed graph G_1
$P_1 = \{v_1, v_2, v_1, v_3, v_4\}$

(b) A path from v_1 to v_4 in
undirected graph G_2
$P_2 = \{v_1, v_2, v_3, v_4\}$

Figure 9.9. *Path between vertices of a graph (see Figure 9.5)*

The *length of a path* is the number of edges on it.

Example

In Figure 9.9, the length of path P_1 is 4 and the length of path P_2 is 3.

A *simple path* is a path in which all the vertices except possibly the first and last vertices are distinct.

Example

In graph G_2 (see Figure 9.5(b)), the path from v_1 to v_4 given by $\{(v_1, v_2), (v_2, v_3), (v_3, v_4)\}$ and written as $\{v_1, v_2, v_3, v_4\}$ is a simple path, whereas the path from v_3 to v_4 given by $\{(v_3, v_1), (v_1, v_2), (v_2, v_3), (v_3, v_4)\}$ and written as $\{v_3, v_1, v_2, v_3, v_4\}$ is not a simple path but a path due to the repetition of vertices.

Also, in graph G_1 (see Figure 9.5(a)) the path from v_1 to v_3 given by $\{<v_1, v_2>, <v_2, v_1>, <v_1, v_3>\}$ written as $\{v_1, v_2, v_1, v_3\}$ is not a simple path but a mere path due to the repetition of vertices. However, the path from v_2 to v_4 given by $\{<v_2, v_1>, <v_1, v_3>, <v_3, v_4>\}$ written as $\{v_2, v_1, v_3, v_4\}$ is a simple path.

A *cycle* is a simple path in which the first and last vertices are the same. A cycle is also known as a *circuit*, *elementary cycle*, *circular path* or *polygon*.

Example

In graph G_2 (see Figure 9.5(b)), the path $\{v_1, v_2, v_3, v_1\}$ is a cycle. Also, in graph G_1 (see Figure 9.5(a)), the path $\{v_1, v_2, v_1\}$ is a cycle or more specifically a **directed cycle**.

Connected graphs

Two vertices v_i, v_j in a graph G are said to be **connected**, only if there is a path in G between v_i and v_j. In an undirected graph, if v_i and v_j are connected, then it automatically holds v_j and v_i as also connected.

An undirected graph is said to be a **connected graph,** if every pair of distinct vertices v_i, v_j are connected.

Example

Graph G_2 (see Figure 9.5(b)) is connected, whereas graph G_3 shown in Figure 9.10 is not connected.

In the case of an undirected graph which is not connected, the maximal **connected subgraph** is called as a **connected component** or simply a **component.**

Example

Graph G_3 (see Figure 9.10) has two connected components, viz., graph G_{31} and G_{32}.

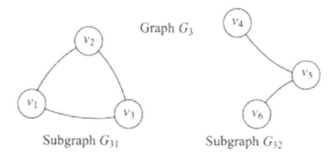

Figure 9.10. *An undirected graph with two connected components*

A directed graph is said to be ***strongly connected*** if every pair of distinct vertices v_i, v_j are connected (by means of a directed path). Thus, if there exists a directed path from v_i to v_j, then there also exists a directed path from v_j to v_i.

Example

Graph G_4 shown in Figure 9.11 is strongly connected.

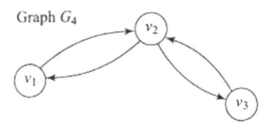

Figure 9.11. *A strongly connected graph*

However, the digraph shown in Figure 9.12 is not strongly connected but is said to possess two ***strongly connected components***. A strongly connected component is a maximal subgraph that is strongly connected.

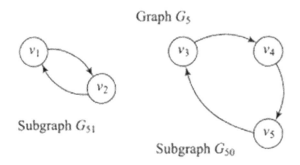

Figure 9.12. *Strongly connected components of a digraph*

Trees

A ***tree*** is defined to be a connected acyclic graph. The following properties are satisfied by a tree:

i) there exists a path between any two vertices of the tree;

ii) no cycles must be present in the tree. In other words, trees are acyclic.

Example

Figure 9.13(a) illustrates a tree. Figure 9.13(b) illustrates graphs which are not trees due to the violation of the property of acyclicity and connectedness respectively.

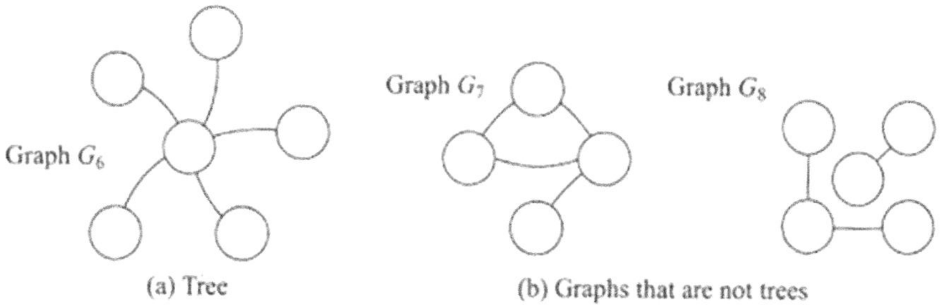

(a) Tree   (b) Graphs that are not trees

Figure 9.13. *Graphs which are trees and not trees*

Note the marked absence of any hierarchical structure and its allied terminologies of parent, child, sibling, ancestor, level, etc., insisted upon in the tree data structure. However, both the definitions of trees – as a data structure and a type of graph – agree on the principles of connectedness and acyclicity.

Degree

The *degree of a vertex* in an undirected graph is the number of edges incident to that vertex. A vertex with degree one is called as a *pendant vertex* or *end vertex*. A vertex with degree zero and hence has no incident edges is called an *isolated vertex*.

Example

In graph G_2 (see Figure 9.5(b)), the degree of vertex v_3 is 3 and that of vertex v_2 is 2.

In the case of digraphs, we define the *indegree* of a vertex v to be the number of edges with v as the head and the *outdegree* of a vertex to be number of edges with v as the tail.

Example

In graph G_1 (see Figure 9.5(a)), the indegree of vertex v_3 is 2 and the out degree of vertex v_4 is 1.

Isomorphic graphs

Two graphs are said to be ***isomorphic*** if they have

i) the same number of vertices;

ii) the same number of edges;

iii) an equal number of vertices with a given degree.

Example

Figure 9.14 illustrates two graphs, which are isomorphic.

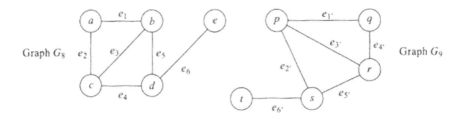

Figure 9.14. *Isomorphic graphs*

The property of isomorphism can be verified on the lists of vertices and edges of the two graphs G_8 and G_9 when superimposed, as shown below. The first two rows of the table illustrate the superimposition of their vertices. Here, vertex a is superimposed on vertex q, vertex b on vertex p and so on. A similar explanation holds with regard to edges listed in the last two rows of the table.

Vertices (G_8)	a	b	c	d	e	
Vertices (G_9)	q	p	r	s	t	
Degree of the vertices	2	3	3	3	1	
Edges (G_8)	e_1	e_2	e_3	e_4	e_5	e_6
Edges (G_9)	e_1'	e_4'	e_3'	e_5'	e_2'	e_6'

Cut set

A *cut set* in a connected graph G is the set of edges whose removal from G leaves G disconnected, provided the removal of no proper subset of these edges disconnects the graph G. Cut sets are also known as *proper cut set* or *cocycle* or *minimal cut set*.

Example

Figure 9.15 illustrates the cut set of the graph G_{10}. The cut set $\{e_1,\ e_4\}$ disconnects the graph into two components as shown in the figure. $\{e_5\}$ is also another cut set of the graph.

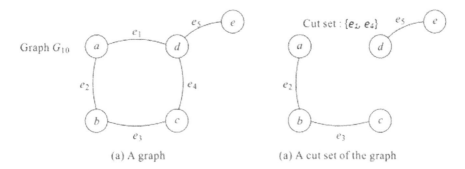

(a) A graph   (a) A cut set of the graph

Figure 9.15. *A cut set of a graph*

Labeled graphs

A graph G is called a *labeled graph* if its edges and/or vertices are assigned some data. In particular, if the edge e is assigned a non-negative number $l(e)$, then it is called the *weight* or *length* of the edge e.

Example

Figure 9.16 illustrates a labeled graph. A graph with weighted edges is also known as a *network*.

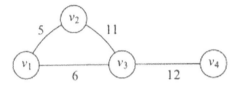

Figure 9.16. *A labeled graph*

Eulerian graph

A walk starting at any vertex going through each edge exactly once and terminating at the start vertex is called an ***Eulerian walk*** or ***Euler line***.

The Koenigsberg bridge problem was in fact a problem of obtaining an Eulerian walk for the graph concerned. The solution to the problem discussed in section 9.1 can be rephrased as, an Eulerian walk is possible only if the degree of each vertex in the graph is even.

Given a connected graph G, G is an ***Euler graph*** iff all the vertices are of even degree.

Example

Figure 9.17 illustrates an Euler graph. $\{e_1, e_2, e_3, e_4\}$ shows an Eulerian walk. The even degree of the vertices may be noted.

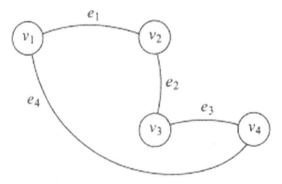

Figure 9.17. *An Euler graph*

Hamiltonian circuit

A *Hamiltonian circuit* in a connected graph is defined as a closed walk that traverses every vertex of *G* exactly once, except of course the starting vertex at which the walk terminates.

A *circuit* in a connected graph G is said to be **Hamiltonian** if it includes every vertex of *G*. If any edge is removed from a Hamiltonian circuit, then what remains is referred to as a **Hamiltonian path**. Hamiltonian path traverses every vertex of *G*.

Example

Figure 9.18 illustrates a Hamiltonian circuit.

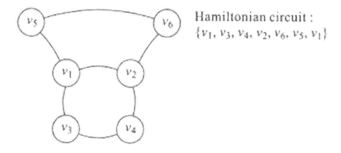

Hamiltonian circuit :
$\{v_1, v_3, v_4, v_2, v_6, v_5, v_1\}$

Figure 9.18. *A Hamiltonian circuit*

9.3. Representations of graphs

The representation of graphs in a computer can be categorized as (i) *sequential representation* and (ii) *linked representation*. Of the two, though sequential representation has several methods, all of them follow a matrix representation thereby calling for their implementation using arrays.

The linked representation of a graph makes use of a singly linked list as its fundamental data structure.

9.3.1. *Sequential representation of graphs*

The sequential or the matrix representation of graphs has the following methods:

i) *adjacency matrix* representation;

ii) *incidence matrix* representation;

iii) *circuit matrix* representation;

iv) *cut set matrix* representation;

v) *path matrix* representation.

Adjacency matrix representation

The *adjacency matrix* of a graph G with n vertices is an $n \times n$ symmetric binary matrix given by $A = \left[a_{ij} \right]$ defined as:

a_{ij} = 1 if the ith and jth vertices are adjacent, that is, there is an edge connecting the ith and jth vertices,

  = 0 otherwise, that is, if there is no edge linking the vertices.

Example

Figure 9.19(a) illustrates an undirected graph whose adjacency matrix is shown in Figure 9.19(b).

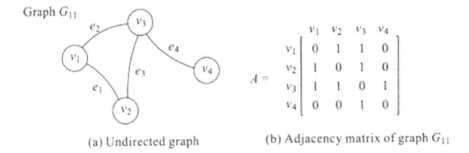

(a) Undirected graph   (b) Adjacency matrix of graph G_{11}

Figure 9.19. *Adjacency matrix of an undirected graph*

It can easily be seen that while adjacency matrices of undirected graphs are symmetric, nothing can be said about the symmetricity of the adjacency matrix of digraphs.

Example

Figures 9.20(a) and (b) illustrate a digraph and its adjacency matrix representation.

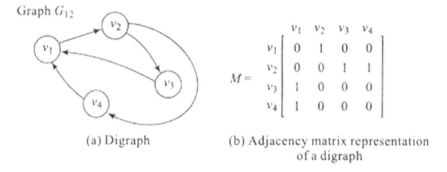

Graph G_{12}

$$M = \begin{array}{c c} & \begin{array}{c c c c} v_1 & v_2 & v_3 & v_4 \end{array} \\ \begin{array}{c} v_1 \\ v_2 \\ v_3 \\ v_4 \end{array} & \left[\begin{array}{c c c c} 0 & 1 & 0 & 0 \\ 0 & 0 & 1 & 1 \\ 1 & 0 & 0 & 0 \\ 1 & 0 & 0 & 0 \end{array} \right] \end{array}$$

(a) Digraph

(b) Adjacency matrix representation of a digraph

Figure 9.20. *Adjacency matrix representation of a digraph*

Incidence matrix representation

Let G be a graph with n vertices and e edges. Define an $n \times e$ matrix $M = [m_{ij}]$ whose n rows correspond to n vertices and e columns correspond to e edges, as:

m_{ij} = 1 if the jth edge e_j is incident on the ith vertex v_i,

= 0 otherwise.

Matrix M is known as the ***incidence matrix*** representation of the graph G.

Example

Consider the graph G_{13} shown in Figure 9.21(a); the incidence matrix representation for the graph is given in Figure 9.21(b).

Graph G_{13}

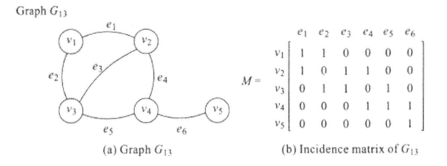

(a) Graph G_{13} (b) Incidence matrix of G_{13}

Figure 9.21. *Incidence matrix representation of a graph*

Circuit matrix representation

For a graph G, let the number of different circuits be t and the number of edges be e. Then the **circuit matrix** $C=[\ C_{ij}\ ]$ of G is a $t \times e$ matrix defined as:

C_{ij} $= 1$ if the ith circuit includes the jth edge,

$= 0$ otherwise.

Example

Consider the graph G_{14} shown in Figure 9.22(a). The circuits for this graph expressed in terms of their edges are 1: $\{e_1,\ e_2,\ e_3\}$, 2:$\{e_3,\ e_4,\ e_5\}$, 3:$\{e_1,\ e_2,\ e_5,\ e_4\}$. The circuit matrix C of order 3×6 is shown in Figure 9.22(b).

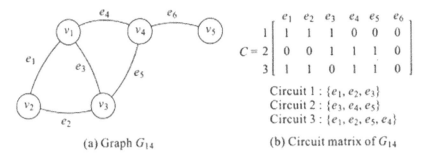

(a) Graph G_{14} (b) Circuit matrix of G_{14}

Figure 9.22. *Circuit matrix representation of a graph*

Cut set matrix representation

For a graph G, a matrix $S = [s_{ij}]$, whose rows correspond to cut sets and columns correspond to edges of the graph, is defined to be a ***cut set matrix*** if

s_{ij} = 1 if the ith cut set contains the jth edge,

        = 0, otherwise.

Example

Consider the graph G_{15} shown in Figure 9.23(a). The cut sets of the graph are $1:\{e_4\}$, $2:\{e_1, e_2\}$, $3:\{e_2, e_3\}$ and $4:\{e_1, e_3\}$. The cut set matrix representation is shown in Figure 9.23(b).

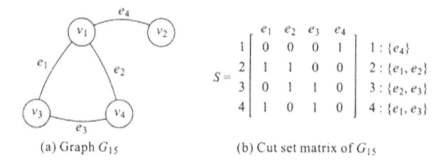

(a) Graph G_{15} (b) Cut set matrix of G_{15}

Figure 9.23. *Cut set matrix representation of a graph*

Path matrix representation

A ***path matrix*** is generally defined for a specific pair of vertices in a graph. If (u, v) is a pair of vertices, then the path matrix denoted as $P(u,v) = [p_{ij}]$ is given by:

p_{ij} = 1 if the jth edge lies in the ith path between vertices u and v,

        = 0 otherwise.

Example

Consider the graph G_{16} shown in Figure 9.24(a). The paths between vertices v_1 and v_4 are $1:\{e_2, e_4\}$ and $2:\{e_1, e_3, e_4\}$. The path matrix representation is shown in Figure 9.24(b).

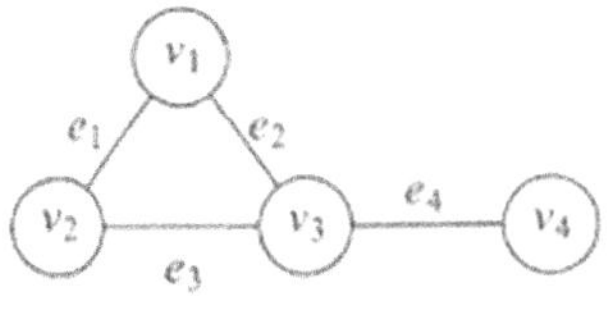

(a) Graph G_{16}

(b) Path matrix between v_1 v_4 of G_{16}

$$P(v_1, v_4) = \begin{array}{c} \\ 1 \\ 2 \end{array} \begin{array}{cccc} e_1 & e_2 & e_3 & e_4 \\ \left[\begin{array}{cccc} 0 & 1 & 0 & 1 \\ 1 & 0 & 1 & 1 \end{array} \right. \end{array}$$

Paths:
1 : $\{e_2, e_4\}$
2 : $\{e_1, e_3, e_4\}$

Figure 9.24. *Path matrix representation*

Of all these sequential representations, adjacency matrix representation best represents the graph and is the most widely used representation. The adjacency matrix A of a graph G with n vertices has an order of $n \times n$. As a result, graph algorithms that make use of the adjacency matrix representation are bound to report a time complexity of $O(n^2)$ since at least $n^2 - n$ entries (excluding the diagonal elements) are to be examined.

9.3.2. *Linked representation of graphs*

The linked representation of graphs is referred to as **adjacency list representation** and is comparatively efficient, with regard to adjacency matrix representation.

Given a graph G with n vertices and e edges, the adjacency list opens n head nodes corresponding to the n vertices of graph G, each of which points to a singly linked list of nodes, which are adjacent to the vertex representing the head node.

Example

Figure 9.25 illustrates a graph and its adjacency list representation.

It can easily be seen that if the graph is undirected, then the number of nodes in the singly linked lists put together is $2e$, whereas in the case of digraphs the number of nodes is just e, where e is the number of edges in the graph.

In contrast to adjacency matrix representations, graph algorithms which make use of an adjacency list representation would generally report a time complexity of $O(n + e)$ or $O(n + 2e)$ based on whether the graph is directed or undirected, respectively, thereby rendering them efficient.

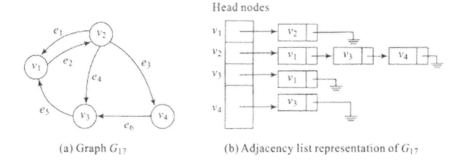

(a) Graph G_{17} (b) Adjacency list representation of G_{17}

Figure 9.25. *Adjacency list representation of a graph*

9.4. Graph traversals

Just as binary tree data structures support traversals of inorder, preorder and postorder, graphs support the following traversals:

– *breadth first traversal*;

– *depth first traversal.*

A traversal, to recall, is a systematic walk, which visits the nodes comprising the data structure (graphs in this case) in a specific order.

9.4.1. Breadth first traversal

We discuss the *breadth first traversal* of an undirected graph in this section. The traversal starts from a vertex u which is said to be visited. Now all nodes v_i, adjacent to u, are visited. The unvisited vertices w_{ij} adjacent to each of v_i are visited next and so on. The traversal terminates when there are no more nodes to visit. The process calls for the maintenance of a **queue** to keep track of the order of nodes whose adjacent nodes are to be visited.

Algorithm 9.1 illustrates the procedure for breadth first traversal of a graph G.

Breadth first traversal as its name indicates traverses the successors of the start node, generation after generation in a horizontal or linear fashion. This "breadth wise" traversal is clearly visible when the traversal is worked over a graph represented as an adjacency list.

Example 9.1 illustrates the breadth first traversal of an undirected graph represented as an adjacency list.

EXAMPLE 9.1.–

Consider the undirected graph G shown in Figure 9.26(a) and its adjacency list representation shown in Figure 9.26(b). The trace of procedure BFT(1), where the start vertex is 1, is shown in Table 9.1.

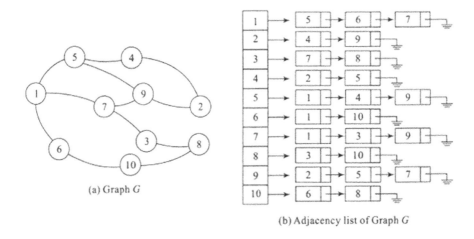

(a) Graph G

(b) Adjacency list of Graph G

Figure 9.26. *A graph and its adjacency list representation to demonstrate breadth first traversal*

The breadth first traversal starts from vertex 1 and visits vertices 5,6,7, which are adjacent to it, while enqueuing them into queue Q. In the next shot, vertex 5 is dequeued and its adjacent, unvisited vertices 4, 9 are visited next and so on. The process continues until the queue Q, which keeps track of the adjacent vertices, is empty.

If an adjacency matrix representation had been used, the time complexity of the algorithm would have been $O(n^2)$ since to visit each vertex, the while loop incurs a time complexity of $O(n)$. On the other hand, the use of adjacency list only calls for the examination of those nodes, which are adjacent to the given node thereby curtailing the time complexity of the loop to $O(e)$.

```
procedure  BFT(s)
/*  s is the start vertex of the traversal in an
undirected graph G */
/* Q is a queue which keeps track of the vertices whose
adjacent nodes are to be visited */
/* Vertices which have been visited have their 'visited'
flags  set to 1  (i.e.) visited (vertex) = 1. Initially,
visited (vertex) = 0 for all vertices of graph G */

    initialize queue Q;
    visited(s) = 1;
    call ENQUEUE (Q,s);       /*  insert s into Q  */
    while not EMPTY_QUEUE(Q) do  /* process until
                                    Q is empty  */
        call DEQUEUE (Q,s)         /* delete s from Q*/
        print(s);         /* output vertex visited  */
        for all  vertices v adjacent to s do
            if  (visited (v) = 0) then
                       {call ENQUEUE (Q,v);
                        visited(v) =1;}
        end
    endwhile
end BFT.
```

Algorithm 9.1. *Breadth first traversal*

9.4.2. *Depth first traversal*

In this section, we discuss the depth first traversal of an undirected graph. The traversal starts from a vertex u, which is said to be visited. Now, all the nodes v_i adjacent to vertex u are collected and the first occurring vertex v_l is visited, deferring the visits to other vertices. The nodes adjacent to v_l, viz., w_{lk}, are collected, and the first occurring adjacent vertex, viz., w_{ll}, is visited deferring the visit to other adjacent nodes and so on. The traversal progresses until there are no more visits possible.

Current Vertex	Queue Q	Traversal output	Status of visited flag of vertices {1, 2, 3, 4, 5, 6, 7, 8, 9, 10} of graph G
1 (Start vertex)	1		1 2 3 4 5 6 7 8 9 10 1 0 0 0 0 0 0 0 0 0
1	5 6 7	1	1 2 3 4 5 6 7 8 9 10 1 0 0 0 1 1 1 0 0 0
5	6 7 4 9	1 5	1 2 3 4 5 6 7 8 9 10 1 0 0 1 1 1 1 0 1 0
6	7 4 9 10	1 5 6	1 2 3 4 5 6 7 8 9 10 1 0 0 1 1 1 1 0 1 1
7	4 9 10 3	1 5 6 7	1 2 3 4 5 6 7 8 9 10 1 0 1 1 1 1 1 0 1 1
4	9 10 3 2	1 5 6 7 4	1 2 3 4 5 6 7 8 9 10 1 1 1 1 1 1 1 0 1 1
9	10 3 2	1 5 6 7 4 9	1 2 3 4 5 6 7 8 9 10 1 1 1 1 1 1 1 0 1 1
10	3 2 8	1 5 6 7 4 9 10	1 2 3 4 5 6 7 8 9 10 1 1 1 1 1 1 1 1 1 1
3	2 8	1 5 6 7 4 9 10 3	1 2 3 4 5 6 7 8 9 10 1 1 1 1 1 1 1 1 1 1
2	8	1 5 6 7 4 9 10 3 2	1 2 3 4 5 6 7 8 9 10 1 1 1 1 1 1 1 1 1 1
8		1 5 6 7 4 9 10 3 2 8	1 2 3 4 5 6 7 8 9 10 1 1 1 1 1 1 1 1 1 1
		1 5 6 7 4 9 10 3 2 8	Breadth first traversal ends

Table 9.1. *Trace of the breadth first traversal procedure on graph G (see Figure 9.26)*

Algorithm 9.2 illustrates a recursive procedure to perform the depth first traversal of graph G.

```
procedure  DFT(s)
  /* s is the start vertex  */
        visited(s) = 1;

        print (s);              /* Output visited vertex  */

        for each vertex v adjacent to s do
            if visited(v) = 0 then
                call DFT(v)
            end
        end
end DFT
```

Algorithm 9.2. *Depth first traversal*

The depth first traversal as its name indicates visits each node that is the first occurring among its adjacent nodes and successively repeats the operation, thus moving "deeper and deeper" into the graph. In contrast, breadth first traversal moves sideways or breadth ways in the graph. Example 9.2 illustrates a depth first traversal of an undirected graph.

EXAMPLE 9.2.–

Consider the undirected graph G and its adjacency list representation shown in Figure 9.26. Figure 9.27 shows a tree of recursive calls which represents a trace of the procedure DFT(1) on the graph G with start vertex 1.

The tree of recursive calls illustrates the working of the DFT procedure. The first call DFT(1) visits start vertex 1 and releases 1 as the traversal output. Vertex 1 has vertices 5, 6, 7 as its adjacent nodes. DFT(1) now invokes DFT(5), visiting vertex 5 and releasing it as the next traversal output. However, DFT(6) and DFT(7) are kept in waiting for DFT(5) to complete its execution. Such procedure calls waiting to be executed are shown in broken line boxes in the tree of recursive calls.

Now DFT(5) invokes DFT(4) releasing vertex 4 as the traversal output while DFT(9) is kept in abeyance. Note that though vertex 1 is an adjacent node of vertex 5, since no DFT() calls to vertices already visited are invoked, DFT(1) is not called for. The process continues until DFT(6) completes its execution with no more nodes left to visit. During recursion the calls made to DFT() procedure are indicated using solid arrows in the forward direction.

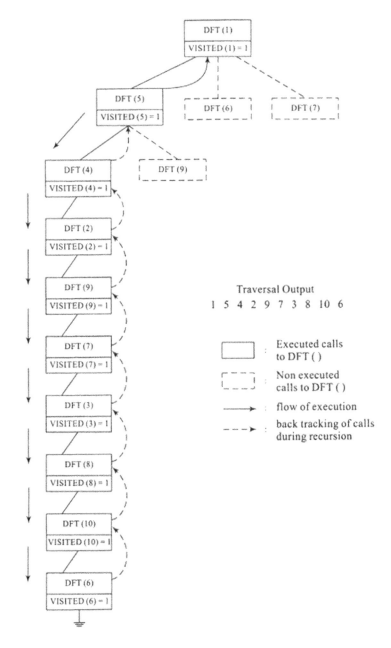

Figure 9.27. *Tree of recursive calls showing the trace of procedure* DFT (1) *on graph G (see Figure 9.26)*

Once DFT(6) finishes execution, backtracking takes place which is indicated using broken arrows in the reverse direction. Once DFT(1) completes execution the traversal output is gathered to be 1 5 4 2 9 7 3 8 10 6.

In the adjacency list representation of graph G, DFT() examines each node in the adjacency list at most once. Since there are *2e* list nodes, the time complexity turns out to be *O(e)*. On the other hand, the adjacency matrix implementation for procedure DFT() records a time complexity of *O(n²)*.

Both breadth first and depth first traversals, irrespective of the vertex they start from, visit all vertices of the graph that are connected to it. Hence, if the graph is connected, both traversals would visit all the vertices of the graph. On the other hand, if the graphs were not connected, both traversals would yield only their connected components. Thus, breadth first and depth first traversal can be useful in testing for the connectivity of graphs. If after executing the traversal algorithms, there are vertices which are left unvisited, then it implies that the graph is disconnected.

9.5. Applications

We illustrate the application of graphs for

i) determination of shortest path (***single source shortest path problem***);

ii) extraction of ***minimum cost spanning trees***.

9.5.1. *Single source shortest path problem*

Given a network of cities and the distances between them, the objective of the *single source shortest path problem* is to find the shortest path from a city (termed *source*) to all other cities connected to it.

The network of cities with their distances is represented as a *weighted digraph*. Algorithm 9.3 illustrates ***Dijkstra's algorithm*** for the single source shortest path problem.

Let *V* be a set of *N* cities (vertices) of the digraph. Here the source is city 1. The set *T* is initialized to city 1. The DISTANCE vector, DISTANCE [2:N] initially records the distances of cities 2 to *N* connected to the source by an edge (not a path!). If there is no edge directly connecting the city to the source, then we initialize its DISTANCE value to ∞. Once the algorithm completes its iterations, the DISTANCE vector holds the shortest distance of cities 2 to *N* from the source city 1.

It is convenient to represent the weighted digraph using its cost matrix $(COST)_{N \times N}$. The cost matrix records the distances between cities connected by an edge.

Dijkstra's algorithm has a complexity of $O(N^2)$, where N is the number of vertices (cities) in the weighted digraph.

```
procedure  DIJKSTRA_SSSP(N, COST)

/*N is the number of vertices labeled { 1, 2, 3,…N} of the
weighted digraph. COST[1:N,1:N] is the cost matrix of the
graph. If there is no edge then COST [i,j] = ∞*/

/* The procedure computes the cost of the shortest  path from
vertex 1 the source,  to every other vertex of the weighted
digraph */

  T = {1};  /* Initialize T to source vertex */
  for  i = 2 to N  do
  DISTANCE[i] = COST[1,i];     /*Initialize DISTANCE
                     vector to the cost of the edges
                     connecting vertex i with the source
                     vertex 1.  If there is no edge then
                     COST [1, i] = ∞*/
  end
  for i = 1 to N-1  do

    Choose a vertex u in V - T such that DISTANCE[u]
    is a minimum;
    Add u to T;
    for each vertex w in V-T do
      DISTANCE[w] = minimum(DISTANCE[w],DISTANCE[u] +
                                        COST[u,w] );
    end
  end

end DIJKSTRA_SSSP
```

Algorithm 9.3. *Dijkstra's algorithm for the single source shortest path problem*

EXAMPLE 9.3.–

Consider the weighted digraph of cities and its cost matrix shown in Figure 9.28. Table 9.2 shows the trace of the Dijkstra's algorithm.

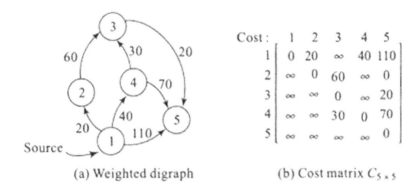

(a) Weighted digraph   (b) Cost matrix $C_{5 \times 5}$

Figure 9.28. *A weighted digraph and its cost matrix*

Iteration	T	u	DISTANCE [2]	DISTANCE [3]	DISTANCE [4]	DISTANCE [5]
Initial	{1}	-	20	∞	40	110
1	{1,2}	2	20	80	40	110
2	{1,2,4}	4	20	70	40	110
3	{1,2,4,3}	3	20	70	40	90
4	{1,2,4,3,5}	5	20	70	40	90

Table 9.2. *Trace of Dijkstra's algorithm on the weighted digraph (see Figure 9.28)*

The DISTANCE vector in the last iteration records the shortest distance of the vertices {2, 3, 4, 5} from the source vertex 1.

To reconstruct the shortest path from the source vertex to all other vertices, a vector PREDECESSOR [1:N], where PREDECESSOR [v] records the predecessor of vertex v in the shortest path, is maintained. PREDECESSOR [v] is initialized to source for all v ≠ source. PREDECESSOR [v] is updated by inserting the statement:

```
if (DISTANCE[u] + COST[u, w]) < DISTANCE[w]
then PREDECESSOR[w] = u
```

soon after DISTANCE [w] = minimum (DISTANCE [w], DISTANCE [u] + COST [u,w]) is computed in procedure DIJKSTRA_SSSP. To trace the shortest path, we move backwards from the destination vertex, hopping on the predecessors recorded by the PREDECESSOR vector until the source vertex is reached.

EXAMPLE 9.4.–

To trace the shortest paths of the vertices from vertex 1 using Dijkstra's algorithm, inclusion of the statement updating PREDECESSOR vector results in the following:

	PREDECESSOR				
	[1]	[2]	[3]	[4]	[5]
Initialization	-	1	1	1	1
Final values after iteration 4		1	4	1	3

To trace the shortest path from source 1 to vertex 5, we move in the reverse direction from vertex 5 (shown in dotted lines) hopping on the predecessors until the source vertex is reached, as illustrated below.

PREDECESSOR(5) = 3 PREDECESSOR(3) = 4 PREDECESSOR(4) = 1

Vertex 5 ← Vertex 3 ← Vertex 4 ← Source Vertex 1

Thus, the shortest path between vertex 1 and vertex 5 is $1 - 4 - 3 - 5$ and the distance is given by DISTANCE[5] = 90.

9.5.2. *Minimum cost spanning trees*

Consider an application where n stations are to be linked using a communication network. The laying of communication links between any two stations involves a cost. The problem is to obtain a network of communication links which, while preserving the connectivity between stations, does it with minimum cost. If the problem were to be modeled as a weighted graph, the ideal solution to the problem would be to extract a subgraph termed ***minimum cost spanning tree***, which while preserving the connectedness of the graph yields minimum cost.

Let $G = (V, E)$ be an undirected connected graph. A subgraph $T = (V, E')$ of G is a ***spanning tree*** of G iff T is a tree.

Example

For the connected undirected graph shown in Figure 9.29(a), some of the spanning trees extracted from the graph are shown in Figure 9.29(b).

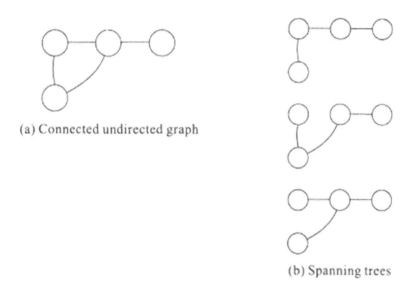

(a) Connected undirected graph

(b) Spanning trees

Figure 9.29. *Spanning trees of a graph*

Given a connected undirected graph, there are several spanning trees that may be extracted from it. Now given $G = (V, E)$ to be a connected, weighted, undirected graph where each edge involves a cost, the extraction of a spanning tree extends itself to the extraction of a minimum cost spanning tree. A *minimum cost spanning tree* is a spanning tree, which has a minimum total cost.

A spanning tree of a graph G with n vertices will have $(n - 1)$ edges. This is due to the property that a tree with n vertices has always $(n - 1)$ edges (refer illustrative problem 9.9). Also, the addition of even one single edge results in the spanning tree losing its acyclicity properties and the removal of one single edge results in losing its connectedness properties.

Algorithm 9.4 illustrates ***Prim's algorithm*** for the extraction of minimum cost spanning trees from a weighted, connected, undirected graph, and Algorithm 9.5 illustrates ***Kruskal's algorithm*** to accomplish the same in a different way.

Prim's algorithm strives to build the minimum cost spanning tree edge by edge, ensuring that the edge selected at each step is of minimum cost, does not form a cycle and at the same time results in the tree remaining connected, during its construction.

On the other hand, Kruskal's algorithm works over a forest of trees (not a single tree) constructed out of minimum cost edges selected one at a time, but finally ensuring that the minimum cost spanning tree is obtained. Kruskal's algorithm therefore necessitates sorting the edges of the graph according to their ascending order of costs so that working over the forest becomes easy.

Thus, while Prim's algorithm associates the number of vertices (n) in the spanning tree with its terminating condition, Kruskal associates the number of edges in the spanning tree (e which is equal to $(n - 1)$) with its terminating condition.

The time complexity of Prim's algorithm is $O(n^2)$ and that of Kruskal's algorithm is $O(e.\ log\ e)$, where n is the number of vertices on the graph and e the number of edges on the graph.

EXAMPLE 9.5.–

Consider the connected, weighted, undirected graph shown in Figure 9.30. Table 9.3 illustrates the trace of algorithm PRIM on the graph.

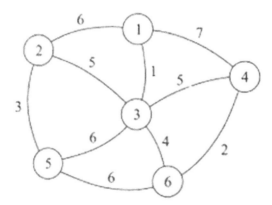

Figure 9.30. *A connected weighted undirected graph for the extraction of a minimum cost spanning tree using Prim's algorithm*

```
procedure  PRIM(G)
/*  G = (V,E) is a weighted, connected undirected graph
and E' is the set of edges which are to be extracted to
obtain the minimum cost spanning tree */

    E' = φ;             /* Initialize  E'  to a null set */
    Select a minimum cost edge (u,v) from E;
    V' = {u}               /* Include  u  in V'  */
    while V' ≠ V do
      Let (u, v) be the lowest cost edge such that
      u is in V' and  v is in V - V';
      Add edge (u,v) to set E';
      Add v to set V';
    endwhile

end PRIM
```

Algorithm 9. 4. *Prim's algorithm to obtain the minimum cost spanning tree from a connected undirected graph*

Edge	Cost of the edge	V'	E'	Spanning tree
(1, 3)	1	1	–	–
(1, 3)	1	{1, 3}	{(1, 3)}	
(3, 6)	4	{1, 3, 6}	{(1, 3), (3, 6)}	
(6, 4)	2	{1, 3, 6, 4}	{(1, 3), (3, 6), (6, 4)}	
(3, 2)	5	{1, 3, 6, 4, 2}	{(1, 3), (3, 6), (6, 4), (3, 2)}	
(2, 5)	3	{1, 3, 6, 4, 2, 5}	{(1, 3), (3, 6), (6, 4), (3, 2), (2, 5)}	

Table 9.3. *Trace of the Prim's algorithm on the connected weighted undirected graph (see Figure 9.30)*

We first initialize V' to a vertex of the lowest cost edge of the graph G. Then with each iteration, we look for the lowest cost edge that has one of its end points in V', all the while ensuring that the edge chosen does not destroy the property of connectedness and acyclicity insisted upon by spanning tree. Once $V' = V$, the algorithm terminates obtaining the minimum cost spanning tree. In this example, the minimum cost spanning tree has a cost of 15.

```
procedure KRUSKAL(G)

/* G = (V, E) is a weighted connected undirected graph
and E' is the set of edges that are to be extracted from
E to construct the minimum cost spanning tree */

/* Sort the edges in E according to their ascending
order of costs*/

  E' = Φ;
  while  (E ≠ Φ  and number of edges in E' ≠ (n-1) )

    Choose the lowest cost edge (v, w) from E;
    Delete (v, w) from E;
    if (v, w) does not create a cycle in E'
    then Add (v, w) to E'
    else discard (v, w)

  endwhile

end KRUSKAL
```

Algorithm 9.5. *Kruskal's algorithm to obtain the minimum cost spanning tree from a weighted connected undirected graph*

EXAMPLE 9.6.–

Consider the connected weighted undirected graph shown in Figure 9.30. Table 9.4 illustrates the trace of Kruskal's algorithm on the graph.

E (Sorted list of edges)	Choice of the lowest cost edge (u, w)	E' (Spanning tree construction)
(1, 3) (4, 6) (2, 5) (3, 6) (3, 4) (2, 3) (3, 5) (5, 6) (1, 2) (1, 4)	(1, 3)	
(4, 6) (2, 5) (3, 6) (3, 4) (2, 3) (3, 5) (5, 6) (1, 2) (1, 4)	(4, 6)	
(2, 5) (3, 6) (3, 4) (2, 3) (3, 5) (5, 6) (1, 2) (1, 4)	(2, 5)	
(3, 6) (3, 4) (2, 3) (3, 5) (5, 6) (1, 2) (1, 4)	(3, 6)	
(3, 4) (2, 3) (3, 5) (5, 6) (1, 2) (1, 4)	(3, 4)	 Discard (3, 4)
(2, 3) (3, 5) (5, 6) (1, 2) (1, 4)	(2, 3)	 Minimum cost Spanning tree construction complete

Table 9.4. *Trace of Kruskal's algorithm on the*
connected, weighted, undirected graph (see Figure 9.30)

As can be observed, the edges are sorted according to their ascending order of costs. The minimum cost edges are selected one at a time with the sole criterion that they do not violate the property of acyclicity of the spanning tree. Unlike Prim's algorithm, the choice of the edges ignores the connectedness property, thereby resulting in the construction of a forest during the early steps of the algorithm execution. The algorithm successfully terminates when the number of edges in the spanning tree equals $(n-1)$. In this example, the cost of the minimum cost spanning tree is 15.

ADT for graphs

Data objects:
 A graph G of vertices and edges. Vertices represent
data.

Operations:
Check if graph G is empty
CHECK_GRAPH_EMPTY (G)   (Boolean function)

Insert an isolated vertex V into a graph G. Ensure
that V does not exist in G before insertion.
INSERT_VERTEX (G, V)

Insert an edge connecting vertices U, V into a graph G.
Ensure that such an edge does not exist in G before
insertion.
INSERT_EDGE(G, U, V)

Delete vertex V and all the edges incident on it from
the graph G. Ensure that such a vertex exists in the
graph before deletion.
DELETE_VERTEX (G, V)

Delete   an edge from the graph G connecting the
vertices U, V. Ensure that such an edge exists before
deletion.
DELETE_EDGE (G, U, V)

Store ITEM into a vertex V of graph G
STORE_DATA(G, V, ITEM)

Retrieve data of a vertex V in the graph G and return
it in ITEM
RETRIEVE_DATA (G, V, ITEM)

Perform Breadth first traversal of a graph G.
BFT (G)

Perform Depth first traversal of a graph G.
DFT(G)

Summary

– Graphs are nonlinear data structures. The history of graph theory originated from the classical Koenigsberg bridge problem.

– A graph $G = (V, E)$ consists of a finite set of vertices V and edges E. Undirected graph, digraph, complete graph, subgraph, tree, isomorphic graphs and labeled graphs are graphs that satisfy special properties.

– Path, simple path, cycle, degree, cut set, pendant vertex, Eulerian walk and Hamiltonian circuit are terminologies associated with graphs.

– For problem solving using computers, graphs are represented using two popular methods, viz., adjacency matrix representation and adjacency list representation, which belong to the class of sequential and linked representations, respectively.

– The other matrix representations for graphs are incidence matrix, circuit matrix, cut set matrix and path matrix.

– Graphs support the traversals of breadth first and depth first. The traversal techniques can be employed to test for the connectedness of the graph.

– Single source shortest path problem and extraction of minimal cost spanning trees using Prim's and Kruskal's algorithms are important applications of graphs.

9.6. Illustrative problems

PROBLEM 9.1.–

Draw the graphs:

$G_1 : V_1 = \{a, b, c, d\}\ E_1 = \{<a, b> <b, c> <d, c><c, a>\}$

$G_2 : V_2 = \{a, b, c, d\}\ E_2 = \{(a, b)\ (b, c)\ (a, d)\ (b, d)\}$

Solution:

Figure P9.1 illustrates the graphs. Here, G_1 is a digraph and G_2 is an undirected graph.

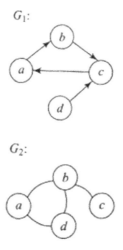

Figure P9.1. *The digraph G₁ and the undirected graph G₂*

PROBLEM 9.2.–

For the graph given in Figure P9.2, find:

i) an isolated vertex;

ii) degree of node b;

iii) a simple path from a to c;

iv) a path which is not simple from a to c;

v) a cycle;

vi) a pendant vertex.

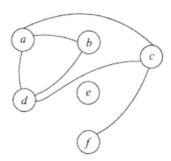

Figure P9.2. *An example graph*

Solution:

i) *e*

ii) *2*

iii) *{a, d, c}* or *{a, b, d, c}*

iv) *{a, b, d, a, c}*

v) *{a, b, d}*

vi) *f*

PROBLEM 9.3.–

For the graph given in Figure P9.3,

a) obtain:

i) the cut sets;

ii) an Eulerian walk;

iii) a Hamiltonian path.

b) Is the graph complete?

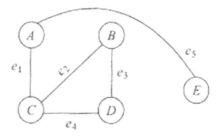

Figure P9.3. *A graph*

Solution:

a)

i) The cut set is {*C*} since removal of the vertex with all the edges incident on it disconnects the graph.

ii) No, an Eulerian walk does not exist since not all nodes have even degree.

iii) A Hamiltonian path is given by D B C A E.

b) No, the graph is not complete since all the 5_{C_2} edges are not available.

PROBLEM 9.4.–

Represent the graph shown in Figure P9.3 using:

i) adjacency matrix;

ii) adjacency list;

iii) incidence matrix.

Solution:

i) Adjacency matrix

$$
\begin{array}{c c}
 & \begin{array}{c c c c c} A & B & C & D & E \end{array} \\
\begin{array}{c} A \\ B \\ C \\ D \\ E \end{array} &
\left(\begin{array}{c c c c c}
0 & 0 & 1 & 0 & 1 \\
0 & 0 & 1 & 1 & 0 \\
1 & 1 & 0 & 1 & 0 \\
0 & 1 & 1 & 0 & 0 \\
1 & 0 & 0 & 0 & 0
\end{array}\right)
\end{array}
$$

ii) Adjacency list

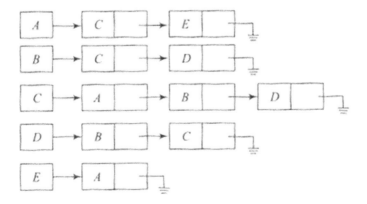

iii) Incidence matrix

$$\begin{array}{c} \\ A \\ B \\ C \\ D \\ E \end{array}\left(\begin{array}{ccccc} e_1 & e_2 & e_3 & e_4 & e_5 \\ 1 & 0 & 0 & 0 & 1 \\ 0 & 1 & 1 & 0 & 0 \\ 1 & 1 & 0 & 1 & 0 \\ 0 & 0 & 1 & 1 & 0 \\ 0 & 0 & 0 & 0 & 1 \end{array}\right)$$

PROBLEM 9.5.–

Show that if d_i is the degree of vertex i in a graph G with n vertices and e edges then:

$$e = \frac{\sum_{i=1}^{n} d_i}{2}$$

Solution:

Since each edge contributes to the degree of its two end vertices,

$$d_1 + d_2 + \ldots d_n = 2e$$

i.e. $e = \dfrac{(d_1 + d_2 + \ldots d_n)}{2}$

$$= \frac{\sum_{i=1}^{n} d_i}{2}$$

Hence the result. This problem is a derived result of **Handshaking lemma**.

NOTE.– [*Handshaking Lemma*] In any finite undirected graph $G = (V, E)$, the sum of the degrees is equal to twice the number of edges in the graph, that is,

$$\sum_{v \in V} \deg(v) = 2.|E|,$$

where $\deg(v)$ denotes the degree of node v and $|E|$ the number of edges in the graph G.

PROBLEM 9.6.–

With the help of the result, $\sum_{i=1}^{n} d_i = 2e$ (proved in illustrative problem 9.5) show that the number of vertices of odd degree is even.

Solution:

$$\sum_{i=1}^{n} d_i = \sum_{\substack{odd \\ vertices}} degree(d_k) + \sum_{\substack{even \\ vertices}} degree(d_j)$$

$$\therefore \sum_{\substack{odd \\ vertices}} degree(d_k) = \quad 2e - \sum_{\substack{even \\ vertices}} degree(d_j)$$

$$\Rightarrow \sum_{\substack{odd \\ vertices}} degree(d_k) = an \quad even \quad number \ c$$

As each d_k of the summation is an odd number, for the summation to be an even number (denoted as c), the number of terms must be even. Hence the number of vertices of odd degree is even.

PROBLEM 9.7.–

There is one and only one path between every pair of vertices in a tree T. Prove this.

Solution:

If there is more than one path between a pair of distinct vertices v_i , v_j in a tree T, then it means that a circuit exists. Hence, T is no longer a tree. Therefore, there exists one and only path between every pair of vertices in a tree T.

PROBLEM 9.8.–

If in a graph G there is one and only one path between every pair of vertices, then G is a tree.

Solution:

For G to be a tree, (i) G should be connected and (ii) G should have no cycles.

i) It is true since there exists a path between every pair of vertices.

ii) It is also true since there is one and only one path between every pair of vertices, which ensures absence of cycles (see illustrative problem 9.7).

Hence, *G* is a tree.

PROBLEM 9.9.–

A tree *T* with *n* vertices has *(n – 1)* edges. Prove this.

Solution:

We can prove this by induction:

For $n = 1$, a tree has no edge or has $(1-1) = 0$ edges.

For $n = 2$, a tree has one edge or has $(2-1) = 1$ edge.

The statement is therefore true for $n = 1$ and $n = 2$. Let us suppose the theorem holds for a tree *T* with $n - 1$ vertices. Now to prove that it is true for a tree *T* with *n* vertices, let us consider a tree *T* with *n* vertices. Remove an edge *e* from *T*. This disconnects *T* and results in two trees T_1, T_2 each with n' and $n-n'$ nodes, respectively, for some n'. Since n' and $n-n'$ are fewer than *n*, the total number of edges in T_1 and T_2 put together is $(n' - 1) + (n - n' - 1) = n - 2$. Replacing *e*, the tree *T* has $(n - 2 + 1) = n - 1$ edges. Thus, this is proof.

PROBLEM 9.10.–

Extract a minimum cost spanning tree for the graph shown in Figure P9.10 using Prim's algorithm.

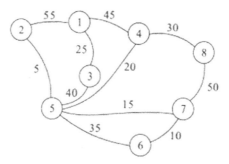

Figure P9.10. *A graph for extraction of minimum cost spanning tree*

Solution:

Table P9.10 illustrates the trace of the Prim's algorithm in obtaining the minimum cost spanning tree.

Total cost of the minimum spanning tree is 145.

Edge	Cost of the edge	V'	E'	Minimum cost Spanning tree
(2, 5)	–	{2}	–	–
(2, 5)	5	{2, 5}	{(2, 5)}	
(5, 7)	15	{2, 5, 7}	{(2, 5), (5, 7)}	
(7, 6)	10	{2, 5, 7, 6}	{(2, 5), (5, 7), (7, 6)}	
(5, 4)	20	{2, 5, 7, 6, 4}	{(2, 5), (5, 7), (7, 6), (5, 4)}	
(4, 8)	30	{2, 5, 7, 6, 4, 8}	{(2, 5), (5, 7), (7, 6), (5, 4), (4, 8)}	
(5, 6) Reject	–	–	–	
(5, 3)	40	{2, 5, 7, 6, 4, 8, 3}	{(2, 5), (5, 7), (7, 6), (5, 4), (4, 8), (5, 3)}	
(1, 3)	25	{2, 5, 7, 6, 4, 8, 3, 1}	{(2, 5), (5, 7), (7, 6), (5, 4), (4, 8), (5, 3), (1, 3)}	

Table P9.10. *Trace of the Prim's algorithm on the graph shown in Figure P9.10*

PROBLEM 9.11.–

Obtain a solution to the single source shortest path problem defined on the digraph, as shown in Figure P9.11.

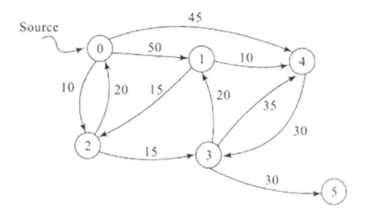

Figure P9.11. *A weighted digraph of a single source shortest problem*

Solution:

Table P9.11 illustrates the trace of the Dijkstra's algorithm on the single source shortest path problem.

Iteration	T	U	DISTANCE					PREDECESSOR				
			[1]	[2]	[3]	[4]	[5]	[1]	[2]	[3]	[4]	[5]
Initialize	{0}	-	50	10	∞	45	∞	0	0	0	0	0
1	{0,2}	2	50	10	25	45	∞	0	0	2	0	0
2	{0,2,3}	3	45	10	25	45	55	3	0	2	0	3
3	{0,2,3,1}	1	45	10	25	45	55	3	0	2	0	3
4	{0,2,3,1,4}	4	45	10	25	45	55	3	0	2	0	3
5	{0,2,3,1,4,5}	5	45	10	25	45	55	3	0	2	0	3

Table P9.11. *Trace of Dijkstra's algorithm on the single source shortest path problem illustrated in Figure P9.11*

The shortest paths and distances are given as:

Source	Destination	Shortest Path	Shortest Distance
0	1	0 – 2 – 3 – 1	45
0	2	0 – 2	10
0	3	0 – 2 – 3	25
0	4	0 – 4	45
0	5	0 – 2 – 3 – 5	55

PROBLEM 9.12.–

Extract a minimum cost spanning tree for the graph shown in Figure P9.10 using Kruskal's algorithm.

Solution:

Table P9.12 illustrates the trace of Kruskal's algorithm during the construction of the minimum cost spanning tree. The total cost of the minimum cost spanning tree is 145.

E (Sorted list of edges)	Choice of the lowest cost edge (v, w)	E' (Spanning tree construction)
(2, 5) (6, 7) (5, 7) (4, 5) (1, 3) (4, 8) (5, 6) (3, 5) (1, 4) (7, 8) (1, 2)	(2, 5)	② ⑤
(6, 7) (5, 7) (4, 5) (1, 3) (4, 8) (5, 6) (3, 5) (1, 4) (7, 8) (1, 2)	(6, 7)	② ⑤ ⑥ ⑦
(5, 7) (4, 5) (1, 3) (4, 8) (5, 6) (3, 5) (1, 4) (7, 8) (1, 2)	(5, 7)	② ⑤ ⑥ ⑦
(4, 5) (1, 3) (4, 8) (5, 6) (3, 5) (1, 4) (7, 8) (1, 2)	(4, 5)	② ⑤ ④ ⑥ ⑦
(1, 3) (4, 8) (5, 6) (3, 5) (1, 4) (7, 8) (1, 2)	(1, 3)	② ⑤ ④ ① ③ ⑦ ⑥
(4, 8) (5, 6) (3, 5) (1, 4) (7, 8) (1, 2)	(4, 8)	② ⑤ ⑧ ① ③ ④ ⑦ ⑥
(5, 6) (3, 5) (1, 4) (7, 8) (1, 2)	(5, 6)	Discard edge (5, 6)
(3, 5) (1, 4) (7, 8) (1, 2)	(3, 5)	40 ② 5 ⑤ ⑧ ① 25 ③ 20 30 15 ④ ⑦ 10 ⑥
		Minimum cost Spanning tree construction done

Table P9.12. *Trace of Kruskal's algorithm on the minimum cost spanning tree illustrated in Figure P9.10*

PROBLEM 9.13.–

A *k*-ary tree is one where every node has either 0 or *k* nodes (see Chapter 8) and hence is a graph. Prove using Handshaking lemma (introduced in illustrative problem 9.5) that $L = (k-1)*I + 1$, where L is the number of leaf nodes in the tree, k is the arity and I the number of internal nodes in the tree.

Solution:

From the Handshaking lemma, we know that sum of the degrees of the *k*-ary tree is equal to twice the number of edges in the tree. Of the I internal nodes in the *k*-ary tree, $(I-1)$ nodes have a degree of $(k+1)$, one internal node which is the root node has a degree of k and the L leaf nodes have a degree of 1. Thus,

$$(I-1)*(k+1)+k+L = 2.e \quad \ldots \tag{i}$$

where e is the number of edges in the *k*-ary tree.

It is already known that a tree T with n vertices has $(n-1)$ edges (see illustrative problem 9.9). Thus, for the *k*-ary tree,

$$I + L - 1 = e \ldots \tag{ii}$$

Substituting (ii) in (i) for e, yields the result

$$(I-1)*(k+1)+k+L = 2.(I+L-1) \ldots \tag{iii}$$

Simplifying (iii) yields $L = (k-1)*I + 1$, which is the result required.

NOTE.– The result when applied to those binary trees which are special cases of *k*-ary trees, that is *k*-ary trees with $k = 2$, yields $L = I + 1$. In other words, the number of leaf nodes in a binary tree whose degrees of the nodes are either 0 or 2 is always one more than that of its non-terminal nodes.

PROBLEM 9.14.–

Level order traversal of a binary tree was discussed in programming assignment 6 of Chapter 8. A level order traversal is nothing but a ***Breadth first traversal*** undertaken on a binary tree.

Trace breadth first traversal on the k-ary tree ($k = 3$) shown in Figure P9.14(a) using Algorithm 9.1. Clearly trace the contents of the queue and the `visited` flag data structure that are employed during the traversal.

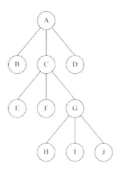

Figure P9.14(a). *A k-ary tree (k = 3)*

Solution:

Table P9.14 illustrates the trace of the breadth first traversal over the k-ary tree ($k = 3$) shown in Figure P9.14(a), beginning with the root node. Figure P9.14(b) shows the adjacency list representation of the k-ary tree.

The breadth first traversal of the k-ary tree yields the output *ABCDEFGHIJ*.

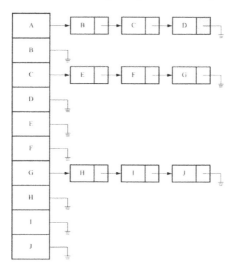

Figure P9.14(b). *Adjacency list representation of the k-ary tree illustrated in Figure 9.14(a)*

Current Vertex	Queue Q	Traversal ouput	Status of visited flag of vertices of the tree									
Start A	A		A B C D E F G H I J									
			1	0	0	0	0	0	0	0	0	0
A	B C D	A	A B C D E F G H I J									
			1	1	1	1	0	0	0	0	0	0
B	C D	A B										
C	D E F G	A B C	A B C D E F G H I J									
			1	1	1	1	1	1	1	0	0	0
D	E F G	A B C D										
E	F G	A B C D E										
F	G	A B C D E F										
G	H I J	A B C D E F G	A B C D E F G H I J									
			1	1	1	1	1	1	1	1	1	1
H	I J	A B C D E F G H										
I	J	A B C D E F G H I										
J		A B C D E F G H I J	A B C D E F G H I J									
			1	1	1	1	1	1	1	1	1	1

Table P9.14. *Trace of the breadth first traversal on the k-ary tree illustrated in Figure 9.14(a)*

Review questions

1) Which of the following does not hold good for the given graph *G*?

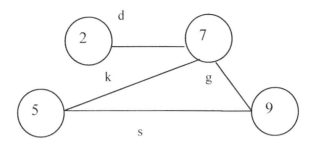

i) An Eulerian walk exists for the graph;

ii) the graph is an undirected graph;

iii) the graph has a cycle;

iv) the graph has a pendant vertex.

a) (i)   b) (ii)   c) (iii)   d) (iv)

2) Which of the following properties is not satisfied by two graphs that are isomorphic?

i) They have the same number of vertices;

ii) they have the same number of edges;

iii) they have an equal number of vertices with a given degree;

iv) there must exist at least one cycle.

a) (i)   b) (ii)   c) (iii)   d) (iv)

3) For the graph shown in review question 1, the following matrix represents its:

$$
\begin{array}{c}
\quad d\ g\ k\ s \\
\begin{array}{c}
2 \\
5 \\
7 \\
9
\end{array}
\begin{bmatrix}
1 & 0 & 0 & 0 \\
0 & 0 & 1 & 1 \\
1 & 1 & 1 & 0 \\
0 & 1 & 0 & 1
\end{bmatrix}
\end{array}
$$

i) adjacency matrix representation;   ii) incidence matrix representation;

iii) circuit matrix representation;   iv) cut set matrix representation.

a) (i)   b) (ii)   c) (iii)   d) (iv)

4) In the context of graph traversals, state whether true or false:

i) Graph traversals could be employed to check for the connectedness of a graph.

ii) For any graph, graph traversals always visit all vertices of the graph.

a) (i) true (ii) true

b) (i) true (ii) false

c) (i) false (ii) true

d) (i) false (ii) false

5) Which among the following properties is not satisfied by a minimum cost spanning tree T extracted from a graph G with n vertices?

i) T has a cycle.

ii) T has $(n-1)$ edges.

iii) T has n vertices.

iv) T is connected.

a) (i)   b) (ii)   c) (iii)   d) (iv)

6) Distinguish between digraphs and undirected graphs.

7) For a graph of your choice, trace its (i) adjacency matrix and (ii) adjacency list representations.

8) Draw graphs that contain (i) an Eulerian walk and (ii) a Hamiltonian circuit.

9) How can graph traversal procedures help in detecting graph connectivity?

10) Discuss an application of minimum cost spanning trees.

11) Trace (i) breadth first traversal and (ii) depth first traversal on the graph shown below, beginning from vertex y:

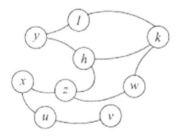

12) For the graph shown below, obtain the shortest path from vertex 1 to all other vertices:

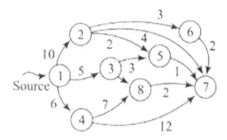

13) For the graph shown below, extract minimum cost spanning trees using Prim's and Kruskal's algorithms:

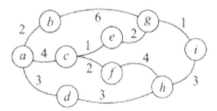

14) A graph G claims that it has 7 edges with each vertex in the graph having a degree of 2. How many vertices does G have?

15) How can depth first traversal be used to detect a cycle in a connected graph? (Hint: Depth first traversal of a connected graph extracts a tree. A back edge from any of the nodes in the tree to its ancestor will create a cycle.)

Programming assignments

1) Execute a program to input a graph $G = (V, E)$ as an adjacency matrix. Include functions to:

    i) test if G is complete;

    ii) obtain a path and a simple path from vertex u to vertex v;

    iii) obtain the degree of a node u, if G is undirected, and indegree and outdegree of node u if G is directed.

2) Execute a program to input a graph $G = (V, E)$ as an adjacency list. Include two functions BFT and DFT to undertake a breadth first and depth first traversal of the graph. Making use of the traversal procedures, test whether the graph is connected.

3) Implement Dijkstra's algorithm to obtain the shortest paths from the source vertex 1 to every other vertex of the graph G given below:

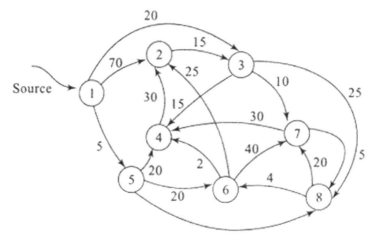

4) Design and implement an algorithm to obtain a spanning tree of a connected, undirected graph using breadth first or depth first traversal.

5) Design and implement an algorithm to execute depth first traversal of a graph represented by its incidence matrix.

6) Design and implement an algorithm to obtain an Eulerian walk of an undirected graph in the event of such a walk being available.

7) Implement the ADT for graphs in a programming language of your choice choosing a linked representation for the graphs.

8) Write a program to detect cycles in a connected graph using depth first traversal.

Binary Search Trees and AVL Trees

10.1. Introduction

In Chapter 8, the tree and binary tree data structures were discussed. Binary search trees and AVL trees are a category of binary trees that facilitate efficient retrievals. In this chapter, the definition of a binary search tree and its operations, viz., retrieval, insertion, and deletion, are discussed. However, binary search trees can have their setbacks too, the rectification of which yields an AVL tree. The definition of the AVL search tree and the operations of retrieval, insertion and deletion on the tree are elaborated in this chapter. The application of the two data structures for the representation of symbol tables in compiler design has been detailed later in the text.

10.2. Binary search trees: definition and operations

10.2.1. *Definition*

A **binary search tree** T may be an empty binary tree. If non-empty, then for a set S, T is a labeled binary tree in which each node u is labeled by an element or key $e(u) \in S$ such that:

i) for each node u in the left subtree of v, $e(u) < e(v)$;

ii) for each node u in the right subtree of v, $e(u) > e(v)$;

iii) for each element $a \in S$, there is exactly one node u such that $e(u) = a$.

In other words, a binary search tree T satisfies the following norms:

i) all keys of the binary search tree must be *distinct*;

ii) all keys in the left subtree of T are less than the root element;

iii) all keys in the right subtree of T are greater than the root element;

iv) the left and right subtrees of T are also binary search trees.

Figure 10.1 illustrates an empty binary search tree and a non-empty binary search tree defined for the set $S = \{G, M, B, E, K, I, Q, Z\}$. It needs to be emphasized here that for a given set S, more than one binary search tree can be constructed.

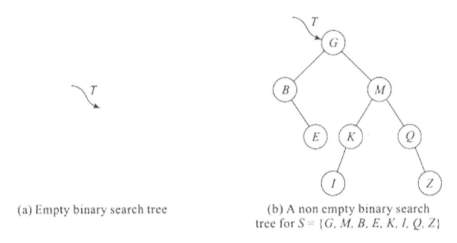

(a) Empty binary search tree

(b) A non empty binary search tree for $S = \{G, M, B, E, K, I, Q, Z\}$

Figure 10.1. *Example binary search trees*

The inorder traversal of a binary search tree T yields the elements of the associated set S in the ascending order. If $S = \{a_i, i = 1,2,\ldots n\}$, then the inorder traversal of the binary search tree yields the elements in its ascending sequence, that is, $a_1 < a_2 < a_3 <\ldots a_n$. Thus, the inorder traversal of the binary search tree shown in Figure 10.1 results in $\{B, E, G, I, K, M, Q, Z\}$, which are the elements of S in the ascending order.

10.2.2. Representation of a binary search tree

A binary search tree is commonly represented using a linked representation in the same way as that of a binary tree (see section 8.5.2). The node structure and the linked representation of the binary search tree shown in Figure 10.1 is illustrated in Figure 10.2. However, the null pointers of the nodes may be emphatically represented using fictitious nodes called **external nodes**. The external nodes labeled as e_i are shown as solid circles in Figure 10.2. Thus, a linked representation of a binary search tree is viewed as a bundle of external nodes, which represent the null pointers and **internal nodes** that represent the keys. Such a binary tree is referred to as an *extended binary tree*. Obviously, the number of external nodes in a binary search tree comprising n internal nodes is $n + 1$. The path from the root to an external node is called as an *external path*.

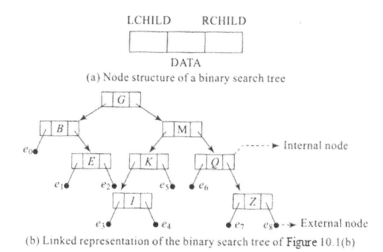

(a) Node structure of a binary search tree

(b) Linked representation of the binary search tree of Figure 10.1(b)

Figure 10.2. *Linked representation of a binary search tree*

10.2.3. Retrieval from a binary search tree

Let T be a binary search tree. To retrieve a key u from T, u is first compared with the root key r of T. If $u = r$, then the search is done. If $u < r$, then the search begins at the left subtree of T. If $u > r$, then the search begins at the right subtree of T. The search is repeated recursively in the respective left and right subtrees with u compared against the respective root keys, until the key u is either found or not found. If the key is found, the search is termed *successful*, and if not found, the search is termed *unsuccessful*.

While all successful searches terminate at the appropriate internal nodes in the binary search tree, all unsuccessful searches terminate only at the external nodes in the appropriate portion of the binary search tree. Hence external nodes are also referred to as *failure nodes*. Thus, if the inorder traversal of a binary search tree yields the keys in the sequence $a_1 < a_2 < a_3 < \ldots a_n$, then the failure nodes $e_0, e_1, e_2, e_3, \ldots e_n$ are all *equivalence classes*, which represent cases of unsuccessful searches on the binary search tree. While e_0 traps all unsuccessful searches of keys that are less than a_1, e_1 traps those that are greater than a_1 and less than a_2 and so on. In general, e_i traps all keys between a_i and a_{i+1}, which are unsuccessfully searched. For example, in Figure 10.2(b), all keys less than B which result in unsuccessful searches terminate at the external node e_0 and those which are greater than Q but less than Z terminate at the external node e_7 and so on.

Algorithm 10.1 illustrates the procedure to retrieve the location LOC of the node containing the element ITEM from a binary search tree T.

```
procedure FIND_BST(T, ITEM, LOC)
/* LOC is the address of the node containing  ITEM
which is to be retrieved from the  binary search tree
T. In case of unsuccessful search the procedure prints
the message "ITEM not found" and returns LOC as NIL*/

if T = NIL then {print(" binary search tree T is
                        empty");
                exit;}              /* exit procedure*/

else
    {LOC = T;
     while (LOC ≠ NIL) do
         case
         :ITEM = DATA(LOC): return (LOC);
                         /* ITEM found in node LOC*/
         :ITEM < DATA(LOC): LOC = LCHILD(LOC);
                             /* search left subtree*/
         :ITEM > DATA(LOC): LOC = RCHILD(LOC);
                             /* search right subtree*/
         endcase
     endwhile
     if (LOC = NIL) then
       {print("ITEM not found");
        return (LOC)}      /* unsuccessful  search*/
    }
end FIND_BST
```

Algorithm 10.1. *Procedure to retrieve*
ITEM from a binary search tree T

10.2.4. Why are binary search tree retrievals more efficient than sequential list retrievals?

For a list of n elements stored as a sequential list, the worst case time complexity of searching an element both in the case of successful search or unsuccessful search is $O(n)$. This is so since in the worst case, the search key needs to be compared with every element of the list. However, in the case of a binary search tree as is evident in Algorithm 10.1, searching for a given key k results in discounting half of the binary search tree at every stage of its comparison with a node on its path from the root downwards. The best case time complexity for the retrieval operation is therefore $O(1)$ when the search key k is found in the root itself. The worst case occurs when the search key is found in one of the leaf nodes whose level is equal to the height h of the binary search tree. The time complexity of the search is then given by $O(h)$. In some cases, binary search trees may grow to heights that equal n, the number of elements in the associated set, thereby increasing the time complexity of a retrieval operation to $O(n)$ in the worst case (see section 10.2.7). However, on average, in assuming random insertions/deletions, we obtain the height h of the binary search tree to be $O(log\ n)$ yielding a time complexity of $O(log\ n)$ for a retrieval operation.

EXAMPLE 10.1.–

Consider the set $S = \{416, 891, 456, 765, 111, 654, 345, 256, 333\}$ whose associated binary search tree T is shown in Figure 10.3.

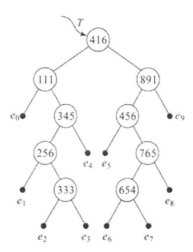

Figure 10.3. *A binary search tree*

Let us retrieve the keys 333 and 777 from the binary search tree. Tables 10.1 and 10.2 show the trace of the algorithm FIND for the retrieval of the two keys, respectively. Here, #(n) where $n \in S$ indicates the location (address) of the node containing the key n. While retrieval of 333 yields a successful search terminating at node #(333), retrieval of 777 results in an unsuccessful search terminating at the appropriate external node.

LOC	ITEM $\overset{<}{\underset{>}{=}}$ DATA(LOC)?	Updated LOC
Initially LOC = T =#(416)	333 < 416	LOC = LCHILD(#(416)) = #(111)
LOC =#(111)	333 > 111	LOC = RCHILD(#(111)) = #(345)
LOC =#(345)	333 < 345	LOC = LCHILD(#(345)) = #(256)
LOC =#(256)	333 > 256	LOC = RCHILD(#(256)) = #(333)
LOC =#(333)	333 = 333	RETURN(#(333)) Element found and node returned!

Table 10.1. *Trace of Algorithm 10.1 for the retrieval of ITEM=333*

LOC	ITEM $\overset{<}{\underset{>}{=}}$ DATA(LOC)?	Updated LOC
Initially LOC = T =#(416)	777 > 416	LOC = RCHILD(#(416)) = #(891)
LOC =#(891)	777 < 891	LOC = LCHILD(#(891)) = #(456)
LOC =#(456)	777 > 456	LOC = RCHILD(#(456)) = #(765)
LOC =#(765)	777 > 765	LOC = RCHILD(#(765)) = NIL
LOC = NIL		Element not found! RETURN(NIL)

Table 10.2. *Trace of Algorithm 10.1 for the retrieval of ITEM=777*

10.2.5. *Insertion into a binary search tree*

The insertion of a key into a binary search tree is similar to the retrieval operation. The insertion of a key u initially proceeds as if it were trying to retrieve the key from the binary search tree, but on reaching the null pointer (failure node), which it is sure to encounter since key u is not present in the tree, a new node containing the key u is inserted at that position.

EXAMPLE 10.2.–

Let us insert keys 701 and 332 into the binary search tree T associated with set $S = \{416, 891, 456, 765, 111, 654, 345, 256, 333\}$, as shown in Figure 10.3. Figure 10.4(a) shows the insertion of 701. Note how the operation moves down the tree in the path shown and when it encounters a failure node e_7, the key 701 is inserted as the right child of node containing 654. Again the insertion of 332, which follows a similar procedure, is illustrated in Figure 10.4(b).

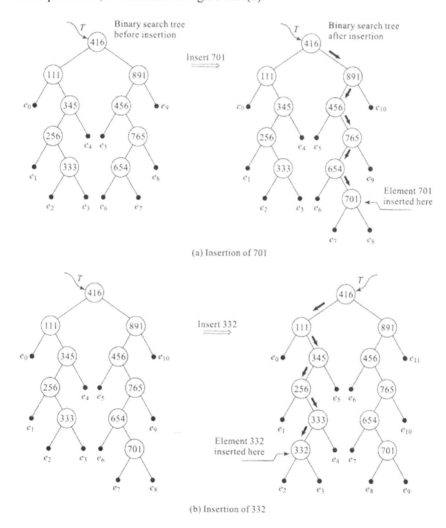

(a) Insertion of 701

(b) Insertion of 332

Figure 10.4. *Insertion of elements 701 and 332 into the binary search tree shown in Figure 10.3*

The algorithm for the insert procedure is only a minor modification of Algorithm 10.1. The time complexity of an insert operation is also $O(log\ n)$.

10.2.6. *Deletion from a binary search tree*

The deletion of a key from the binary search tree is comparatively not as straight as the insertion operation. We first search for the node containing the key by undertaking a retrieval operation. But once the node is identified, the following cases are tested before the node containing the key u is appropriately deleted from the binary search tree T:

i) key u is a leaf node;

ii) key u has a lone subtree (left subtree or right subtree only);

iii) key u has both left subtree and right subtree.

Case (i)

If the key u to be deleted is a leaf node, then the deletion is trivial since the appropriate link field of the parent node of key u only needs to be set as NIL. Figure 10.5(a) illustrates this case.

Case (ii)

If the key u to be deleted has either a left subtree or a right subtree (but not both), then the link of the parent node of u is set to point to the appropriate subtree. Figure 10.5(b) illustrates the case.

Case (iii)

If the key u to be deleted has both a left subtree and a right subtree, then the problem is complicated. In this case, since the right subtree comprises keys that are greater than u, the parent node of key u is now set to point to the right subtree of u. Now where do we accommodate the left subtree of u? Since all the keys of the left subtree of u are less than that of the right subtree of u, we move as far left as possible in the right subtree of u until an empty left subtree is found and link the left subtree of u at that position. Figure 10.5(c) illustrates the case.

The other methods of deletion in this case include replacing the key u with either the largest key l occurring in the left subtree of u or the smallest key s in the right subtree of u. It is guaranteed that l or u will turn out to be a node with either empty subtrees or any one non-empty subtree. After replacing *u* with *l* or *s* as the case may be, the nodes carrying *l* or *s* are deleted from the tree using the appropriate procedure (Case (i) or Case (ii)).

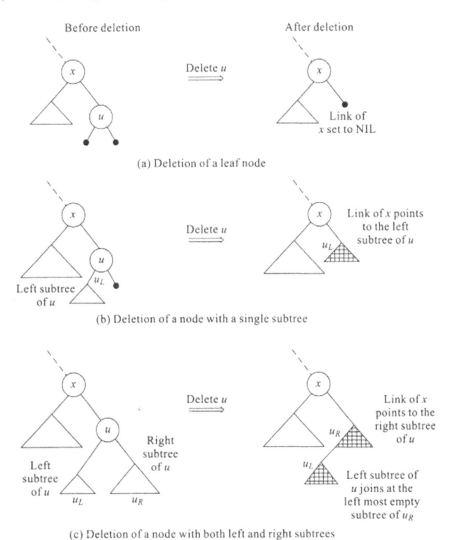

(a) Deletion of a leaf node

(b) Deletion of a node with a single subtree

(c) Deletion of a node with both left and right subtrees

Figure 10.5. *Deletion of a key from a binary search tree*

EXAMPLE 10.3.–

Delete keys 333, 891 and 416 in the order given, from the binary search tree T associated with set $S = \{416, 891, 456, 765, 111, 654, 345, 256, 333\}$ shown in Figure 10.3.

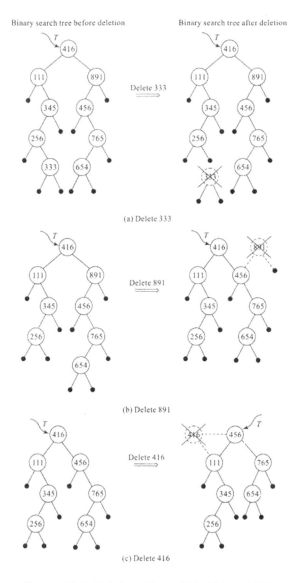

Figure 10.6. *Deletion of keys 333, 891 and 416 from the binary search tree shown in Figure 10.3*

Deletion of 333, a leaf node, illustrates Case (i). The RCHILD link of node #(256) is set to NIL. Figure 10.6(a) shows the deletion.

Deletion of 891, a node with a single subtree (left subtree), illustrates Case(ii). In this case, the RCHILD link of node #(416) is set to point to node #(456). Figure 10.6(b) illustrates the deletion.

Lastly, the deletion of 416, the root node with both the left and right subtrees intact, results in node #(456) taking over as the root. However, the left subtree of the root, viz., the subtree with node #(111) as the root, attaches itself as far left of the right subtree of node #(416). It therefore attaches itself to the LCHILD of node #(456). Figure 10.6(c) illustrates this case.

Algorithm 10.2 illustrates the deletion procedure on a binary search tree given NODE_U, the node to be deleted and NODE_X its parent. For simplicity, the procedure illustrates only the deletion operation for all non-empty nodes NODE_U other than the root. A general procedure to delete any ITEM from a binary search tree T can be easily attempted (see programming assignment 1). The time complexity of the delete operation on a binary search tree is $O(log\ n)$.

10.2.7. *Drawbacks of a binary search tree*

Though binary search trees in comparison to sequential lists report a better performance of $O(log\ n)$ time complexity for their insert, delete and retrieval operations, they are not without their setbacks. As pointed out in section 10.2.4, there are instances where binary search trees may grow to heights that equal n, the number of elements to be represented as the tree, thereby deteriorating their performance. This may occur due to a sequence of insert operations or delete operations. Examples 10.4 and 10.5 illustrate instances of when the height of a binary search tree reaches n.

EXAMPLE 10.4.–

Let us construct binary search trees for the sets $S_1 = \{A, B, C, D, E, F, G, H, I, J, K, L, M\}$ and $S_2 = \{M, L, K, J, I, H, G, F, E, D, C, B, A\}$. It can be seen that while the elements of S_1 are in the ascending order of the alphabetical sequence, those in S_2 are in the descending order of the sequence. The respective binary search trees are shown in Figure 10.7.

procedure DELETE(NODE_U, NODE_X)
/* *NODE_U is the node which is to be deleted from the*
binary search tree. NODE_X is the parent node for which
NODE_U may be the left child or the right child.
Procedure DELETE is applicable for deletion of all non empty
nodes other than the root (i.e.) NODE_U ≠ NIL and NODE_X ≠
*NIL */*

  case
  :LCHILD(NODE_U)= RCHILD(NODE_U)= NIL:
                        /* *NODE_U is a leaf node*/
        Set RCHILD(NODE_X) or LCHILD(NODE_X)to NIL
        based on whether NODE_U is the right
        child or left child of NODE_X respectively;
        call RETURN(NODE_U); /* *dispose node to the*
                        Available space list/

  :LCHILD(NODE_U)<> NIL **and** RCHILD(NODE_U)<> NIL:
                        /* *NODE_U has both left*
                                and right subtrees/
                        /* *attach right subtree of*
                                *NODE_U to NODE_X */
        Set RCHILD(NODE_X) or LCHILD(NODE_X)to
        RCHILD(NODE_U) based on whether NODE_U is
        the right child or left child of NODE_X
        respectively;
                        /* *attach left subtree of*
                        NODE_U as far left of the right
                        subtree of NODE_U as possible/
        TEMP = RCHILD(NODE_U);
        while (LCHILD(TEMP) <> NIL) **do**
            TEMP = LCHILD(TEMP);
        endwhile

        LCHILD(TEMP)= LCHILD(NODE_U);
        call RETURN(NODE_U);

```
:LCHILD(NODE_U)<> NIL and RCHILD(NODE_U)= NIL:
                /*NODE_U has only  left subtree*/
        TEMP = LCHILD(NODE_U);
        Set RCHILD(NODE_X) or LCHILD(NODE_X)to TEMP
        based on whether NODE_U is the  right child
        or left child of NODE_X respectively;
        call RETURN(NODE_U);


:LCHILD(NODE_U)= NIL and RCHILD(NODE_U)<> NIL:
                /*NODE_U has only right subtree*/
        TEMP = RCHILD(NODE_U);
        Set RCHILD(NODE_X) or LCHILD(NODE_X)to TEMP
        based on whether NODE_U is the  right child
        or left child of NODE_X respectively;
        call RETURN(NODE_U);
endcase

end DELETE
```

Algorithm 10.2. *Procedure to delete a node NODE_U from a binary search tree given its parent node NODE_X*

Figure 10.7. *Binary search trees for the sets S_1 = { A, B, C, D, E, F, G, H, I, J, K, L , M} and S_2 = {M, L, K, I, H, G, F, E, D, C, B, A}*

Observe that the two binary search trees are right skewed and left skewed, respectively. In such a case, the height h of the binary search tree is equal to n and hence a search operation on these binary search trees in the worst case would yield $O(n)$ time complexity.

EXAMPLE 10.5.–

Consider a skeletal binary search tree shown in Figure 10.8(a). Deletion of node y in the tree yields the one shown in Figure 10.8(b). Here again it may be seen that the binary search tree after deletion has yielded a left skewed binary tree once again resulting in $O(n)$ time complexity in the event of a search operation.

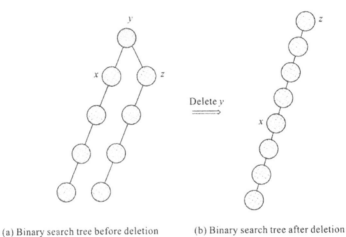

(a) Binary search tree before deletion   (b) Binary search tree after deletion

Figure 10.8. *Deletion from a binary search tree resulting in a skewed binary tree*

It is clear from the above examples that if the height of the binary search tree is left unchecked for, it can result in skewed binary trees deteriorating in their performance. In other words, it is essential that the binary search trees are maintained so as to have a **balanced height**. Trees whose height in the worst case yields $O(log\ n)$ are known as **balanced trees**. **AVL trees** are one such trees and is discussed in section 10.3.

10.2.8. Counting binary search trees

Given n elements, counting the number of binary search trees that can be constructed out of the n elements turns out to be a problem in **combinatorial** *mathematics*. Fortunately, many counting problems in combinatorial mathematics have been successfully solved using what are called *Catalan numbers*.

Catalan numbers, named after the Belgian mathematician Eugène Charles Catalan (1814–1894), form a sequence of natural numbers that occur in various counting problems in combinatorial mathematics and often involve recursively defined objects.

The nth Catalan number is given by:

$$C_n = \frac{(2.n)!}{(n+1)!.n!}$$

The Catalan numbers for $n = 0, 1, 2, 3, 4$, for instance, are given by:

$C_0 = 1, C_1 = 1, C_2 = 2, C_3 = 5, C_4 = 14$, and so on.

Catalan numbers are also recursively defined as:

$$C_{n+1} = \sum_{i=0}^{n} C_i.C_{n-i}, \quad n \geq 0$$
$$C_0 = 1$$

The total number of binary search trees with n different keys is given by:

$$\text{COUNT}_{\text{BST}}(n) = \text{Catalan number } C_n = \frac{(2.n)!}{(n+1)!.n!}.$$

EXAMPLE 10.6.–

Table 10.3 illustrates the counting of different binary search trees constructed out of the given element list.

The total number of binary trees with n different keys is given by:

$$\text{COUNT}_{\text{BT}}(n) = \text{COUNT}_{\text{BST}}(n)*n!$$

n	List	Binary search trees constructed	Catalan Number $C_n = \dfrac{2n!}{(n+1)!\, n!}$
0	{ }	Empty binary search tree	$C_0 = 1$
1	{ a }	a	$C_1 = 1 = \dfrac{2!}{2!\, 1!}$
2	{ a, b }	a b	$C_2 = 2 = \dfrac{4!}{(3!)\,(2!)}$
3	{ a, b, c }	c a b	$C_3 = 5 = \dfrac{6!}{(4!)\,(3!)}$

Table 10.3. *Counting of binary search trees – a demonstration*

10.3. AVL trees: definition and operations

In section 10.2.7, it was pointed out how binary search trees can reach heights equal to n, the number of elements in the tree, thereby deteriorating its performance. To eliminate this drawback, it is essential that during an insert or delete operation which can affect the structure of the tree and hence the height of the tree, it is ensured that the binary search tree remains of balanced height. In other words, there needs to be a mechanism to ensure that an insert or delete operation does not turn the tree into a skewed one. As mentioned earlier, trees whose height in the worst case turns out to be $O(log\ n)$ are known as **balanced trees** or **height-balanced trees**. One such balanced tree, viz., AVL tree, is discussed in this section. AVL trees were proposed by Adelson-Velskii and Landis in 1962.

10.3.1. Definition

An empty binary tree is an **AVL tree**. If non-empty, the binary tree T is an AVL tree iff

i) T_L and T_R, the left and right subtrees of T are also AVL trees;

ii) $|h(T_L) - h(T_R)| \leq 1$, where $h(T_L)$ and $h(T_R)$ are the heights of the left subtree and right subtree of T, respectively.

For a node u, $bf(u) = (h(u_L) - h(u_R))$, where $h(u_L)$ and $h(u_R)$ are the heights of the left and right subtrees of the node u, respectively, is known as the **balance factor** (*bf*) of the node u. In an AVL tree, every node u has a balance factor $bf(u)$, which may be either 0 or +1 or –1.

A binary search tree T, which is an AVL tree, is referred to as an **AVL search tree**. This section elaborates on the operations of insert, delete and retrieval performed on AVL search trees.

Figure 10.9 illustrates examples of AVL trees and AVL search trees. The balance factor of each of the nodes is indicated by the side of the node within parentheses. Note how the balance factors of the nodes in the AVL trees are either 0 or +1 or –1.

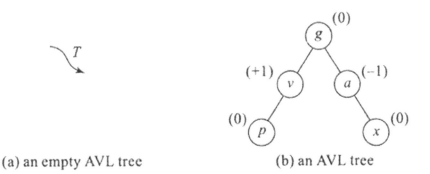

(a) an empty AVL tree   (b) an AVL tree

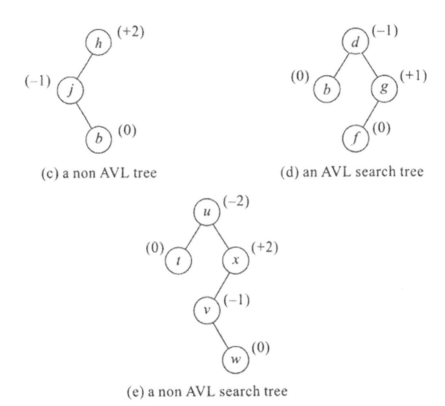

(c) a non AVL tree   (d) an AVL search tree

(e) a non AVL search tree

Figure 10.9. *Examples of AVL trees and non-AVL trees*

AVL trees and AVL search trees just like binary trees or binary search trees may be represented using a linked representation adopting the same node structure (see sections 8.5.2 and 10.2.2). However, to facilitate efficient rendering of insert and delete procedures, a field termed BF may be included in the node structure to record the balance factor of the specific node.

10.3.2. *Retrieval from an AVL search tree*

The retrieval of a key from an AVL search tree is in no way different from the retrieval operation on a binary search tree. Algorithm 10.1, illustrating the find operation on a binary search tree *T*, may be utilized for retrieval of an element from an AVL search tree as well. However, since the height of the AVL search tree of *n* elements is $O(log\ n)$, the time complexity of the find procedure when applied on AVL search trees does not exceed $O(log\ n)$.

10.3.3. *Insertion into an AVL search tree*

The insertion of an element u into an AVL search tree T proceeds exactly as one would to insert u in a binary search tree. However, if after insertion the balance factors of any of the nodes turn out to be anything other than 0 or +1 or –1, then the tree is said to be **unbalanced**. To balance the tree, we undertake what are called **rotations**. Rotations are mechanisms that shift some of the subtrees of the unbalanced tree to obtain a balanced tree.

With regard to rotations, there are some important observations, which are helpful in the implementation of the operations on AVL trees. For the initiation of rotations, it is required that the balance factors of all nodes in the unbalanced tree are limited to –2, –1, 0, 1 and +2. Also, the rotation is initiated with respect to an ancestor node A that is closest to the newly inserted node u and whose balance factor is either +2 or –2. If a node w after insertion of node u reports a balance factor of $bf(w) = +2$ or –2, respectively, then its balance factor before insertion should have been +1 or –1, respectively. The insertion of a node can only change the balance factors of those nodes on the path from the root to the inserted node. If the closest ancestor node A of the inserted node u has a balance factor $bf(A) = +2$ or –2, then prior to insertion the balance factors of all nodes on the path from A to u must have been 0. In fact, these observations are vital to determine the closest ancestor A after insertion of u.

The four different types of rotations are listed below. The classification is based on the position of the inserted node u with respect to the ancestor node A, which is closest to the node u and reports a balance factor of –2 or +2.

i) **LL rotation**: Node u is inserted in the left subtree (**L**) of left subtree (**L**) of A.

ii) **LR rotation**: Node u is inserted in the right subtree (**R**) of left subtree (**L**) of A.

iii) **RR rotation**: Node u is inserted in the right subtree (**R**) of right subtree (**R**) of A.

(iv) **RL rotation**: Node u is inserted in the left subtree (**L**) of right subtree (**R**) of A.

Each of the four classes of rotations is illustrated with examples.

LL rotation

Figure 10.10 illustrates a generic representation of *LL* type imbalance and the corresponding rotation that is undertaken to set right the imbalance. After insertion of node u, the closest ancestor node of node u, viz., node A, reporting an imbalance $(bf(A) = +2)$ is first found out. For simplicity of discussion, the generic tree shown in

Figure 10.10(a) has been chosen to have the ancestor node A occurring at the root. In reality, the ancestor node A may occur anywhere down the tree. Now with reference to the ancestor node A, we find that the node u has been inserted in the left subtree (L) of left subtree (L) of A. This implies there is an LL type of imbalance and to balance the tree an LL rotation is to be called for. The AVL tree before insertion of u (see Figure 10.10(a)), the unbalanced tree after insertion of u (see Figure 10.10(b)) and the balanced tree after the LL rotation (see Figure 10.10(c)) have been illustrated.

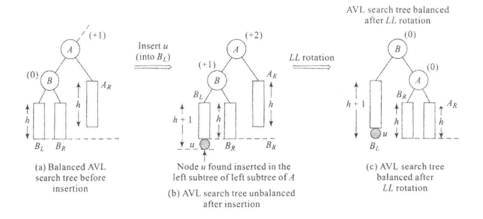

(a) Balanced AVL search tree before insertion

(b) AVL search tree unbalanced after insertion

Node u found inserted in the left subtree of left subtree of A

(c) AVL search tree balanced after LL rotation

Figure 10.10. *Generic representation of an* LL *rotation*

Here, u is found inserted in the left subtree of B, viz., B_L, where B is in the left subtree of A. We assume the heights of the generic subtrees A_R, B_L and B_R to be h. Observe the imbalance in the balance factor of A after insertion of u. $bf(A)$ which was +1 before insertion of u changes to +2 after insertion. To balance the tree, the LL rotation pushes B up as the root of the AVL tree, which results in node A slumping downwards to its left along with its right subtree A_R. Now the tree is rearranged by shifting the right subtree of B viz., B_R to join A as its left subtree, leaving B_L (holding the inserted node u) undisturbed as the left subtree of B.

EXAMPLE 10.7.–

Consider the AVL search tree shown in Figure 10.11(a). Let us insert C into the AVL search tree. To facilitate ease of understanding, the notations employed in the generic tree of Figure 10.10 have been mapped to the given tree. Note how C finds itself inserted in the left subtree of left subtree of M, the closest ancestor node of C that shows $bf(M)$ = +2 after insertion.

The *LL* rotation pushes *F* up to become the root of the tree and shifts the subtree with node *K*, which was originally the right subtree of *F*, to the left subtree of *M*.

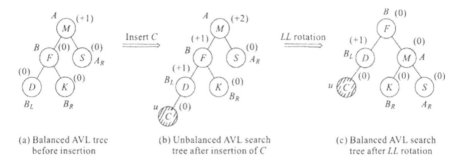

(a) Balanced AVL tree
before insertion

(b) Unbalanced AVL search
tree after insertion of *C*

(c) Balanced AVL search
tree after *LL* rotation

Figure 10.11. *An example of* LL *rotation*

LR rotation

Figure 10.12 illustrates the generic representation of an *LR* type of imbalance and the corresponding rotation that is undertaken to set right the imbalance. Here, the node *u* on insertion finds *A* to be its closest ancestor node that is unbalanced and with reference to node *A* is inserted in the right subtree of left subtree of *A*. This therefore is an *LR* type of imbalance and calls for *LR* rotation to balance the tree. The AVL tree before insertion of *u* (see Figure 10.12(a)), the unbalanced tree after insertion of *u* (see Figure 10.12(b)) and the balanced tree after the *LR* rotation (see Figure 10.12(c)) have been illustrated.

Here, *u* finds itself inserted in the right subtree of left subtree of *A*, the closest ancestor node. The heights of the subtrees A_R, B_L, B_R, C_L and C_R are as shown in the figure. Let us suppose *u* is found in C_L the left subtree of *C*. The procedure is no way different if *u* is found in C_R the right subtree of *C*. The *LR* rotation rearranges the tree by first shifting *C* to the root node. Then the left subtree C_L of *C* is shifted to the right subtree of *B* and C_R the right subtree of *C* is shifted to the left subtree of *A*. The rearranged tree is balanced. In the case of *LR* rotation, the following observations hold:

If *BF(C)* = 0 after insertion of new node, then *BF(A)* = *BF(B)* = 0 after rotation.

If *BF(C)* = −1 after insertion of new node, then *BF(A)* = 0, *BF(B)* = +1 after rotation.

If *BF(C)* = +1 after insertion of new node, then *BF(A)* = −1, *BF(B)* = 0 after rotation.

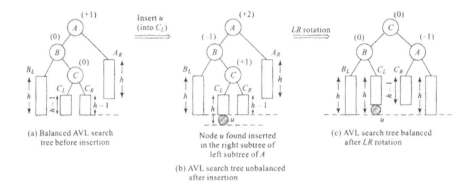

(a) Balanced AVL search tree before insertion

Node *u* found inserted in the right subtree of left subtree of *A*

(b) AVL search tree unbalanced after insertion

(c) AVL search tree balanced after *LR* rotation

Figure 10.12. *Generic representation of an* LR *rotation*

EXAMPLE 10.8.–

Consider the AVL search tree shown in Figure 10.13(a). The subtrees C_L and C_R of node C in the generic representation shown in Figure 10.12 are mapped to empty subtrees in this tree. In other words, the node labeled L has empty left and right subtrees. Let us insert H into the AVL search tree. Note how H gets inserted into the right subtree of left subtree of S, the closest ancestor node of H that shows $bf(S) = +2$. The LR rotation rearranges the tree by first pushing node L to be the root. As a result, node S slumps to its right along with its right subtree comprising the element W. Thereafter, the original left subtree of L holding the newly inserted node H is attached to F as its right subtree. In the absence of a right subtree for L (which was so before rotation), only an empty tree is attached as the left subtree of S.

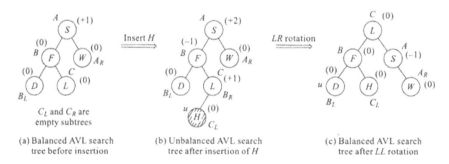

(a) Balanced AVL search tree before insertion

C_L and C_R are empty subtrees

(b) Unbalanced AVL search tree after insertion of *H*

(c) Balanced AVL search tree after *LL* rotation

Figure 10.13. *An example of* LR *rotation*

RR rotation

The *RR* rotation is symmetric to the *LL* rotation. Figure 10.14 illustrates the generic representation of the *RR* rotation scheme. Observe how node *u* finds itself inserted in the right subtree of right subtree of *A*, the closest ancestor node that is unbalanced and the rotation is merely a mirror image of the *LL* rotation scheme.

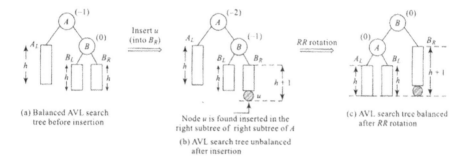

(a) Balanced AVL search tree before insertion

Node *u* is found inserted in the right subtree of right subtree of *A*

(b) AVL search tree unbalanced after insertion

(c) AVL search tree balanced after *RR* rotation

Figure 10.14. *Generic representation of an* RR *rotation*

EXAMPLE 10.9.–

Consider the AVL search tree shown in Figure 10.15(a). The insertion of *Z* calls for an *RR* rotation. The unbalanced AVL search tree and the balanced tree after *RR* rotation have been shown in Figures 10.15(b) and (c), respectively.

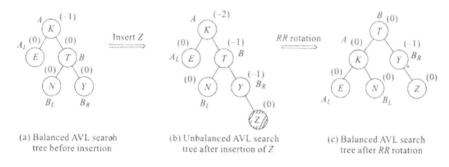

(a) Balanced AVL search tree before insertion

(b) Unbalanced AVL search tree after insertion of *Z*

(c) Balanced AVL search tree after *RR* rotation

Figure 10.15. *An example of* RR *rotation*

RL rotation

RL rotation is symmetric to *LR* rotation. Figure 10.16 illustrates the generic representation of the *RL* rotation scheme. Here, node *u* finds itself inserted in the left subtree of right subtree of node *A*, which is the closest ancestor node that is unbalanced. Note how the *RL* rotation is the mirror image of the *LR* rotation scheme. As pointed out for the *LR* rotation scheme, the rotation procedure for *RL* remains the same irrespective of u being inserted in C_L or C_R, the left subtree and right subtree of C, respectively.

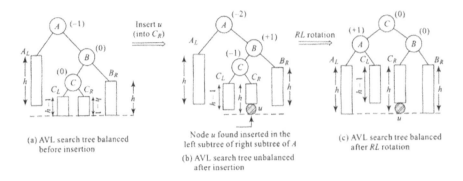

(a) AVL search tree balanced before insertion

(b) AVL search tree unbalanced after insertion

Node u found inserted in the left subtree of right subtree of A

(c) AVL search tree balanced after *RL* rotation

Figure 10.16. *Generic representation of an* RL *rotation*

EXAMPLE 10.10.–

Consider the AVL search tree shown in Figure 10.17(a). The insertion of M calls for an *RL* rotation. The unbalanced AVL search tree and the balanced tree after *RL* rotation have been shown in Figures 10.17(b) and (c), respectively.

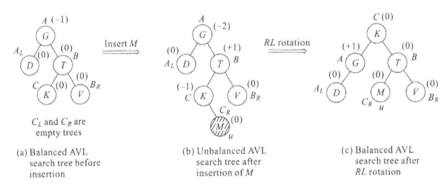

(a) Balanced AVL search tree before insertion

(b) Unbalanced AVL search tree after insertion of M

(c) Balanced AVL search tree after *RL* rotation

Figure 10.17. *An example of* RL *rotation*

In the above classes of rotations, *LL* and *RR* are called as **single rotations** and *LR* and *RL* are called as **double rotations**. An *LR* rotation is a combination of *RR* rotation followed by an *LL* rotation and *RL* rotation is a combination of *LL* rotation followed by an *RR* rotation.

Algorithm 10.3 illustrates a skeletal procedure to insert an element into an AVL search tree. The procedure initially tries to identify the most recent ancestor node A of the inserted element whose $bf(A) = \pm 1$. If no such node A is found, then all nodes in the path from the root to the newly inserted node have a balance factor of 0 at the time of insertion and hence the tree cannot go unbalanced due to the insertion. In such a case, we only update the balance factors of the nodes in the path from the root to the newly inserted node by updating the BF value of the node to +1 if ITEM is inserted in its left subtree and to -1 if it is inserted in its right subtree.

```
procedure INSERT(T, ITEM)

/*Steps to insert an ITEM into  an AVL search tree T. The node
structure  comprises  the  fields  LCHILD,  DATA,  BF  and  RCHILD
representing left child link, data, balance factor and  right
child link*/

    call GETNODE(X); /* get ready new node X containing
                      ITEM*/
    DATA(X) = ITEM;
    LCHILD(X) = RCHILD(X) = NIL and BF(X)=0;
                      /* AVL search tree T is empty*/
    if (T = NIL)
    then  {Set T to X;
           exit;
          }

/*AVL search tree T is non empty and ITEM is  distinct from
other elements in T */

    Find node P where ITEM is to be inserted as either
    the left child or right child of P by following a
    path from the root onwards. Also, while
    traversing down the tree in search of the point of
    insertion  of ITEM, take note of the most recent
    ancestor node A whose BF(A)= ±1;

    Insert node X carrying ITEM as the left or right
    child of node P;

/*if no ancestor node A is found the balance factors of all
nodes on the path from the root to the node containing ITEM is
0.  The  tree  will  therefore  remain  balanced  even  after
insertion of ITEM. Merely  update the BF fields of all the
nodes on the path from the root to node P after insertion of
ITEM and exit*/
```

```
if   (node A not found) then
     {TEMP = T;
                        /* update BF field of node to +1 if    ITEM
                        is inserted in its left subtree   and to -1
                        if inserted in its right   subtree*/
        while (TEMP <> X) do
          if (DATA(X) > DATA(TEMP))
          then
                 {BF(TEMP)=-1;
                   TEMP = RCHILD(TEMP);
                 }

          else {BF(TEMP) = +1;
                 TEMP= LCHILD(TEMP);
                 }
        endwhile
        exit;
     }
```

/*if node A exists and BF(A)= +1 with ITEM inserted in
the right subtree of A or BF(A)=-1 with ITEM inserted in
the left subtree of A, then set BF(A)= 0. Update the
balance factors of all nodes in the path from node A to the
inserted node X*/

```
if (node A found)
then
     {if (BF(A)= +1 and ITEM was inserted in the right
             subtree of A) or
        (BF(A)= -1 and ITEM was inserted in the left
             subtree of A)

     then   {BF(A)=0;
             Update the balance factors of all nodes   in the
             path from node A to the inserted node X;
             exit;
             }
     }
else
/* AVL search tree T is unbalanced. Classify the imbalance
and perform the appropriate rotations*/
     {
        Identify  the   type   of   imbalance   and   apply   the
        appropriate rotations.   Update  the  balance  factors
        of the nodes   as required by the rotation   scheme
        as well as reset the LCHILD and RCHILD links of the
        appropriate nodes.
     }
end INSERT
```

Algorithm 10.3. *Skeletal procedure to insert an ITEM into an AVL search tree T*

If node A exists and $bf(A) = +1$ and the insertion is done in the right subtree of A or if $bf(A) = -1$ and the insertion is done in the left subtree of A, then we set $bf(A) = 0$. Also, we update the balance factors of all nodes in the path from the node A to the newly inserted node. In all other cases, the type of imbalance is identified and the appropriate rotations are carried out. This may call for updating the balance factors of the involved nodes as well as resetting the link fields of the relevant nodes after identifying the appropriate B, C, A_L, B_L, B_R, C_L and C_R relevant to the rotation scheme.

The time complexity of the insert operation is $O(height) = O(log\ n)$.

10.3.4. Deletion from an AVL search tree

To delete an element from an AVL search tree, we discuss the operation based on whether the node t carrying the element to be deleted is either a leaf node or one with a single non-empty subtree or with two non-empty subtrees. A delete operation just like an insert operation may also imbalance an AVL search tree. Just as $LL/LR/RL/RR$ rotations are called for to rebalance the tree after insertion, a delete operation also calls for rotations categorized as L and R. While the L category is further classified as $L0$, $L1$ and $L-1$ rotations, the R category is further classified as $R0$, $R1$ and $R-1$ rotations. The **Classify rotations for deletion** section of Algorithm 10.4 details the mode of classification of the L and R rotations. However, it needs to be remembered that not all deletions call for rotations.

Considering the complex nature of the operation, we present its skeletal work procedure in two algorithms, viz., Algorithms 10.4 and 10.5. While Algorithm 10.4 illustrates the case when node t is a leaf node or one with a single non-empty subtree, Algorithm 10.5 illustrates the case when node t is one with two non-empty subtrees. For the invocation of the algorithms, we assume that the node holding the ITEM which is to be deleted from the AVL search tree T, viz., node t, has already been found.

Rotation free deletion of a leaf node

In the case of deletion of node t which is a leaf node, we physically delete the node and make the child the link of its parent, viz., node p null. Now update the balance factor of node p based on whether the deletion occurred to its right or left. If it had occurred to the right then we increase bf(node p) by 1 else decrease bf(node p) by 1. The new updated value of bf(node p) is now tested against Rules 1–4 of Algorithm 10.4 for updating the balance factors of its ancestor nodes. In the event of any imbalance, the appropriate rotations, viz., **L0/R0**, **L1/R1** or **L-1/R-1**, are called for rendering the tree balanced.

EXAMPLE 10.11.–

Consider the balanced AVL search tree shown in Figure 10.18. Deleting 30 is a case of deleting a leaf node. Figure 10.18(a) shows the balanced tree after deletion. Observe how the parent of node 30, viz., the node holding 25, resets its RCHILD link to NIL after the physical deletion of the node holding 30. Now how are the balance factors of the other nodes updated?

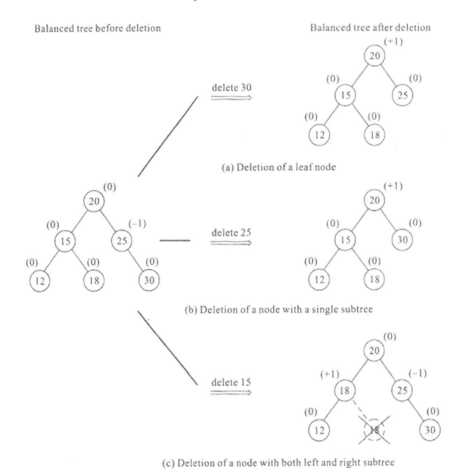

Figure 10.18. *Rotation free deletion of nodes in an AVL search tree*

Since the deletion of key 30 occurred to the right of key 25, *bf*(25) is increased by 1. Hence, the new updated *bf*(25) is 0. As per Rule 2 outlined in Algorithm 10.4, this calls for the update of the balance factors of all ancestor nodes of key 25. Since the root (key 20) is the only ancestor node available and the deletion took place to its right, $bf(20)$ is increased by 1 which yields the new value as $bf(20) = +1$. We now see that the tree is automatically balanced and in this case no rotations were called for.

Rotation free deletion of a node having a single subtree

In the case of deletion of node t with a single subtree, just as before we reset the child link of the parent node, node p, to point to the child node of node t. The balance factors of node p and/or its ancestor nodes are updated using Rules 1–4 of Algorithm 10.4.

EXAMPLE 10.12.–

Deletion of key 25 illustrated in Figure 10.18(b) is a case of deletion of a node with a single subtree. Observe how the RCHILD link of node 20 (the root) is reset to point to node 30, the right child of node 25. Since the deletion occurred to the right of node 20, $bf(20)$ is updated to $+1$. Again, the deletion does not call for any rotation to balance the tree.

Rotation free deletion of a node having both the subtrees

In the case of deletion of node t which has both its subtrees to be non-empty, the deletion is a little more involved (see Algorithm 10.5). We first replace DATA (node t) with the smallest key of the right subtree of node t or with the largest key of the left subtree of node t. Algorithm 10.4 illustrates a replacement using the smallest key on the right subtree of node t. The smallest key of the right subtree of node t can be obtained by moving right and then moving deep left until the left child link is NIL. Similarly, moving left and then moving deep right until an empty right child link is seen will yield the largest element in the left subtree of node t. An important observation here is that the node representing the smallest value of the right subtree or the largest value of the left subtree will turn out to be either leaf nodes or nodes with a single subtree. Now we physically delete the node holding this replacement value using the procedure discussed for the deletion of a leaf node or a node with a single subtree (see Algorithm 10.4).

EXAMPLE 10.13.–

Deletion of node 15 from the balanced AVL search tree shown in Figure 10.18 yields the balanced tree shown in Figure 10.18(c). Here, the *value 15* in the respective node is *replaced by 18*, the smallest value in the right subtree of node 15. Now we physically delete the leaf node holding 18 using the case discussed earlier.

Observe how *bf*(18) (the balance factor of the node which earlier had the value 15 but now holds the replaced value 18) is updated to +1 and applying Rule 3 of Algorithm 10.4, the balance factors of no other ancestor nodes are changed. The example once again illustrates a case of rotation free deletion.

procedure DELETE1(T, node t)

/*Steps to delete an ITEM from a non-empty AVL search tree T. node t that holds ITEM and is either a leaf node or one with a single non empty subtree has been identified. The node structure comprises the fields LCHILD, DATA, BF and RCHILD representing left child link, data, balance factor and right child link respectively */

if node t is a leaf node **or** a node with a single child
then
        { Let node p be its parent node;
          Delete node t and reset the links of node p appropriately so as to either have a null link or to point to the lone child of node t as is the case;
        }
else
        call DELETE2(T, node t); /* call procedure
                          DELETE2(T, node t)*/

Update balance factors:

Rule 1: With regard to node p, if node t's deletion occurred in its right subtree then bf(p) increases by 1 and if it occurred in its left subtree then bf(p) decreases by 1.
Rule 2: If the new bf(p)=0 then the height of the tree is decreased by 1 and therefore this calls for updating the balance factors of its parent node and/or its ancestor nodes.
Rule 3: If the new bf(p) = ±1, then the height of the tree is the same as it was before deletion and therefore the balance factors of the ancestor nodes remains unchanged.
Rule 4: If the new bf(p)= ±2, then the node p is unbalanced and the appropriate rotations need to be called for.

Classify rotations for deletion:

While propagating the balance factor updates from the node p upwards to the root node there may be nodes whose balance factors are updated to ±2. Let A be the first such node on the path from node p to the root.

If the deletion took place on the right of A
then classify the rotation as R else classify it as L;

For the R classification, if $bf(A)=+2$ then it should have been +1 before deletion and A should have a left subtree with root B. Based on $bf(B)$ being either 0 or +1 or -1, classify the R rotations further as R0, R1 and R-1 respectively (Sec. 10.3.5).

For the L classification, if $bf(A)= -2$ then it should have been -1 before deletion and A should have a right subtree with root B. Based on $bf(B)$ being either 0 or +1 or -1, classify the L rotations further as L0, L1 and L-1 respectively (Sec. 10.3.6).

Perform rotation:
Perform the appropriate rotations to balance the tree.

end DELETE1.

Algorithm 10.4. *Skeletal procedure to delete an ITEM from a non-empty AVL search tree T where node t in T holding ITEM is either a leaf node or one with a single subtree*

procedure DELETE2 (T, node t)

```
/*Steps to delete an ITEM from  a non-empty  AVL search tree
T. node t holding ITEM and which has both a left and a right
non-empty subtree has been identified.   The node structure
comprises the fields LCHILD, DATA, BF and RCHILD representing
left child link, data, balance factor and  right child link.
*/
```

if node t is one with a non-empty left and right subtree
then

```
{
    Find the smallest key in the right subtree of
    node t. This is obtained by moving down the
    RCHILD link of node t to reach node u and
    traversing the LCHILD links of the left subtree
    of node u until it is empty;

    Let node v be the last node reached while
    traversing the left subtree of node u down the
    left child nodes.

    Now, LCHILD(node v) = NIL.
    Let SUCC = DATA(node v);
    Replace DATA(node t) with SUCC;
    Delete node v using procedure
    DELETE1(T, node v), since node v will
    either be a leaf node or one with a single
    subtree.
}
```

end DELETE2.

Algorithm 10.5. *Skeletal procedure to delete an ITEM from a non-empty AVL search tree T where node t in T holding ITEM is one with both a left and a right subtree*

As pointed out in Rule 4 of Algorithm 10.4, during the propagation of balance factor updates from the specific node to the root upwards, there could be cases of imbalance among the nodes. To set right the imbalance, it is essential that the category of rotation, viz., *L* or *R*, is identified before sub-classifying it further as *L0/R0*, *L1/R1* or *L-1/R-1*. All the rotations are performed with regard to the first ancestor node *A* encountered on the path to the root node and whose $bf(A) = \pm 2$. Each of the *R* category and *L* category of rotations is illustrated with examples.

10.3.5. *R category rotations associated with the delete operation*

R0 rotation

Figure 10.19 illustrates the generic representation of an *R0* rotation. Node *t* is to be deleted from a balanced tree with *A* shown as the root (for simplicity) and with A_R as its right subtree. *B* is the root of *A*'s left subtree and has two subtrees B_L and B_R. The heights of the subtrees are as shown in the figure. Now the deletion of node *t* results in an imbalance with $bf(A) = +2$. Since deletion of node *t* occurred to the right of *A* and since *A* is the first node on the path to the root, the situation calls for an R rotation with respect to A. Again since $bf(B) = 0$, the rebalancing needs to be brought about using an $R0$ rotation only. Here, B pushes itself up to occupy A's position pushing node A to its right along with A_R. While B retains B_L as its left subtree, B_R is handed over to node A to function as its left subtree. Observe how the tree regains its balance.

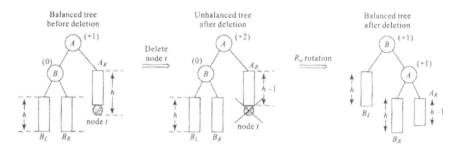

Figure 10.19. *Generic representation of an R0 rotation*

EXAMPLE 10.14.–

Figure 10.20 illustrates the deletion of key 65 from the balanced tree shown. Since 65 occurred to the right of 55, $bf(55)$ is updated to 0. This implies the balance factors of its ancestors nodes need to be updated. When we proceed to the node holding 50, $bf(50)$ is updated to +2. This calls for an $R0$ rotation with respect to node 50. The notations of the generic representation (see Figure 10.19) have been mapped to the given tree for ease of understanding. At the end of the rotation, the tree is balanced with 30 as its root and the tree appropriately rearranged.

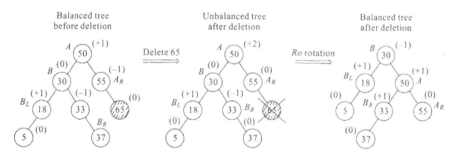

Figure 10.20. *Deletion of a node calling for R0 rotation*

R1 rotation

Figure 10.21 illustrates the generic representation of an *R1* rotation. Deletion of node *t* occurs to the right of *A*, the first ancestor node whose $bf(A) = +2$. But $bf(B) = +1$ classifies it further as *R1* rotation. The rotation is similar to the *R0* rotation and yields a balanced tree.

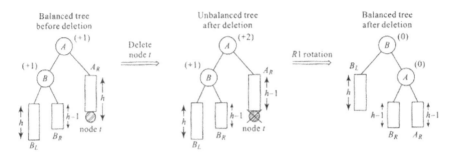

Figure 10.21. *Generic representation of an R1 rotation*

EXAMPLE 10.15.−

Figure 10.22 shows the deletion of key 80 from the given balanced AVL search tree. The deletion occurs to the right of 76 and while updating the balance factors of the ancestor nodes yields $bf(76) = +2$, which is the first and only ancestor node reporting imbalance. *R1* rotation yields 60 as the root with the tree accordingly rearranged to balance it.

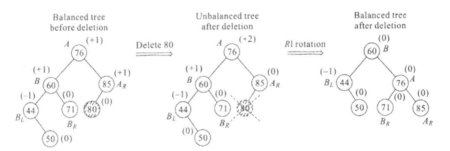

Figure 10.22. *Deletion of a node calling for R1 rotation*

R-1 rotation

The generic representation of an R-1 rotation is shown in Figure 10.23. As in the other rotations deletion of node t results in the imbalance of the tree with regard to A and also leaves $bf(B) = -1$ calling for R-1 rotation. Here, let C be the root of the right subtree of B and C_L and C_R its left and right subtrees, respectively. During the rotation, C elevates itself to become the root pushing A along with its right subtree A_R to its right. The tree is now rearranged with C_L as the right subtree of B and C_R as the left subtree of A. The tree automatically gets balanced. R-1 rotation is a case of double rotation where the rotation is once applied over B and then again over A.

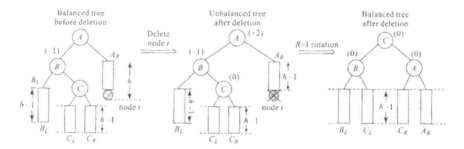

Figure 10.23. *Generic representation of an R-1 rotation*

EXAMPLE 10.16.–

Figure 10.24 illustrates the deletion of key 40 from the given balanced AVL search tree. Since 40 occurs to the left of the key 46, $bf(46)$ is updated to 0 triggering an update of $bf(35)$ which yields +2. Since $bf(21) = -1$, we resort to R-1 rotation. The rest of the steps in the rotation follow those shown in the generic representation (see Figure 10.23).

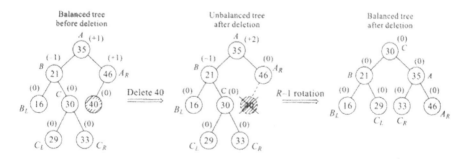

Figure 10.24. *Deletion of a node calling for R-1 rotation*

10.3.6. *L category rotations associated with the delete operation*

If the deletion of node t occurs to the left of A, the first ancestor node on the path to the root reporting $bf(A) = -2$, then the category of rotation to be applied is L. As in R rotations, based on $bf(B) = +1, -1$ or 0 the L rotation is further classified as *L1, L-1* and *L0*, respectively. The generic representations of the *L0, L1* and L-1 rotations are shown in Figure 10.25. An illustrative example for the L category of rotations is presented in illustrative problem 10.9.

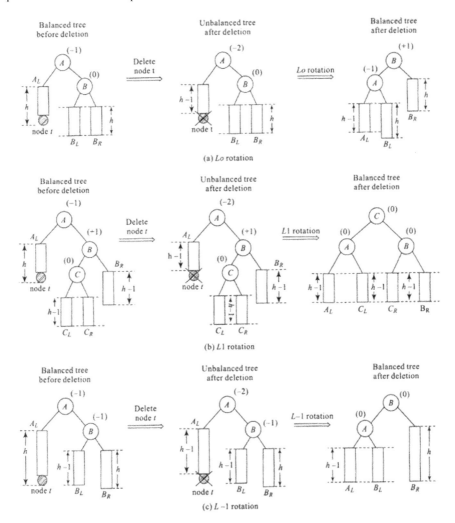

Figure 10.25. *Generic representations of L0, L1 and L-1 rotations*

Unlike insertion, to rebalance a tree after a deletion it may be that more than one rotation is required. In fact, the number of rotations required is $O(log\ n)$. It can be observed that there are similarities between the *LL, LR, RL* and *RR* rotations undertaken during insertion and the *L0/R0, L1/R1* and *L-1/R-1* rotations undertaken during deletion.

10.4. Applications

10.4.1. *Representation of symbol tables in compiler design*

Compilers are translators that translate a source programming language code into a target programming language code, viz., machine code or assembly level language code. The various phases in the design of compilers include *lexical analysis, syntactic analysis, semantic analysis, intermediate code generation, code optimization* and *code generation*.

During lexical analysis, which is the first phase of the compiler, the source program is scanned character by character to identify the keywords, user identifiers, constants, labels, etc., which are termed as *tokens*. These tokens are stored in data structures called *symbol table*s, which store information pertaining to the tokens as a *name-attribute* pair. Thus, there are individual symbol tables for keywords, user identifiers, constants, etc.

Symbol tables which are constructed for a fixed set of data already known in advance and calling for no insert or delete operations after construction, but are only susceptible to search or retrieval operations are known as *static tables*. On the other hand, those symbol tables which support insertion and deletion operations besides search are known as *dynamic tables*. While a keyword table is an example of a static symbol table, a user identifier table is an example of a dynamic table.

With regard to the keywords that are fixed for a given source language, a compiler stores them using a static symbol table using an appropriate data structure that favors efficient retrievals. This is so since the lexical analyzer distinguishes a keyword token k, from a user identifier token u, by undertaking a search of the tokens k and u on the keyword table. While the search for k in the keyword table would yield a successful search, the same for u would yield an unsuccessful search. Those appropriately selected tokens which yield an unsuccessful search in the keyword table are classified as user id tokens and stored separately in a user id table. It is here that one sees the application of binary search trees and we terminate any further discussion on compilers at this point.

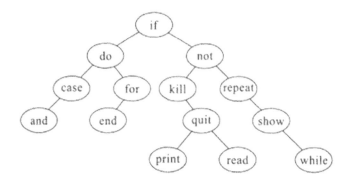

Figure 10.26. *Representation of a sample keyword table using binary search trees*

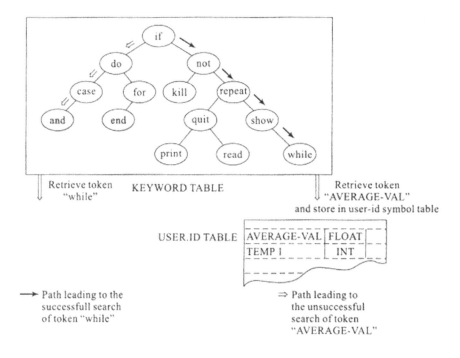

Figure 10.27. *Searching for a keyword and a user id from a keyword symbol table represented using a binary search tree*

Since the keyword and user id tokens need searching for the presence or the absence of their respective tokens in the keyword table, it is essential that the keyword table is represented using a data structure that supports efficient retrievals.

A binary search tree is an excellent candidate for the representation of both static and dynamic symbol tables considering its $O(log\ n)$ average case complexity for insert, delete and retrieval operations. Figure 10.26 shows a sample keyword table represented using a binary search tree. Figure 10.27 illustrates a successful and an unsuccessful search of a token on the tree shown in Figure 10.26. While the retrieval of token "while" yields success in five comparisons, the retrieval of "AVERAGE-VAL" which is a user id results in an unsuccessful search in four comparisons and hence find its place in the user id table shown.

The application of binary search trees for the representation of keyword symbol table in compiler design can be probed further to bring in the application of AVL search trees as well. It is known that for a given set K of keywords, a finite set of binary search trees may be constructed. However, the problem now is to look for the most efficient representation among the binary search trees. Though a procedure to construct an *optimal binary search tree*, viz., a binary search tree which reports the minimum cost (see illustrative problem 10.4), the optimal binary search tree may lead to inefficient retrievals comparatively due to the imbalance of nodes. It is in such a case that the application of AVL search trees becomes visible. Representing the keyword table as an AVL search tree ensures the retrieval of tokens in $O(log\ n)$ time in the worst case.

Summary

– Binary search trees may be empty or if otherwise are labeled binary trees where the left child key is less than its parent node key and right child key is greater than the parent node key. All the keys forming a binary search tree are distinct. Binary search trees are represented using linked representations. However, in many cases, it is convenient to represent them as extended binary trees.

– A search or retrieval operation on a binary search tree is of $O(log\ n)$ complexity and hence is more efficient than the same over a sequential list. The insert and delete operations are also of $O(log\ n)$ complexity.

– The insertion of a key in a binary search tree is similar to that of searching for the key (unsuccessfully) and inserting it at the appropriate position as a leaf node. The deletion of a binary search tree is discussed depending on whether the deleted node is a leaf node or a node with a single subtree or a node with two subtrees.

– Binary search trees suffer from the drawback of becoming skewed especially when the keys are inserted in their sorted order.

– The total number of binary search trees with n different keys can be determined using Catalan numbers.

– AVL trees are height-balanced trees with the balance factor of the nodes being either 0, 1 or –1. AVL search trees are height-balanced binary search trees.

– The search or retrieval operation on an AVL search tree is similar to that on a binary search tree.

– The insertion operation on an AVL search tree is similar to that of a binary search tree but when it leads to imbalance of the tree, any one of the rotations, viz., *LL, LR, RL* and *RR*, are undertaken to rebalance the tree.

– The deletion operation on an AVL search tree is classified as that of a leaf node, or a node with a single subtree or a node with two subtrees. In the event of any imbalance in the tree, the *R* category of rotations, viz., *R0, R1, R*-1, and the *L* category of rotations, viz., *L0, L1* and *L*-1 or a combination, are called for to rebalance the tree.

– Binary search trees and AVL search trees find application in the representation of symbol tables in compiler design.

10.5. Illustrative problems

PROBLEM 10.1.–

a) Construct a binary search tree T for the following set S of elements in the order given:

S = { INDIGO, GREEN, CYAN, YELLOW, RED, ORANGE, VIOLET}

b) How many comparisons are made for the retrieval of "YELLOW" from the tree corresponding to the one drawn in Figure P10.1(a)?

c) For what arrangements of elements of S will the associated binary search tree turn out to be skewed?

d) For the binary search tree(s) constructed in Figure P10.1(c), how many comparisons are made for the retrieval of "YELLOW"?

Solution:

a) The binary search tree constructed for *S* with the elements considered in the order given is shown in Figure P10.1(a).

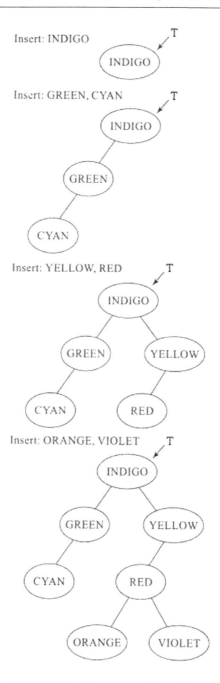

Figure P10.1(a). *The binary search tree T constructed for list S given in illustrative problem 10.1(a)*

Ascending order of S: {CYAN, GREEN, INDIGO, ORANGE, RED, VIOLET, YELLOW}

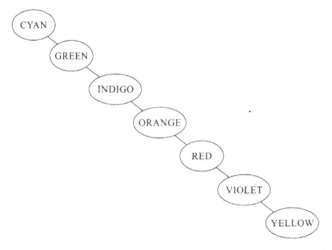

Descending order of S: {YELLOW, VIOLET, RED, ORANGE, INDIGO, GREEN, CYAN}

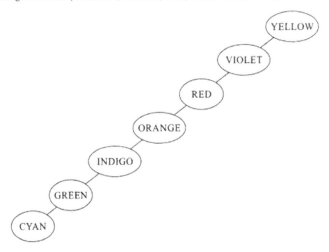

Figure P10.1(b). *Skewed binary search trees associated
with list S given in illustrative problem 10.1(a)*

b) The number of comparisons for the retrieval of "YELLOW" is 2. The search key "YELLOW" is first compared with the root, which is "INDIGO" and since "YELLOW" is greater than "INDIGO", the search moves to the right of "INDIGO", where it is found entailing one more comparison.

c) If the elements of S are sorted either in the ascending or in the descending order, then the associated binary search tree will be either right skewed or left skewed, respectively. Figure P10.1(b) illustrates the trees.

d) In the case of the left skewed tree, the number of comparisons for "YELLOW" is 1 and in the case of the right skewed tree, the number of comparisons is 7.

PROBLEM 10.2.–

Given the following binary search trees, draw the same after the deletion of the specified elements in the respective binary search trees.

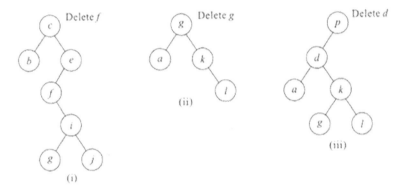

Solution:

Deletion of *f* is a case of deletion of a node with a single non-empty subtree with root *i*. Hence simply delete *f* and link the node *e* with node *i*.

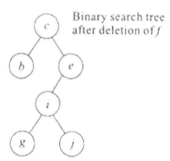

Binary search tree after deletion of *f*

Deletion of *g* is a case of deletion of a node with two non-empty subtrees. Delete *g* and push *k* along with its subtree to be the root. *a* joins as the left child of *k*.

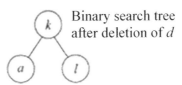

Binary search tree after deletion of *d*

Deletion of *d* is again a case of deletion of a node with two non-empty subtrees. After the deletion of *d*, *k* along with its subtrees moves up. *a* joins *g* as its left child.

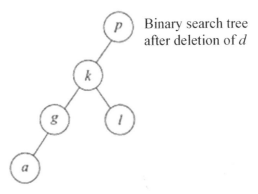

Binary search tree after deletion of *d*

PROBLEM 10.3.–

On the binary search tree shown in Figure P10.1(a), perform the following operations in the order shown:

Insert GREY, Insert PINK, Delete YELLOW, Delete RED

Solution:

The trees after the two insert operations and two delete operations in the given sequence are shown below:

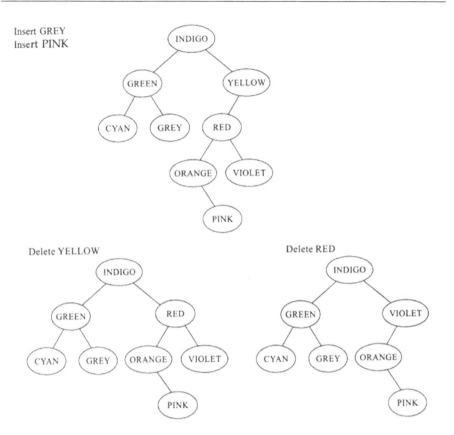

PROBLEM 10.4.–

[**Optimal binary search trees**] Let $S = \{a_1, a_2, a_3, \ldots a_n\}$ be a set of elements and T_k be the set of associated binary search trees that can be constructed out of S. Let p_i $1 \leq i \leq n$, be the probability with which a_i is searched for (probability of successful search) and let q_j $0 \leq j \leq n$ be the probability with which a key X, $a_j \leq X \leq a_{j+1}$ is unsuccessfully searched for (probability of an unsuccessful search) on a binary search tree T_k. As explained in section 10.2.2, the search for such an X will end up in an appropriate external node e_j. The cost of a binary search tree is given by:

$$\sum_{1 \leq i \leq n} p_i \cdot level(a_i) + \sum_{0 \leq j \leq n} q_j \cdot (level(e_j) - 1)$$

An optimal binary search tree is a tree $T \in T_k$ such that cost(T) is the minimum. The term $\sum_{0 \le j \le n} q_j \cdot (level(e_j) - 1)$ when q_j $0 \le j \le n$ represent weights associated with the external nodes is known as weighted external path length.

Consider a set S = {end, goto, print, stop}, let $\{p_1, p_2, p_3, p_4\} = \left\{\frac{1}{20}, \frac{1}{5}, \frac{1}{10}, \frac{1}{20}\right\}$ and $\{q_0, q_1, q_2, q_3, q_4\} = \left\{\frac{1}{5}, \frac{1}{10}, \frac{1}{5}, \frac{1}{20}, \frac{1}{20}\right\}$. Find the cost of the following binary search trees and show which of the two have the minimum cost?

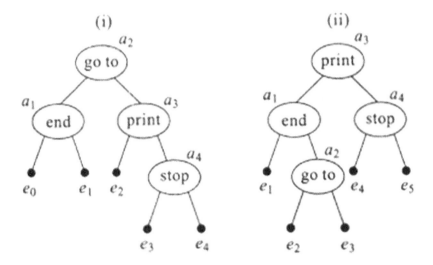

Solution:

The cost of tree (i) is given by:

$$\left\{\frac{1}{20} \cdot 2 + \frac{1}{5} \cdot 1 + \frac{1}{10} \cdot 2 + \frac{1}{20} \cdot 3\right\} + \left\{\frac{1}{5} \cdot 2 + \frac{1}{10} \cdot 2 + \frac{1}{5} \cdot 2 + \frac{1}{20} \cdot 3 + \frac{1}{20} \cdot 3\right\}$$

$$= \frac{13}{20} + \frac{26}{20} = \frac{39}{20}$$

The cost of tree(ii) is given by:

$$\left\{\frac{1}{20} \cdot 2 + \frac{1}{5} \cdot 3 + \frac{1}{10} \cdot 1 + \frac{1}{20} \cdot 2\right\} + \left\{\frac{1}{5} \cdot 2 + \frac{1}{10} \cdot 3 + \frac{1}{5} \cdot 3 + \frac{1}{20} \cdot 2 + \frac{1}{20} \cdot 2\right\}$$

$$= \frac{18}{20} + \frac{30}{20} = \frac{48}{20}$$

Hence, among the two binary search trees, tree(i) is a minimum cost binary search tree.

PROBLEM 10.5.–

Which of the following is an AVL tree?

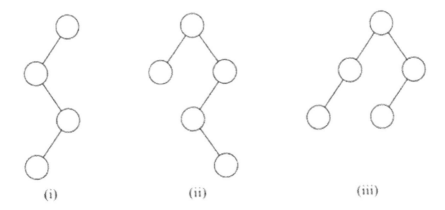

(i)   (ii)   (iii)

Solution:

The one shown in (iii).

PROBLEM 10.6.–

Construct an AVL search tree using the following data. Perform the appropriate rotations to rebalance the tree.

OS/2, LINUX, DOS, UNIX, XENIX, MAC

Solution:

The construction of the AVL search tree is as shown below:

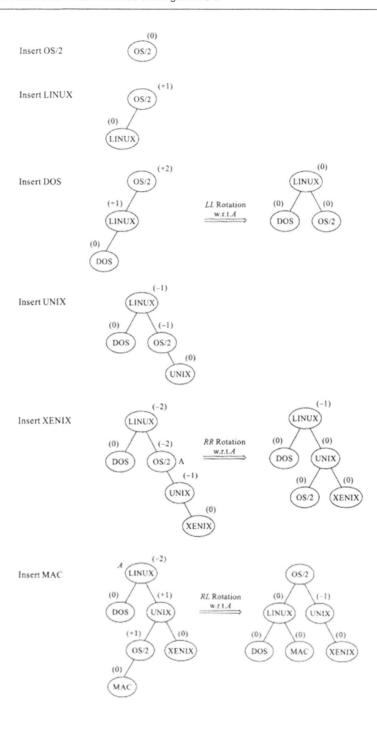

PROBLEM 10.7.–

For the AVL search tree constructed in illustrative problem 10.6, perform the following operations using the original tree for each operation:

Delete DOS, Delete UNIX, Delete OS/2.

Solution:

Each of the delete operations as performed on the original tree is illustrated below:

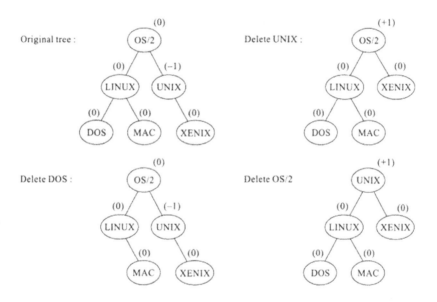

Observe that each of the three cases are examples of deletion of a leaf node, a node with a single subtree and a node with both subtrees, respectively. Also the deletion operations are rotation free.

PROBLEM 10.8.–

For the following AVL search tree, undertake the following deletions in the sequence shown:

Delete I, Delete B, Delete H

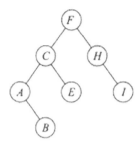

Solution:

The balanced tree after the execution of the three operations in a sequence is shown below:

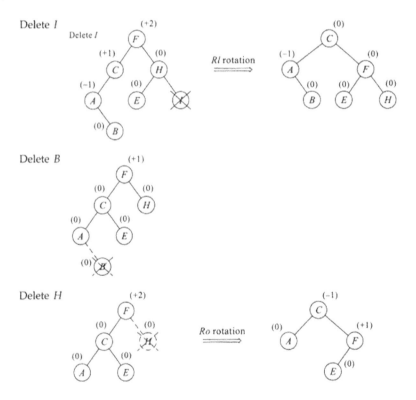

Here, while Delete I and Delete H called for *R1* and *R0* rotations, respectively, Delete B did not call for any rotations.

PROBLEM 10.9.–

Perform the following deletions on the given AVL search trees:

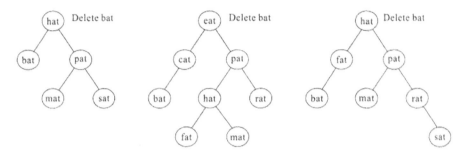

Solution:

This problem is an illustration of *L category rotations*. Hence, the notations A, B, C, A_L, A_R, B_L, B_R, C_L and C_R employed in the generic representations of the L rotations (see section 10.3.6) have been used in the tree for ease of understanding.

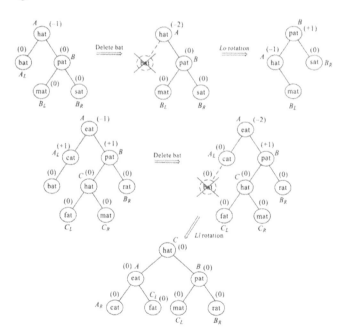

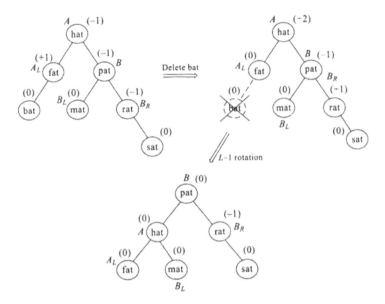

PROBLEM 10.10.–

Delete 75 from the following AVL search tree:

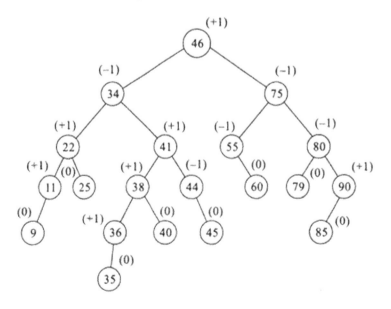

Solution:

The deletion of 75 leads to deletion of 79 and calls for two rotations, viz., *L1* and *R*-1, to set right the imbalance. The various steps during the deletion are shown below:

Step 1: Delete 75
leads to
Delete 79

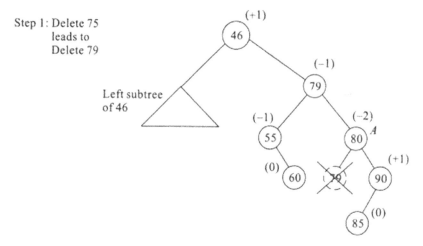

Step 2: Call *L1* rotation

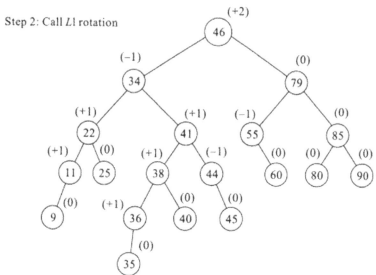

Step 3: Call $R-1$ rotation

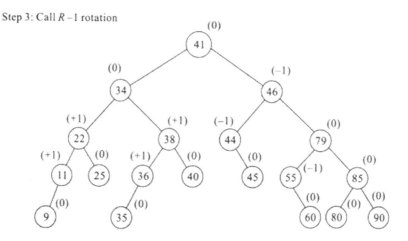

PROBLEM 10.11.–

Given a binary search tree T, how can the minimum and maximum elements in the binary search tree be obtained? What would be the time complexity if the binary search tree T was a left skewed or a right skewed tree?

Solution:

Traversing the binary search tree T beginning with the root node and recursively moving left until a leaf node is reached yields the minimum element that is represented by the leaf node. A similar traversal beginning with the root node and recursively moving right until a leaf node is reached yields the maximum element that is represented by the leaf node.

If the binary search tree T comprising n nodes was left skewed, then the minimum element retrieval would yield a time complexity of $O(n)$ and the maximum element retrieval a time complexity of $O(1)$. On the other hand, if the binary search tree T was right skewed, then the time complexity of retrieving the minimum element would be $O(1)$ and the same for retrieval of maximum element would be $O(n)$.

PROBLEM 10.12.–

Count the number of binary search trees that can be constructed out of the list {56, 110, 44, 75}.

Solution:

Since the list contains $n = 4$ distinct elements, the number of distinct binary search trees that can be constructed using Catalan number is $C_4 = 14$. Table P10.12 shows the distinct binary search trees constructed.

$n = 4$ list {56, 110, 44, 75}   Catalan number

$$C_4 = 14 = \frac{8!}{5!\,4!}$$

binary search trees:

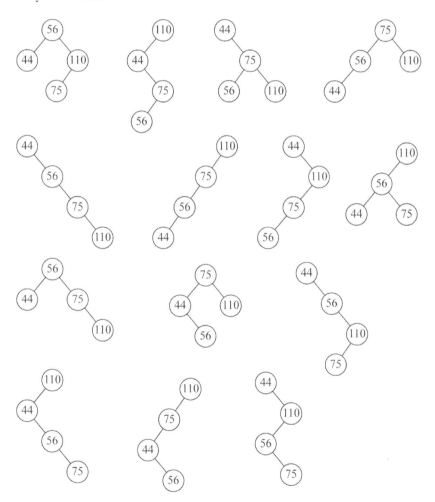

Table P10.12. *The distinct binary search trees constructed for the list {56, 110, 44, 75}*

Review questions

1) Which among the following norms is not satisfied by a binary search tree *T*?

i) All keys of the binary search tree need not be distinct.

ii) All keys in the left subtree of *T* are less than the root element.

iii) All keys in the right subtree of *T* are greater than the root element.

iv) The left and right subtrees of *T* are also binary search trees.

a) (i)   b) (ii)   c) (iii)   d) (iv)

2) State whether true or false:

In the case of a binary search tree with *n* nodes,

i) the number of external nodes is $(n-1)$;

ii) an inorder traversal yields the keys of the nodes in the ascending order.

a) (i) true, (ii) true   b) (i) true, (ii) false

c) (i) false, (ii) true   d) (i) false, (ii) false

3) Which among the following deteriorates the performance of a binary search tree *T* with *n* nodes?

i) When there are a large number of deletions to *T*.

ii) When the number of external nodes becomes $(n+1)$.

iii) When the height of *T* becomes *n*.

iv) When the height of *T* becomes $log_2 n$.

a) (i)   b) (ii)   c) (iii)   d) (iv)

4) The balance factor of any node in an AVL tree cannot be:

a) 0   b) +1   c) –1   d) +3

5) In an AVL tree, during the deletion of node *t* which is a leaf node and whose parent node is node *p*, which among the following does not happen during the sequence of operations?

i) Physically delete node *t* and make the child link of its parent, viz., node *p* null.

ii) Make the child link of node p point to the child node of node t and then physically delete node t.

iii) Update the balance factor of node p based on whether the deletion occurred to its right or left.

iv) Update the balance factors of the ancestor nodes of node p.

a) (i)   b) (ii)   c) (iii)   d) (iv)

6) If a key u to be deleted from a binary search tree has only a left subtree and if it were the right child of its parent node, then

i) set both the links of its parent node to NIL;

ii) allow the right link of its parent node alone to be NIL;

iii) allow the left link of its parent node to point to the left subtree of key u;

iv) allow the right link of its parent node to point to the left subtree of key u.

a) (i)   b) (ii)   c) (iii)   d) (iv)

7) How are binary search tree representation of lists advantageous over their sequential list representations?

8. How is the deletion of a node that has both left and right subtrees undertaken in a binary search tree?

9) What is the need for an AVL tree?

10) How is the rotation free deletion of a node having both the subtrees done in an AVL search tree?

11) Outline the generic representation of an LL type imbalance in an AVL search tree and the corresponding rotation.

12) For the following list of data, construct a binary search tree:

LINUX, OS2, DOS, XENIX, SOLARIS, WINDOWS, VISTA, XP, UNIX, CPM.

Undertake the following operations on the binary search tree:

(i) Insert   MAC   (ii) Delete WINDOWS   (iii) Delete UNIX

13) Represent the data list shown in review question 12 as a sequential list. Tabulate the number of comparisons undertaken for retrieving the following keys:

(i) LINUX   (ii) XENIX   (iii) DOS   (iv) UNIX   (v) CPM

14) For the data list {AND, BEGIN, CASE, DO, END, FOR, GOTO, IF, IN, LET, NOT, OR, QUIT, READ, REPEAT, RESET, THEN, UNTIL, WHILE, XOR}

(i) Construct a binary search tree. What are your observations?

(ii) Construct an AVL search tree.

15) For the AVL search tree constructed in review question 14, delete the following keys in the order given:

XOR, READ, END, AND.

16) Given a list of 10 distinct elements, how many distinct binary search trees and binary trees can be constructed out of it?

Programming assignments

1) Implement a menu-driven program to perform the following operations on a binary search tree:

i) Construct a binary search tree (construction begins from an empty tree).

ii) Insert element(s) into a non-empty binary search tree.

iii) Delete element(s) from a non-empty binary search tree.

iv) Search for an element in a binary search tree.

2) Write a function to retrieve the elements of a binary search tree in the sorted order.

3) Execute a programming project to illustrate the construction of an AVL search tree. Demonstrate the construction, insertion and deletion operations using graphics and animation.

4) [*Huffman Coding*] D Huffman applied binary trees with minimal external path length to obtain an optimal set of codes for messages M_j $0 \leq j \leq n$. Each message is encoded using a binary string for transmission. At the receiving end, the messages are decoded using a binary tree in which external nodes represent messages and the external path to the node represents the binary string encoding of the message. Thus, if 0 labels a left branch and 1 a right branch, then a sample decode tree given below can decode messages M_0, M_1, M_2, M_3 represented using codes {0, 100, 101, 11}. These codes are called *Huffman codes*. The expected decode time is given by $\sum_{0 \leq i \leq n} q_i \cdot d_i$, where d_i is the distance of the external node representing message M_i from the root node and q_i is the relative frequency with which the message M_i is transmitted. It is obvious that the cost of decoding a message is dependent on the number of bits in the binary code of the message and

hence on the external path to the node representing the message. Therefore, the problem is to look for a decode tree with minimal weighted external path length to speed up decoding.

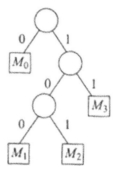

i) Investigate the algorithm given by D Huffman to obtain a decode tree with minimal weighted external path length.

ii) Implement the algorithm given a sample set of weights q_i.

5) Implement an algorithm which given an AVL search tree T and a data item X splits the AVL search tree into two AVL search trees T_1, T_2 such that all the keys in tree T_1 are less than or equal to X and all the keys in tree T_2 are greater than X, respectively.

6) Write a program to check if a binary tree is a binary search tree or not. (Hint: In order traversal.)

7) Write a program that will consider two binary search trees each with m and n nodes and insert the smaller of the two trees to the larger one by inserting each of the nodes in the smaller tree one by one into the larger tree. What is the time complexity of this algorithm?

11

B Trees and Tries

11.1. Introduction

In this chapter, we discuss data structures pertaining to *multi-way trees*. Multi-way trees are tree data structures with more than two branches at a node. The data structures of *m-way search trees*, *B trees* and *tries* belong to this category of tree structures.

AVL search trees, which are height-balanced versions of binary search trees, no doubt promote efficient retrievals and storage operations. The complexity of insert, delete and search operations on AVL search trees is $O(log\ n)$. However, while considering applications such as file indexing, where the entries in an index may be very large, maintaining the index as m-way search trees provides a better option than AVL search trees, which are only balanced binary search trees. While binary search trees are 2-way search trees, m-way search trees, which are extended binary search trees, are multi-way search trees and hence are beneficial for more efficient retrievals.

B trees are height-balanced versions of m-way search trees and hence command their own merits. For all search trees which deal with key-based storage and retrievals, it is essential that the keys are of fixed size for efficient storage management. In other words, these data structures do not recommend the representation of keys with varying sizes. Tries are tree-based data structures that support keys with varying sizes. While other search trees indulge in searching based on the whole key, tries also have the benefit of being based on searching only a portion of the key before the whole key is retrieved or stored.

The definition and operations of the three data structures, that is, m-way search trees, B trees and tries, are detailed in this chapter. Finally, the application of the data structures to file indexing and spell checking are discussed.

11.2. *m*-way search trees: definition and operations

m-way search trees are extensions of binary search trees. Binary search trees indulge in, at most, two-way branching at every node with the left subtree of the node representing elements less than the key value of the node and the right subtree representing elements, which are greater than the key value of the node. On the other hand, each node of an *m*-way search tree can hold at most *m* branches. Thus, *m*-way search trees adopt multi-way branching extending the above-mentioned characteristic of binary search trees.

11.2.1. *Definition*

An *m*-way search tree T may be an empty tree. If T is non-empty, then the following properties must hold true:

i) For some integer m, known as the order of the tree, each node has at most m child nodes. In other words, each node in T is of degree at most m. Thus, a node of degree m will be represented as,

$C_0, (K_1, C_1), (K_2, C_2), (K_3, C_3) \ldots (K_{m-1}, C_{m-1})$ where $K_i, 1 \leq i \leq m - 1$ are the keys and $C_j, 0 \leq j \leq m - 1$ are pointers to the root nodes of the m subtrees of the node.

ii) If a node has k child nodes, $k \leq m$, then the node has exactly *(k–1)* keys $K_1, K_2, K_3, \ldots K_{k-1}$ where $K_i < K_{i+1}$ and each of the keys K_i partitions the keys in the subtrees into k subsets.

iii) For a node $C_0, (K_1, C_1), (K_2, C_2), (K_3, C_3) \ldots (K_{m-1}, C_{m-1})$, all key values in the subtree pointed to by C_i are less than the key $K_{i+1}, 0 \leq i \leq m - 2$ and the key values in the subtree pointed to by C_{m-1} are greater than K_{m-1}.

iv) The subtrees pointed to by $C_i, 0 \leq i \leq m - 1$ are also *m*-way search trees.

11.2.2. *Node structure and representation*

An *m*-way search tree is conceived to be an extended tree with its null pointers represented by external nodes. Although this method of representation is useful for its definition and discussion of its operations, the external nodes, as in the case of any general tree, are only fictional and not physically represented.

Figure 11.1 illustrates a general structure of a node in an *m*-way search tree. The node has $(m - 1)$ key elements and hence exactly m child pointers to the root nodes of the *m* subtrees. Those pointers to subtrees, which are empty, are indicated by external nodes, represented as solid circles emanating from gray-shaded fields.

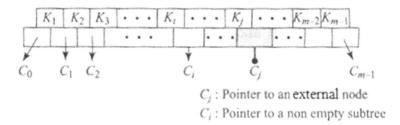

C_j : Pointer to an **external** node

C_i : Pointer to a non empty subtree

Figure 11.1. *Structure of a node in an* m-way search tree

EXAMPLE 11.1.–

An example of 4-way search tree is shown in Figure 11.2. Observe how each node has at most four child nodes, some of which are external nodes. Also note that every node has exactly $(p - 1)$ keys if the number of child nodes it has is p. The root node, for example, has four child pointers and hence four subtrees. The number of keys in the root node is therefore three, that is, [34, 56, 84]. The first subtree of the root node contains keys, which are less than 34; the second subtree, which contains keys greater than 34 and less than 56, is empty; the third subtree contains keys greater than 56 and less than 84; and finally the last subtree contains keys greater than 84. A similar concept is extended to every other node in the subtrees.

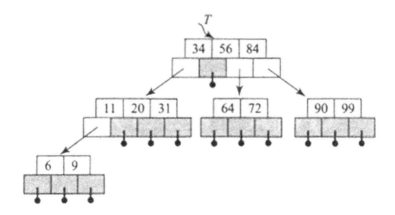

Figure 11.2. *An example of a 4-way search tree*

11.2.3. *Searching an* m-*way search tree*

Searching for a key K in an m-way search tree T is an extension of the method by which the key would have been searched for in a binary search tree. K is first sequentially searched against the key elements of the root node $[K_i, K_{i+1}, \ldots K_t]$. If $K = K_j$, then the search is done. If $K > K_j$ and $K < K_{j+1}$ for some j, then the search moves down to the root node of the corresponding subtree T_j. The search progresses in a similar fashion until the key is obtained, in which case the search is termed successful. If it is not found, it is termed unsuccessful.

Consider the sample 4-way search tree shown in Figure 11.2. Searching for key 6 calls for moving down the first subtree of the root [34, 56, 84], since 6 < 34. The search further moves down the first subtree of the node [11, 20, 31] since 6 < 11. Now the node [6, 9] is reached. A mere sequential search of the key in the list of elements reports the presence of 6. The path traced by the search for the successful search of 6 is shown in Figure 11. 3. Let us now search for key 66 in the tree shown in Figure 11.2. Since 66 > 56 and 66 < 84, the search moves down the third subtree of the root node. Here, the node [64, 72] is encountered and it is sequentially searched for 66. Since 66 > 64 and 66 < 72, the search moves down the second subtree of the node [64, 72], which is an external node. Here, the search terminates and the search is termed unsuccessful since the element 66 is not found in the tree. The path traced by the search is shown in Figure 11.3.

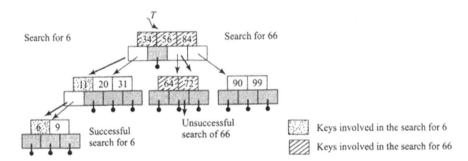

Figure 11.3. *Search for keys 6 and 66 in the 4-way search tree shown in Figure 11.2*

11.2.4. *Inserting into an* m-*way search tree*

The insertion of a key into an m-way search tree proceeds as we would to search for the key. The search is bound to fall off at some node in the tree. At that position, the key may be either inserted as an element if the node can accommodate the key or may be inserted as a new node in the next level.

Consider the insertion of key 95 in Figure 11.2. Searching for 95 results in falling off the tree at the node [90, 99]. Since the tree is a 4-way search tree, every node in the tree can accommodate at most three keys. Therefore, we merely insert 95 in the node [90, 99] to obtain [90, 95, 99]. Accordingly, observe the change in the pointer fields of the node. Let us now insert 25 into the same tree. In this case, searching for 25 results in falling off the tree at an external node belonging to [11, 20, 31]. Since the node is already full with three elements, we insert 25 as a new node in the subtree of [11, 20, 31]. Figure 11.4 illustrates the insertion of keys 95 and 25 in the given 4-way search tree.

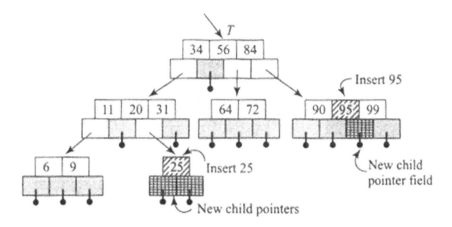

Figure 11.4. *Insertion of keys 95 and 25 into the 4-way search tree shown in Figure 11.2*

11.2.5. *Deleting from an* m-*way search tree*

The delete operation as always is complicated when compared to its insert operation counterpart. To delete a key, we proceed as usual to find the key in the tree. Now let us suppose the key K is found in a node with its left subtree pointer as C_i and its right subtree pointer as C_j. Based on the following cases (**Dm** indicates **D**eletion in an **m**-way search tree), the deletion of K is undertaken:

Case Dm. 1: $C_i = C_j = $ NIL. If the left and right subtrees of key K are NIL, then we simply delete the key K and adjust the number of pointer fields in the node.

Case Dm. 2: $C_i = $ NIL and $C_j \neq $ NIL. If the left subtree of key K is empty and the right subtree is not, choose the smallest key K' from the right subtree of K and replace K with K'. This in turn may recursively call for the appropriate deletion of K' from the tree following one or more of the four cases.

Case Dm. 3: $C_i \neq$ NIL and $C_j =$ NIL. If the right subtree of key K is empty and the left subtree is not, choose the largest key K'' from the left subtree of K and replace K with K''. This in turn may recursively call for the appropriate deletion of K'' from the tree following one or more of the four cases.

Case Dm. 4: $C_i \neq$ NIL and $C_j \neq$ NIL. If the left subtree and the right subtree of key K are non-empty, then choose either the largest key from the left subtree or the smallest key from the right subtree. Call it K'''. Replace key K with the same and as before undertake appropriate steps to delete K''' from the tree.

Let us delete 9 from the 4-way search tree shown in Figure 11.2. The deletion belongs to *Case Dm. 1* where both the left and right subtrees of key 9 are empty. We simply delete 9 from the node.

The delete operation of 11 belongs to *Case Dm. 3* where the left subtree of key 11 is non-empty and its right subtree is empty. We replace 11 with the largest key from its left subtree, that is, 9 and delete 9 following *Case Dm. 1*.

Finally, deleting 84 illustrates *Case Dm. 4* where both its left and right subtrees are non-empty. In such a case, we choose to replace 84 with the smallest key from the right subtree of 84, that is, 90. The deletion of 90 in turn follows *Case Dm. 1*.

The 4-way search tree after the deletion of 9, 11 and 84 are illustrated in Figures 11.5(a–c). The affected nodes and the pointer fields during the deletions have been marked in the figure.

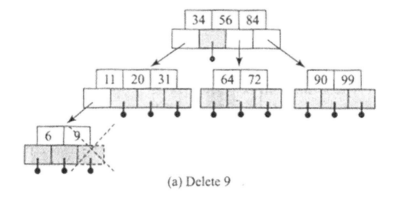

(a) Delete 9

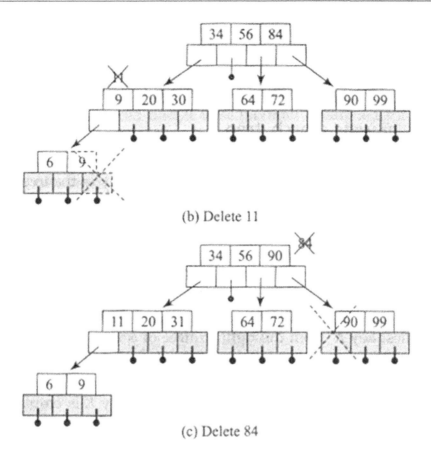

(b) Delete 11

(c) Delete 84

Figure 11.5. *Deletion (independent) of keys 9, 11 and 84 from the 4-way search tree shown in Figure 11.2*

EXAMPLE 11.2.–

Consider a 5-way search tree, shown in Figure 11.6. Let us insert B, Y and L in the sequence given into the original tree. Figure 11.7 illustrates the insertions. While B and L call for insertion of the keys in the existing nodes, Y needs a new node to be opened since the node $[S, T, X, Z]$ is full.

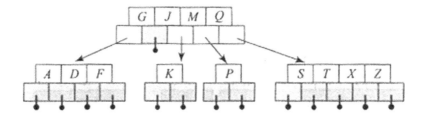

Figure 11.6. *An example of 5-way search tree*

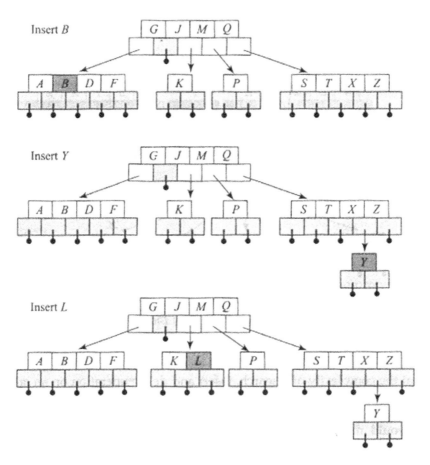

Figure 11.7. *Insertion of B, Y, L into the 5-way search tree shown in Figure 11.6*

EXAMPLE 11.3.–

In the 5-way search tree shown in Figure 11.6, let us delete *T, G, Q* with each deletion independent of the other and performed on the original tree.

Deleting *T* follows *Case Dm. 1* of section 11.2.5. We simply delete *T* and change the pointer fields accordingly. Deleting *G* follows *Case Dm. 3*. We replace *G* with the largest key value chosen from its left subtree, that is, *F*. *F* is deleted from its original position following *Case Dm. 1*. Deleting *Q* follows *Case Dm. 4*. *Q* is replaced by the smallest element in the right subtree of *Q*, that is, *S*. *S* is deleted from its original position following *Case Dm. 1*. Figure 11.8 illustrates each of the three deletions.

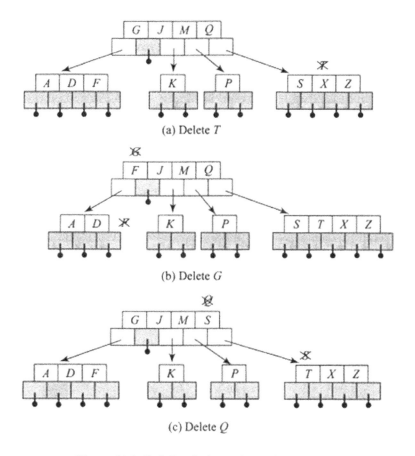

(a) Delete *T*

(b) Delete *G*

(c) Delete *Q*

Figure 11.8. *Deletion (independent) of T, G and Q from the 5-way search tree shown in Figure 11.6*

11.2.6. *Drawbacks of* m-*way search trees*

It is evident that the complexity of a search, insert and delete operation on an *m*-way search tree of height *h* (excluding external nodes) is given by $O(h)$. An *m*-way search tree of height *h* can have elements whose number lies between a minimum of *h* and a maximum of $m^h - 1$. A minimum of *h* elements would mean having one node with one element per node at each level. The maximum would be possible when each level has *m* child nodes and each node on each level has $(m - 1)$ elements. This would imply the maximum number of nodes in any level *i* to be given by m^{i-1}. The total number of nodes in an *m*-way search tree of height *h* would be given by $\sum_{i=1}^{h} m^{i-1} = \frac{(m^h - 1)}{(m-1)}$. Hence, the maximum number of elements in the *m*-way search tree of height *h* would be given by $\frac{(m^h - 1)}{(m-1)} \cdot (m - 1) = (m^h - 1)$.

Since the number of elements in an *m*-way search tree of height *h* varies from a minimum of *h* to a maximum of $m^h - 1$, if the tree represents *n* elements then the height varies from a minimum of $log_m(n + 1)$ to a maximum of *n*. Thus, in the worst case the height of the *m*-way search tree representing *n* elements may be $O(n)$, resulting in poor performance. Hence, it is essential that even *m*-way search trees are maintained with balanced heights. B trees are height-balanced *m*-way search trees and this data structure is detailed in the next section.

11.3. B trees: definition and operations

As mentioned in section 11.2.6, if the growth of the *m*-way search trees is left unchecked, then this may result in trees which yield a complexity of $O(n)$ in the worst case, thereby deteriorating their performance. There is therefore the need for balanced *m*-way search trees, which are known as **B trees of order m**. B trees assure a complexity of $O(\log n)$ for their search, insert and delete operations.

11.3.1. *Definition*

A *B tree of order m* is an *m*-way search tree and hence may be empty. If non-empty, then the following properties are satisfied on its extended tree representation:

i) the root node must have *at least two child nodes* and at most *m* child nodes;

ii) all internal nodes other than the root node must have *at least* $\left\lceil \frac{m}{2} \right\rceil$ non-empty child nodes and at most *m* non-empty child nodes;

iii) the number of keys in each internal node is one less than its number of child nodes, and these keys partition the keys of the tree into subtrees in a manner similar to that of *m*-way search trees;

iv) all external nodes are at the same level.

The node structure and representation of a B tree of order *m* is similar to that of an *m*-way search tree (section 11.2.2). Figure 11.9 illustrates a B tree of order 5. The properties of B trees may be easily verified on the example tree.

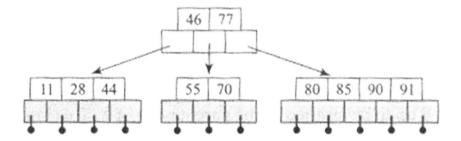

Figure 11.9. *A B tree of order 5*

All internal nodes of the tree except the root have at least $\left\lceil \frac{m}{2} \right\rceil = \left\lceil \frac{5}{2} \right\rceil = 3$ child nodes and hence have at least two keys in their respective nodes. The root node [46, 77] has at least two child nodes. All the external nodes indicated by solid circles are on the same level. The keys in each of the nodes partition the tree into subtrees following the principle of 5-way search trees.

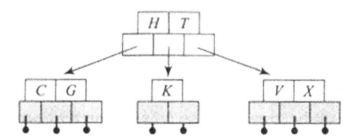

Figure 11.10. *A B tree of order 3 (2-3 tree)*

B trees of order 3 are known as *2-3 trees* since each of their internal nodes have only two or three child nodes. Figure 11.10 illustrates a B tree of order 3. B trees of order 4 are called *2-4 trees* or *2-3-4 trees*. Rudolf Bayer (1972) who first discussed a 2-4 tree called it a *symmetric binary B tree*.

11.3.2. *Searching a B tree of order* m

The search procedure for a B tree of order m is same as the one applied on m-way search trees. The complexity of a search procedure is given by $O(h)$, where h is the height of the B tree of order m (see section 11.3.5).

11.3.3. *Inserting into a B tree of order* m

Inserting a key into a B tree of order m proceeds as we would to search for the key. However, at the point where the search falls off the tree, the key is inserted based on the following norms (***IB*** indicates *I*nsertion in a ***B*** tree):

Case IB. 1: If the node X of the B tree of order m, where the key K is to be inserted, can accommodate K, then it is inserted in the node and the number of child pointer fields is appropriately upgraded.

Thus, if node X is given by $[C_0, (K_1, C_1), (K_2, C_2), \dots (K_i, C_i), (K_{i+1}, C_{i+1}) \dots (K_p, C_p)]$, $p < (m-1)$ and K is such that $K_i < K < K_{i+1}$, then we merely insert (K, C) where C is the child pointer field, at the appropriate position in the node X. The updated node X is given by $[C_0, (K_1, C_1), (K_2, C_2), \dots (K_i, C_i), (K, C), (K_{i+1}, C_{i+1}) \dots (K_p, C_p)]$.

Figure 11.11(b) illustrates *Case IB. 1* type of insertion in the generic node shown in Figure 11.11(a).

Case IB. 2: If the node X where the key K is to be inserted is full, then we apparently insert K into the list of elements and split the list into two at its median K_{median}. The keys which are less than K_{median} form a node X_{left} and those greater than K_{median} form another node X_{right}. The median element K_{median} is pulled up to be inserted in the parent node of X. This insertion may in turn call for *Case IB. 1* or *Case IB. 2* depending on whether the parent node can accommodate K_{median} or not.

Figure 11.11(c) illustrates *Case IB. 2* type of insertion in the generic node shown in Figure 11.11(a).

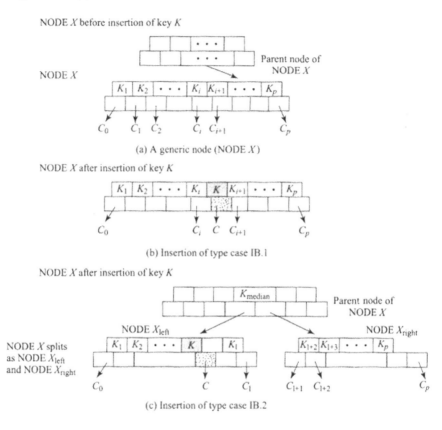

(a) A generic node (NODE X)

(b) Insertion of type case IB.1

(c) Insertion of type case IB.2

Figure 11.11. *Insertion of a key* K *in a* B *tree of order m*

Let us insert 29 into the B tree of order 5 shown in Figure 11.9. The search for 29 falls off the tree at the node [11, 28, 34]. Since the node can accommodate a further element, 29 is inserted into the node with appropriate changes made in the number of child pointers. Figure 11.12(a) illustrates the B tree after the insertion of 29.

On the other hand, the insertion of 96 into the B tree results in the search falling off at the node [80, 85, 90, 91]. However, the node is full. We now apparently insert 96 into the list to obtain [80, 85, 90, 91, 96] and split the list into two at its median, that is, 90. While [80, 85] form one node, [91, 96] form another node and the median element 90 is pulled up to be inserted in the parent node [46, 77]. Since the parent which is also the root can accommodate up to two more elements, 90 is inserted into the node to obtain the new root [46, 77, 90]. Figure 11.12(b) illustrates the insertion of 96 in the B tree.

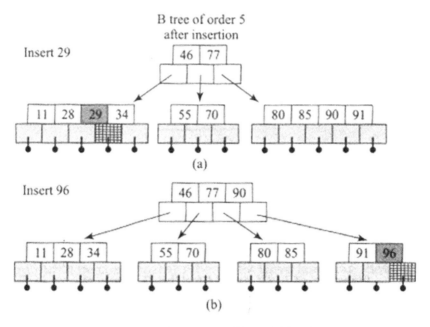

Figure 11.12. *Insertion of 29 and 96 in the B tree of order 5 shown in Figure 11.9*

EXAMPLE 11.4.–

For the 2-3 tree shown in Figure 11.13, let us perform the following operations in the sequence given: insert *L*, insert *W* and insert *M*.

Inserting *L* is a *Case IB. 1* type of insertion and is accommodated straightaway in node [*K*]. Inserting *W* on the other hand is more involved. It calls for the application of *Case IB. 2* twice. *W* is virtually inserted into the node [*V*, *X*] to obtain the list [*V*, *W*, *X*]. The list [*V*, *W*, *X*] splits into two nodes [*V*] and [*X*], pulling *W* up to be inserted in the node [*H*, *T*]. This again triggers a split of the list [*H*, *T*, *W*] into two nodes [*H*] and [*W*] with [*T*] further pulled up to act as the new root. Inserting *M* triggers *Case IB.2* to obtain the nodes [*K*] and [*M*] with *L* accommodated in its parent as [*H*, *L*].

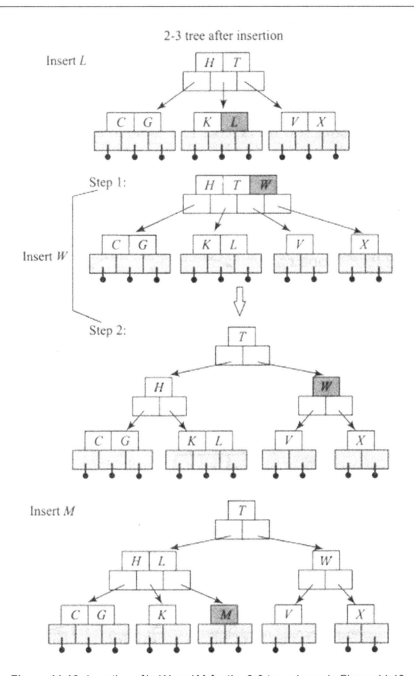

Figure 11.13. *Insertion of* L, W *and* M *for the 2-3 tree shown in Figure 11.13*

11.3.4. *Deletion from a B tree of order* m

The deletion of a key K from a B tree of order m may trigger various cases. It may be as simple as the cases *DB. 1-2* or as complicated as cases *DB. 3-4* (here **DB** indicates **D**eletion from a **B** tree).

Case DB. 1: Key K belongs to a leaf node and its deletion does not result in the node having less than its minimum number of elements. This deletion is the simplest of the cases. In such a case, we merely delete the element from the leaf node and adjust the child pointers accordingly.

Case DB. 2: Key K belongs to a non-leaf node. In such a case, replace K with the largest key (K') in the left subtree of K or the smallest key (K'') from the right subtree of K and follow steps to delete K' or K'' from the node. K' or K'' is bound to occur in a leaf node (why?) and hence triggers *Case DB. 1* for their deletion.

Consider the B tree of order 5 shown in Figure 11.9. Let us delete 80 and 77, both undertaken independently on the original B tree. Note that the deletion of 80 follows *Case DB.1*. We merely delete 80 and adjust the child pointers.

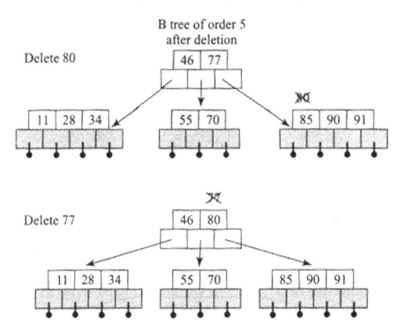

Figure 11.14. *Deletion of 80 and 77 from the B tree of order 5 shown in Figure 11.9*

The deletion of 77, on the other hand, follows *Case DB. 2*. We replace 77 with 80, the smallest key in its right subtree. The deletion of 80 now follows *Case DB.1*. Figure 11.14 shows the deletion of 80 and 77 from the B tree of order 5 (Figure 11.9).

Deletions may turn out to be complicated when they leave less than the minimum number of elements in the nodes concerned. *Cases DB. 3-4* illustrate these instances.

Case DB. 3: When the deletion of a key K from a node X leaves it with less than its minimum number of elements, elements are borrowed from one of its left or right sibling nodes. Thus, if the left sibling node has elements to spare, move the largest key K' in the left sibling node to the parent node. The intervening element P in the parent node is moved down to set right the vacancy created by the deletion of K in node X.

If the left sibling node has no element to spare it would be a waste of time to move to the right sibling node to check if there is an element to spare. What if after the check we were to realize that there were no elements to be spared by the right sibling node as well? In such a case, we proceed to *Case DB. 4* which covers the case when either of the sibling nodes have no elements to offer.

Case DB. 4: When the deletion of a key K from a node X leaves its elements to be less than the stipulated minimum number and if the first tested sibling node (left or right) or both the sibling nodes are unable to spare an element, node X is merged with one of the sibling nodes along with the intervening element P in the parent node. We shall choose to test for the availability of element from the left sibling node first. If there is no element available to be spared, then the elements of the left sibling node are merged with those of node X and the intervening parent element P to create a new node. This in turn calls for the deletion of element P, which may trigger one or more of the cases discussed above.

Consider the deletion of 44 from the B tree of order 5 shown in Figure 11.15(a). This is a direct illustration of *Case DB. 3*. The operation would leave the node [36, 44] with less than its minimum number of keys and therefore we borrow 18 from the left sibling node, which has an element to spare. Now 18 replaces the intervening parent element 20 and 20 moves down to fill the space created by the deletion of 44 in the node. Figure 11.15(b) illustrates the deletion of 44.

Let us proceed to delete 36 from the resulting B tree of order 5 shown in Figure 11.15(b). Note this is a direct illustration of *Case DB.4*. Since the left sibling node has no elements to spare, we merge the left sibling node with the intervening parent element 18 and the node containing the only element after the deletion of 36, that is, [20]. The new node [11, 12, 18, 20] is now a prospective child node. To decide on its appropriate parent, we proceed to delete 18 from the parent node. Again the deletion of 18 from its node is problem-free since the parent node can afford to do the same. Thus, we obtain [55, 76] to be the updated parent node. The new node [11, 12, 18, 20] joins the root as its first subtree.

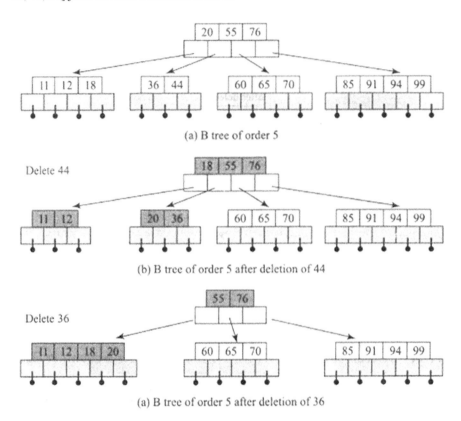

Figure 11.15. *Deletion of 44 and 36 from a B tree of order 5*

EXAMPLE 11.5.–

Consider the B tree of order 3 shown in Figure 11.10. Let us delete V and T, both undertaken independently on the original tree.

Deletion of V is a direct illustration of *Case DB. 1.* We merely delete V and adjust the child pointers of the node. Figure 11.16(a) shows the B tree after deletion of V. Deletion of T illustrates *Case DB. 2* and hence replaces T with V, the largest key in the right subtree. Deletion of V from its original position in the node follows *Case DB. 1.* Figure 11.16(b) illustrates the B tree after deletion of T.

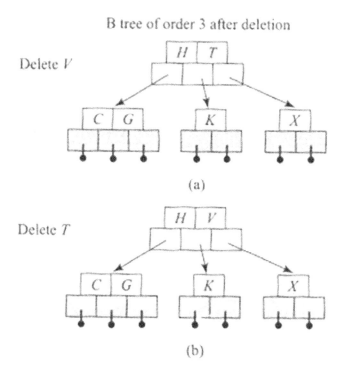

Figure 11.16. *Deletion of V and T from the B tree of order 3 shown in Figure 11.10*

EXAMPLE 11.6.–

Given the B tree of order 3 shown in Figure 11.17, let us delete *M*. To avoid clutter, the snapshots of the B trees during the delete process are shown without pointer fields. Observe how the deletion triggers *Case DB.4* repeatedly before the tree gets balanced. *M* is a single key in a leaf node and its deletion would leave the node with zero elements. To borrow from the node [*G*] is futile and hence we undertake a merge operation, as discussed in *Case DB. 4*, and this yields [*G, K*]. This leaves the parent node concerned with no elements and hence once again triggers *Case DB.4*. The new parent node is [*B, F*]. Observe the rearrangement of the child pointers of the node. *Case DB. 4* is once again triggered with regard to the empty parent of [*B, F*]. Finally, the tree balances itself by settling on [*O, T*] as its root.

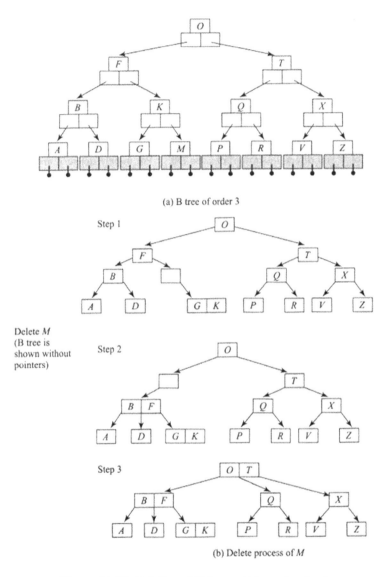

(a) B tree of order 3

Delete M
(B tree is
shown without
pointers)

(b) Delete process of M

Figure 11.17. *Deletion of M from a B tree of order 3*

11.3.5. *Height of a B tree of order* m

If a B tree of order m and height h has n elements, then n satisfies $n \le m^h - 1$. This is true since a B tree of order m is basically an m-way search tree (section 11.2.6). Now having determined the upper bound of n, what is its lower bound? In other words, what is the minimum number of elements that a B tree of order m and height h can hold? To obtain this, let us find out what are the minimum number of nodes in levels $1, 2, ... (h + 1)$. Here, $(h + 1)$ is the level at which the external nodes reside. Since each internal node other than the root has a minimum of $\left\lceil\frac{m}{2}\right\rceil$ child nodes and the root has just one node, the minimum number of nodes in each level beginning from 1 and ending at $(h + 1)$ in the sequential order would be $1, 2, 2 . \left\lceil\frac{m}{2}\right\rceil$, $2 . \left\lceil\frac{m}{2}\right\rceil^2 .....2 . \left\lceil\frac{m}{2}\right\rceil^{h-1}$, respectively. Thus, the number of external nodes on level $(h+1)$ would be $2 . \left\lceil\frac{m}{2}\right\rceil^{h-1}$. Since the number of elements in the B tree is one less than the number of external nodes, the lower bound of n is given by $n \geq 2 . \left\lceil\frac{m}{2}\right\rceil^{h-1} - 1$. Hence, we have $2 . \left\lceil\frac{m}{2}\right\rceil^{h-1} - 1 \leq n \leq m^h - 1$. From this, we can easily infer that $log_m(n + 1) \leq h \leq log_{\left\lceil\frac{m}{2}\right\rceil}\left(\frac{n+1}{2}\right) + 1$. This determines the best case and worst case complexities of a search, insert and delete operation on B trees, which is generally given by $O(h)$, the height of the B tree.

11.4. Tries: definition and operations

Search trees in general favor keys which are of fixed size, since this leads to efficient storage management. However, in the case of applications which are retrieval-based and which call for keys of varying length, tries provide better options. Search trees indulge in multi-way branching based on the whole key and hence searching is done based on key comparisons. In contrast, though tries are also multi-way branched trees, searching is based only on a portion of a key and not on the whole, before it is completely retrieved or stored.

Tries are also called *lexicographic search trees*. The name *trie* (pronounced "try") originated from the word "re*trie*val".

11.4.1. *Definition and representation*

A trie of order m may be empty. If non-empty, then it consists of an ordered sequence of exactly m tries of order m. The branching at any level of the trie is determined only by a portion and not by the whole key.

Alphabetical keys require a trie of order 27 (26 letters of the alphabet + a blank (" ")) for their storage and retrieval. Each branch of the trie partitions the keys into groups beginning with the specific alphabet.

Thus, tries have two categories of node structures, that is, **branch node** and **information node**. A branch node is merely a collection of LINK fields, each pointing either to a branch node or to an information node. An information node holds the key that is to be stored in the trie. For example, in the case of alphabetical keys, each branch node has 27 LINK fields, one for each of the 26 alphabet characters and one for a blank (" "). The keys are stored in the information nodes. To access an information node containing a key, we need to move down a branch node or a series of branch nodes following the appropriate branch based on the alphabetical characters composing the key. All LINK fields that neither point to a branch node nor to an information node are represented using null pointers. To avoid clutter, null pointers have not been represented using any special notations.

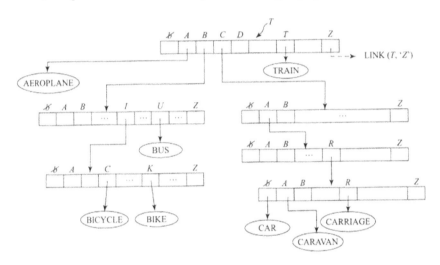

Figure 11.18. *An example trie*

Figure 11.18 illustrates an example trie for alphabetical keys. The trie stores the keys CAR, CARRIAGE, CARAVAN, BIKE, BUS, TRAIN, BICYCLE and AEROPLANE. The information nodes wholly store the keys. To access these information nodes, we follow a path beginning from a branch node moving down each level depending on the characters forming the key, until the appropriate information node holding the key is reached. Thus the depth of an information node in a trie depends on the similarity of its first few characters (*prefix*) with its fellow keys. Here, while AEROPLANE and TRAIN occupy shallow levels (level 1 branch node) in the trie, CAR, CARRIAGE and CARAVAN have moved down by four levels of branch nodes due to their uniform prefixes "CAR". Observe how we move down each level of the branch node with the help of the characters forming the key. The role played by the blank field in the branch node is evident when we move down the trie to access CAR. While the information node pertaining to CAR positions itself under the blank field, those of CARAVAN and CARRIAGE attach themselves to pointers from A and R, respectively, of the same branch node.

11.4.2. Searching a trie

To search for a key K in a trie T, we begin at the root which is a branch node. Let us suppose the key K is made up of characters $k_1 k_2 k_3 \dots k_n$. The first character of the key K, that is, k_1, is extracted and the LINK field corresponding to the letter k_1 in the root branch node is spotted. If LINK(T, k_1), the LINK field of character k_1 corresponding to the branch node T, is equal to NIL, then the search is unsuccessful, since no such key is found. If LINK(T, k_1) is not equal to NIL, then the LINK field may either point to an information node or a branch node. If the information node holds K, then the search is done. The key K has been successfully retrieved. Otherwise, it implies the presence of key(s) with a similar prefix. We extract the next character, k_2 of key K and move down the LINK field corresponding to k_2 in the branch node encountered at level 2 and so on until the key is found in an information node or the search is unsuccessful. The deeper the search, the more there are keys with similar but longer prefixes.

EXAMPLE 11.7.–

Consider the trie T shown in Figure 11.18. Let us search for the keys TRAIN and CARAVAN. To search for the key TRAIN, we extract the first character "T" and move down the LINK field corresponding to "T" in the root branch node. The retrieval is successful since the information node corresponding to the LINK holds the key TRAIN. Let us proceed to retrieve CARAVAN. The first character C urges the search process to move down LINK(T, 'C') in the first branch node. The second character A again leads one to move down to the next level and so does R. At level four, the LINK field corresponding to the fourth character, that is, "A", leads to an information node holding the key CARAVAN. The path can be easily traced on the trie shown.

11.4.3. Insertion into a trie

To insert a key K into a trie, we begin as we would to search for the key K, possibly moving down the trie, following the appropriate LINK fields of the branch nodes, corresponding to the characters of the key. At the point where the LINK field of the branch node leads to NIL, the key K is inserted as an information node.

EXAMPLE 11.8.–

Consider the trie shown in Figure 11.18. Let us insert SHIP and TRAM into the tree. The insertion of SHIP is simple and straightforward. The LINK field corresponding to the first character S in the root node is NIL and hence we insert SHIP as an information node in the appropriate place of the root branch node. In the case of TRAM, the LINK field corresponding to "T" in the root branch node points to an information node holding TRAIN. This implies that there is already a key with a uniform prefix available in the trie. We now remove TRAIN and instead open a branch node to accommodate both TRAIN and TRAM. And lo! the second character of the two keys matches and so does the third! Since the matching prefixes of TRAIN and TRAM ("TRA") is of length 3, the situation now calls for opening three levels of branch nodes other than the root node. It is only at level 4 that TRAIN and TRAM can be inserted as information nodes corresponding to the LINK fields of I and M, respectively. Figure 11.19 illustrates the insertion of SHIP and TRAM in the trie shown in Figure 11.18.

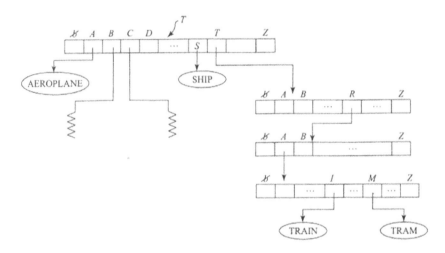

Figure 11.19. *Insertion of SHIP and TRAM into the trie shown in Figure 11.18*

11.4.4. *Deletion from a trie*

The deletion of a key K from a trie proceeds as we would to search for the key. On reaching the information node (NODE I) holding K, this is deleted. However, deletion does not merely stop with this. We need to check whether the branch node to which NODE I is linked is linked to other information nodes as well! If there are more than one information nodes linked to the branch node concerned or if there is at least one LINK field to another branch node or both, then the deletion is done. We merely delete the information node holding the key. On the other hand, if after deletion of NODE I, it leaves the branch node with just one more key (information node NODE I'), then there is no reason why the branch node should be retained at all. We delete the branch node and push NODE I' to a level higher. If the situation leads to NODE I' being the only non-empty node in the current branch node, once again we delete the branch node and push NODE I' higher until it finds a position in a branch node that makes the best use of its LINK fields. Since the deletions are sensitive to the number of keys (information nodes) that are present in a branch node, it would be prudent to include a COUNT field in each branch node recording the number of information nodes that are attached to the branch node.

EXAMPLE 11.9.–

Let us delete CAR and BIKE from the trie shown in Figure 11.18. To delete CAR, we search for it moving down four levels of branch nodes and spot it at an information node before deleting the same. This leaves us with the specific branch node holding two more keys, that is, CARAVAN and CARRIAGE. Therefore, there is nothing that can be done to the branch node and the deletion of CAR is deemed complete.

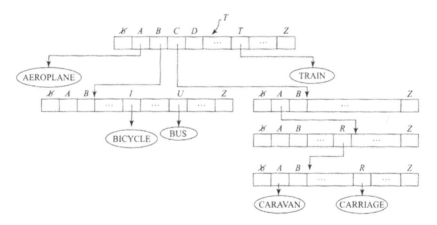

Figure 11.20. *Deletion of CAR and BIKE from the trie shown in Figure 11.18*

In the case of BIKE, we proceed as before and delete the information node holding the key. However, note this leaves the branch node with a single key BICYCLE. We therefore delete the branch node and proceed to accommodate BICYCLE in the branch node that is a level higher. The current branch node holds the key BUS in the LINK field corresponding to "U". The key BICYCLE is attached to it corresponding to the LINK field of I. Figure 11.20 shows the deletion of CAR and BIKE from the trie shown in Figure 11.18.

11.4.5. *Some remarks on tries*

The performance of search trees is determined by the number of keys that form the tree. Recall that the complexities of the search, delete and insert operations were given by $O(h)$ where the height h is dependent on the number of keys represented in the search tree. In contrast, the performance of the trie is dependent on the length of the key – the number of characters forming the key – rather than the number of keys itself. Thus, for example, if the length of the keys of a trie is equal to 7, then the trie can represent $(26)^7 = 8,031,810,176$ combinations of keys and, with the maximum length of uniform prefixes within the keys being 6, can retrieve keys in at most seven comparisons. In contrast, a search tree such as a binary search tree would need approximately $log_2((26)^7) \approx 33$ comparisons for the same!

In general, most applications involve keys of large lengths and the number of keys to be represented in the trie may be sparse when compared to its capacity. In such a case, tries may be expected to perform less well than their search tree counterparts. It is therefore recommended that tries which are multi-way trees are used in judicious combinations with other search trees.

11.5. Applications

Most of the data structures including search trees such as binary search trees and AVL trees are suitable for *internal searching*, that is, searching related to small files that can be accommodated in the internal memory of the computer. In the case of applications that call for very large files or data bases with voluminous records, the files cannot be accommodated in the internal memory of the computer. Hence, these need to be stored in *external memory* or what are called *auxiliary storage* or *external storage devices* such as hard disks, drums and so on. While internal memory access is very fast, the problem with these external devices are that accesses are time consuming. For example, to retrieve a record residing in a hard disk, the block in which the record resides is first to be accessed, then the entire block of records needs to be read and finally the required record is to be retrieved. Therefore, it is essential that files stored in the external memory resort to strategies and techniques resulting in their efficient retrieval and storage. Chapter 14 (Volume 3) details methods of file organization. It is in this context that multi-way trees such as m-way search trees, B trees and tries find their application.

11.5.1. *File indexing*

Retrieval of records from large files or data bases stored in external memory is time consuming. To promote efficient retrievals, *file indexes* are maintained. An *index* is a *<key, address>* pair. The purpose of indexing is to expedite the search process or retrieval of a record. Though there are more than one file management techniques that employ indexing, *indexed sequential access method (ISAM)*-based files have been the foremost in using indexing for efficient retrievals (see section 14.7 of Chapter 14, Volume 3). The records of the file are sequentially stored and for each block of records, the largest key and the block address is stored in an index. To retrieve a record whose key is K, the index is first searched to obtain the address of the block and thereafter a sequential search of the block should yield the desired record. Figure 11.21 illustrates an ISAM file structure. However, if the file is too large, then an index over indexes may have to be built.

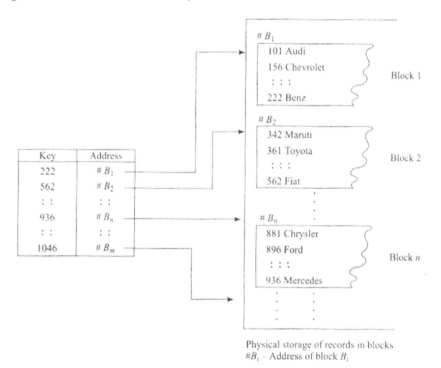

Figure 11.21. *An ISAM file structure*

From the above, it is clear that efficient retrievals are now dependent on the indexes. Though indexes are basically look up tables, it is essential that they are represented using efficient data structures to expedite retrievals. It is here that one finds the application of multi-way trees such as *m*-way search trees, B trees and tries.

B trees as file indexes

B trees are ideally suited for storing file indexes. Each internal node of the B tree stores the *<key, address>* pair. Their balanced heights call for fewer node accesses during the retrievals. Once the key is found, the address of the record is also accessed along with it, thereby speeding up the retrieval process.

B^+ trees as file indexes

B^+ **trees** are descendants of B trees. They satisfy all the properties of B trees but for a modification in the structure of the leaf nodes. While leaf nodes in B trees hold null pointers (external nodes, in fact), the leaf nodes of B^+ trees point to storage areas that contain records having the appropriate key values or pointers to each of these records. Therefore, in a B^+ tree, to retrieve a record given its key, it is essential that the search traverses down to a leaf node to retrieve its address. The non-leaf nodes only serve to help the search process traverse downwards towards the appropriate leaf node. Figure 11.22 illustrates a file index stored as a B^+ tree.

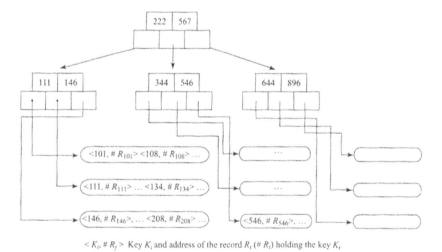

$< K_i, \# R_j >$ Key K_i and address of the record R_i (# R_i) holding the key K_i

Figure 11.22. B^+ *tree representation of a file index*

In comparison to B^+ trees, B trees are more efficient for the following reasons:

i) The <key, address> pair of the records are stored directly in the internal nodes of the B trees only once, thereby saving on storage. In contrast, B^+ trees store the keys in duplicate, once in the internal nodes and the next in the storage areas pointed to by the leaf node pointers.

ii) Unlike B$^+$ trees, to access the <key, address> pair in a B tree, there is no need to traverse down the whole tree to reach the leaf node. The <key, address> pair may be found directly in the respective internal nodes. Therefore, the keys may be accessed in fewer accesses when compared to B+ trees.

11.5.2. *Spell checker*

Most word processing software embeds spell checking which is provided online. Any incorrectly spelled word is automatically highlighted. Tries find an application in this problem. The words of a dictionary are stored as a trie and remembered in the memory of the computer. Every time a word is typed, the word is searched for in the trie and anything which does not lead to an information node is highlighted as an incorrectly spelled word. However, practical considerations call for curtailing the size and storage requirements of the trie since the whole trie needs to be present in the memory at the time of spell checking.

Summary

– *m*-way search trees, B trees of order *m* and tries are examples of multi-way search trees.

– *m*-way search trees are extensions of binary search trees. Searching for a key in an *m*-way search tree is similar to that in a binary search tree. Insertion of a key in a node is directly done if the node has less than its maximum number of elements ($m - 1$). On the other hand, if the node is full, then we insert the key as a new node in the next level at the appropriate position.

– To delete a key from an *m*-way search tree, if both the key's left and right subtrees are empty, then merely delete the key. If either one of the subtrees are non-empty or both are non-empty, then we replace the key to be deleted by either the smallest key in its left subtree or the largest key in its right subtree, as the case may be.

– Since the height of an *m*-way search tree of n elements varies from a minimum of $log_m(n + 1)$ to a maximum of n, the worst case performance of the tree may yield O(n). Hence the need for height-balanced *m*-way search trees.

– B trees of order *m* are height-balanced *m*-way search trees. The insertion of an element in a B tree is direct if the node is partially full. If the node is full, the key is virtually inserted into the list of keys in the node and this node is split into two nodes at its median element. The median element is pushed up to be accommodated in the parent node. This in turn may trigger further adjustments among the key elements of the parent node.

– The deletion of a key from a leaf node in a B tree is direct if it does not leave the node with less than its minimum number of elements. If the deletion belongs to a non-leaf node then it is replaced with either the largest key in its left subtree or the smallest in its right subtree. If the deletion leaves a node with less than its minimum number of elements, then an element is borrowed either from the left sibling node or the right sibling node, provided they have an element to spare. Otherwise, merge the node with one of its sibling nodes along with the intervening parent element to form a new node. This calls for the deletion of the intervening parent element concerned.

– Tries are search trees based on searching with portions of keys rather than the whole keys themselves. The search, insert and delete operations proceed down the trie along the branch nodes to reach the information node where the appropriate operation is carried out.

– B trees find applications in file indexing and tries in spell checking.

11.6. Illustrative problems

PROBLEM 11.1.–

For the 5-way search tree shown in Figure P11.1 perform the following operations in the sequence shown:

Insert *u*, Delete *z*, Insert *b*, Delete *p*

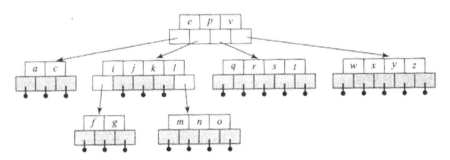

Figure P11.1. *A 5-way search tree*

Solution:

For the insertion of u, the node $[q, r, s, t]$ is full and hence cannot accommodate u. Therefore, we create a new node $[u]$. For the delete z operation, since the left and right subtree pointers of z are NIL, we can easily delete z from the node $[w, x, y, z]$. Inserting b accommodates b into the node $[a, c]$ to form the node $[a, b, c]$. Lastly, deleting p calls for the case where the left and right subtrees of the key to be deleted are not NIL. We choose the smallest key of its right subtree, that is, q and replace p with q. In turn, q is deleted from its node directly since its left and right subtree pointers are NIL. The snapshots of the 5-way search tree for the given operations are shown below.

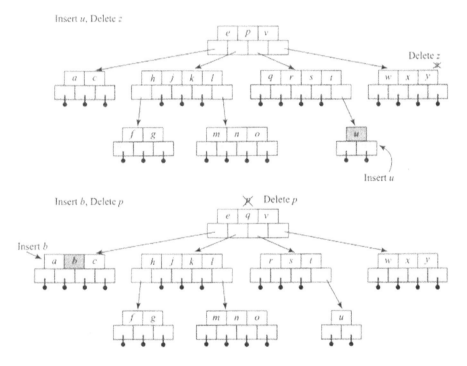

PROBLEM 11.2.–

What is the maximum and minimum number of elements a 100-way search tree of height 3 can hold? What is its maximum and minimum height if $(100)^2$ elements are represented in the tree?

Solution:

Following the discussion of section 11.2.6, the maximum number of elements a 100-way search tree of height 3 can hold is $(100)^3 - 1$ while the minimum number it can hold is equal to its height which is given to be 3. If the tree were to represent $(100)^2$ elements, then the maximum height of the search tree would be $(100)^2$ and the minimum height would be $log_{100}((100)^2 + 1) \cong 2$.

PROBLEM 11.3.–

For the 5-way search tree shown in Figure P11.1, how many comparisons are needed to search for the elements n and z?

Solution:

Searching for n requires eight comparisons and searching for z requires seven comparisons.

Problem 11.4.–

Which of the following is a B tree of order 7? If so, why?

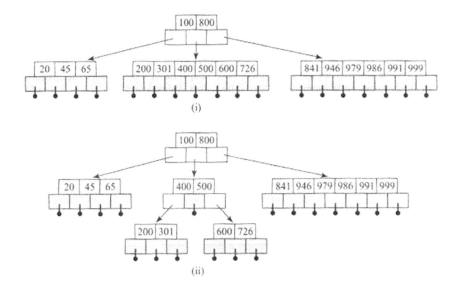

(i)

(ii)

Solution:

The tree shown in (i) is a B tree of order 7, since the following properties appropriate to the tree are satisfied:

i) The root node must have at least two child nodes and that of the given tree has 3 child nodes.

ii) All internal nodes other than the root have at least $\left\lceil \frac{7}{2} \right\rceil = 4$ child nodes.

iii) Each node of p child nodes has $(p-1)$ key elements.

iv) All external nodes are at the same level.

The tree shown in (ii) is not a B tree of order 7 (but possibly a 7-way search tree) since all the external nodes are not on the same level and some of the internal nodes have less than $\left\lceil \frac{7}{2} \right\rceil = 4$ child nodes.

PROBLEM 11.5.–

In the tree shown in Figure (i) of illustrative problem 11.4, undertake the following operations:

Insert 456 and Insert 97.

Solution:

To insert 456 into the B tree of order 7 shown in Figure (i) of illustrative problem 11.4, we arrive at the node [200, 301, 400, 500, 600, 726] while searching for it. Since the node is full we virtually insert 456 into the node and split the node into two at its median, which is 456. While 456 is absorbed in the root which can accommodate it, the split nodes are [200, 301, 400] and [500, 600, 726].

The insertion of 97 is simple and straight. It is accommodated in the node [20, 45, 65]. The B tree after the two insertions is shown below.

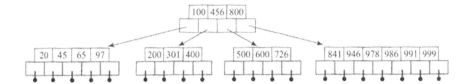

PROBLEM 11.6.–

In the B tree of order 7 obtained in illustrative problem 11.5, perform the following operations in the sequence given:

Delete 600, Delete 800 and Delete 20.

Solution:

Deleting 600 leaves the node [500, 600, 726] with fewer than its minimum number of elements. To borrow an element from its sibling (left sibling) is futile, since it would leave the sibling node concerned with less than its minimum number of elements. Therefore, the left sibling node [200, 301, 400] is merged with [500, 726] along with its intervening parent element 456.

The deletion of 800 in the resulting tree is done by merely replacing 800 by the smallest key in its right subtree, that is, 841. The deletion of 20 is simple and direct. The key 20 is merely removed from its node. The B tree after the three deletions have been carried out is shown below.

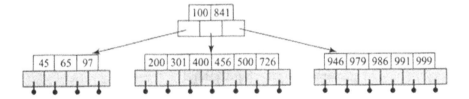

PROBLEM 11.7.–

The *preorder traversal of a B tree of order m* is undertaken by visiting all entries of the root node first, followed by traversing each of the subtrees from left to right in preorder. A *postorder traversal of a B tree of order m* is undertaken by first traversing all its subtrees from left to right in post order and finally visiting all the entries in the root node.

For the final snapshot of the 2-3 tree shown in Figure 11.17(b) in this chapter, undertake preorder and postorder traversals.

Solution:

The preorder traversal of the 2–3 tree yields:

O T B F A D G K Q P R X V Z

The postorder traversal of the 2–3 tree yields:

A D G K B F P R Q V Z X O T

PROBLEM 11.8.–

Construct a trie for the binary keys 011, 111, 101, 001.

Solution:

The trie for the binary keys is as given below:

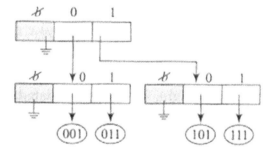

Problem 11.9.–

Perform the following operations on the trie constructed in illustrative problem 11.8:

Insert 01, Insert 11, Delete 011 and Delete 001.

Solution:

The trie after the insert operations is as follows:

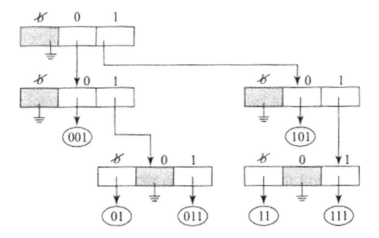

The relevant portion of the trie after the deletion of 011 is as given below:

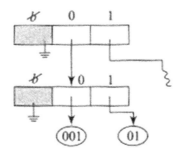

The relevant portion of the trie after the deletion of 001 is as given below:

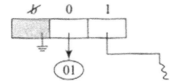

Problem 11.10.–

Construct (i) a 2-3 tree and (ii) a trie for the following keys in the order of their appearance:

CAT, CAN, PAN, PAT, MAN, MAT, MAP

Solution:

i) The snapshots of the 2-3 tree during its construction are shown below:

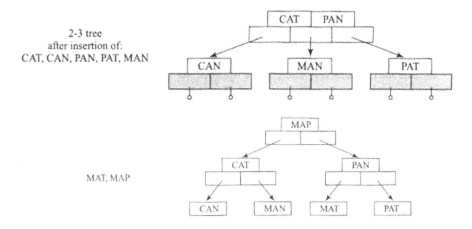

ii) The trie after insertion of the key elements is shown below:

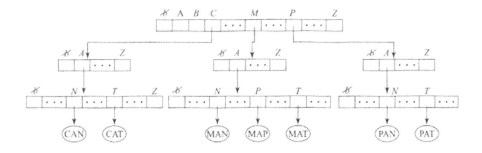

Review questions

1) Which among the following properties does not hold true for an *m*-way search tree?

i) Each node has at least m child nodes.

ii) If a node has k child nodes, $k \leq m$, then the node has exactly $(k-1)$ keys and each of the keys K_i partitions the keys in the subtrees into k subsets.

iii) For a node $C_0, (K_1, C_1), (K_2, C_2), (K_3, C_3) \ldots (K_{m-1}, C_{m-1})$, all key values in the subtree pointed to by C_i are less than the key $K_{i+1}, 0 \leq i \leq m-2$ and the key values in the subtree pointed to by C_{m-1} are greater than K_{m-1}.

iv) The subtrees pointed to by $C_i, 0 \leq i \leq m-1$ are also m-way search trees.

a) (i)   b) (ii)   c) (iii)   d) (iv)

2) To delete key K found in a node of an m-way search tree, with its left subtree empty and right subtree non-empty,

i) simply delete the key K;

ii) choose the smallest key K' from the right subtree of K and replace K with K', which in turn may recursively call for the appropriate deletion of K' from the tree;

iii) choose the largest key K'' from the left subtree of K and replace K with K'', which in turn may recursively call for the appropriate deletion of K'' from the tree;

iv) choose either the largest key from the left subtree or the smallest key from the right subtree (K''') and replace key K with K''', which in turn may recursively call for the appropriate deletion of K''' from the tree.

a) (i)   b) (ii)   c) (iii)   d) (iv)

3) Which among the following properties is not satisfied by a B tree of order m?

i) The root node must have at least m child nodes, $m \geq 1$.

ii) All internal nodes other than the root node must have *at least* $\left\lceil \frac{m}{2} \right\rceil$ non-empty child nodes and at most m non-empty child nodes.

iii) The number of keys in each internal node is one less than its number of child nodes and these keys partition the keys of the tree into subtrees in a manner similar to that of m-way search trees.

iv) All external nodes are at the same level.

a) (i)   b) (ii)   c) (iii)   d) (iv)

4) In the context of insertion of a key K into a B tree of order m, state whether true or false:

i) If the node X of the B tree of order m, where the key K is to be inserted, can accommodate K, then it is inserted in the node and the number of child pointer fields is appropriately upgraded.

ii) If the node X where the key K is to be inserted is full, then we apparently insert K into the list of elements and split the list into two at its median K_{median}.

a) (i) true (ii) true   b) (i) true (ii) false

c) (i) false (ii) true   d) (i) false (ii) false

5) Which among the following properties is not satisfied by a B-tree of order m?

i) Keys are stored in the information nodes.

ii) The depth of an information node in a trie always depends on the length of the key.

iii) To access an information node containing a key, we need to move down a branch node or a series of branch nodes following the appropriate branch based on the alphabetical characters composing the key.

iv) A branch node is merely a collection of pointers to either a branch node or an information node.

a) (i)   b) (ii)

c) (iii)   d) (iv)

6) What are the merits of m-way search trees over AVL search trees?

7) What are the demerits of m-way search trees?

8) What is the need for B trees?

9) Distinguish between 2-3 trees and 2-4 trees.

10) What is the height of a B tree of order m?

11) What is the need for tries?

12) When do tries perform less better than search trees?

13) Insert the following elements in the order given into an empty B tree of order (i) 3 (ii) 4 and (iii) 7.

ZRTADFHQWCVBSEOPLJKMNUTX

Undertake the following operations on the B trees:

(i) Delete Q   (ii) Delete A
(iii) Delete M   (iv) Delete S

14) For the data list shown in review question 13, construct a 3-way search tree. Insert G and delete J K and Z from the search tree.

15) For the following data list construct a trie:

ANT ANTELOPE BEAR BUG ELEPHANT ZEBRA BEETLE TIGER ANTEATER BISON MONKEY ORANGUTANG CHIMPANZEE KOALA KOEL

Perform the following operations on the trie:

(i) Delete CHIMPANZEE, (ii) Delete ANTELOPE, (iii) Insert RHINOCEROS, (iv) Insert MONGREL, (v) Delete ANTEATER

Programming assignments

1) Implement a menu driven program to

i) construct an *m*-way search tree for a specific order *m*;

ii) insert elements into the *m*-way search tree;

iii) delete elements from the *m*-way search tree.

2) Implement a menu-driven demonstration of all the functions pertaining to insert, delete and search operations of B trees of order *m*.

3) Implement a function to delete a key *K* from a trie *T*. Assume that each of the branch nodes has a COUNT field which records the number of information nodes in the sub-trie for which it is the root.

4) Implement functions to traverse a B tree of order *m* by inorder, preorder and postorder traversals.

5) Execute a function to gather all the information nodes beginning with a specific alphabet from a trie representing alphabetical keys.

12

Red-Black Trees and Splay Trees

The data structures of *red-black trees* and *splay trees* are discussed in this chapter. Red-black trees, which are special forms of binary search trees, have their origins in B trees of order 4 but are more efficient than the latter, by way of performance and storage considerations.

Splay trees are binary search trees with a self-adjusting mechanism that renders a better performance with regard to what is known as amortized analysis. They are more efficient when compared to their binary search tree or AVL tree counterparts.

12.1. Red-black trees

12.1.1. *Introduction to red-black trees*

B trees of order m were discussed in Chapter 11. It was shown how B trees are balanced trees efficient for use in applications such as file indexing since they serve to reduce disk accesses. To recall, the node structure of the B trees appears as shown in Figure 12.1. A simple implementation of the node may call for using sequential data structures such as arrays to hold the keys and the pointers to the child nodes. Thus, a B tree of order m may have each of their nodes represented by using two arrays of maximum dimension m and $m - 1$ corresponding to the child pointers and keys, respectively. This entails wastage of space in the worst case scenario. Also, to search for or insert a key demands sequentially searching for the element in the nodes, determines the child pointers of the nodes for the search to move down the tree, before it eventually reaches the key or inserts the key, as the case may be. If the order of the B tree is small, then an effective solution would be to maintain the keys of each of the nodes in the B tree as a binary search tree. However, it needs to ensure that the branches linking the nodes of the binary search tree are distinguished from the same linking the nodes of the B tree.

With regard to B trees of order 4, also referred to as 2-4 trees or 2-3-4 trees, it can be shown that a binary search tree representation of each of its nodes yields a concept that forms the basis for a special kind of binary search tree called the *red-black tree*. Consider the 2-4 tree shown in Figure 12.2(a), a binary search tree representation of each of the nodes is shown in Figure 12.2(b). Here, thin lines indicate branches which link the nodes of the binary search tree and thick lines the same between the nodes of the original B tree. Now, if the thin lines and the nodes hanging from them were shaded light (**red**) and the thick lines and the nodes hanging from them were shaded gray (**black**), the resulting tree would be as shown in Figure 12.2(c). Note that *the root node is always shaded black*. Such a tree is what is known as the *red-black tree*.

A node with two keys in the 2-4 tree may be represented as a binary search tree in either of the two ways as shown in Figure 12.3(a). For example, the root node of the 2-4 tree [10, 70] may be represented in any one of the two ways as shown in Figure 12.3(b).

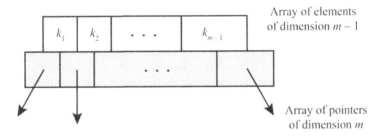

Figure 12.1. *Node structure of a B tree of order m and its representation*

12.1.2. Definition

A *red-black tree* is an extended binary search tree in which the nodes and the edges from which these nodes emanate are either *red* or *black* and satisfy the following properties:

i) The root node and the external nodes are always black nodes.

ii) [*Red Condition*] No two red nodes can occur consecutively on the path from the root node to an external node.

iii) [*Black Condition*] The number of black nodes on the path from the root node to an external node must be the same for all external nodes.

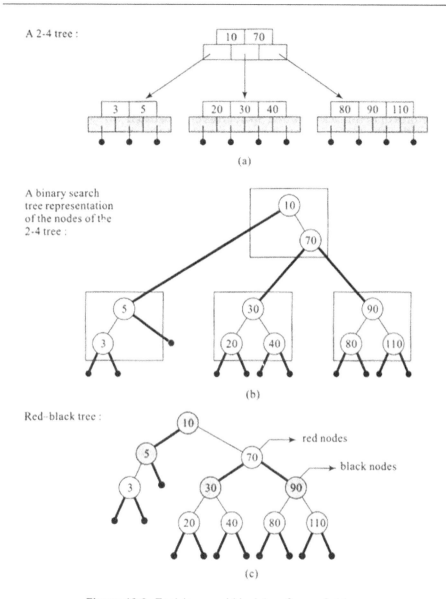

Figure 12.2. *Evolving a red-black tree from a 2-4 tree*

Since the color of the node is same as the color of the edge from which the node emanates, the red and black conditions may be expressed in terms of the edges as well. The red condition could be alternatively defined as no two red pointers or edges which can occur consecutively on a path from the root node to an external node. The black condition could be redefined as all paths from the root node to external nodes must have the same number of black pointers. Besides the above mentioned conditions, all pointers linking internal nodes with the external nodes must be black.

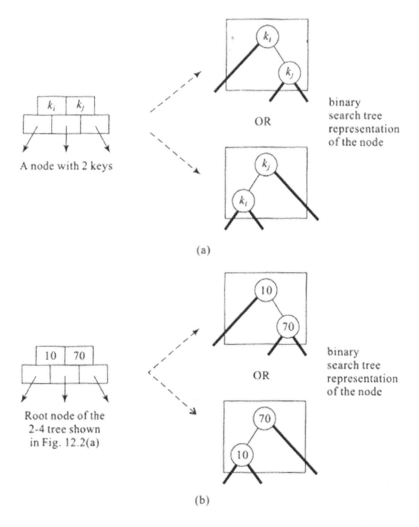

Figure 12.3. *Possible binary search tree representations of a node with two keys*

The number of black nodes or edges on the path from a node to an external node is called the *rank* of the node. The rank of all external nodes is 0.

In this chapter, all red nodes and edges will be represented using empty circles and thin lines and all black nodes and edges will be represented using shaded circles and thick lines, respectively.

EXAMPLE 12.1.–

Figure 12.4 illustrates a red-black tree. Observe the tree as an extended binary search tree with its root and external nodes being black. The red condition where no two consecutive red nodes can occur is satisfied on all the paths from the root to the external nodes. Also, the black condition where all root-to-external node paths must contain the same number of black nodes is also true. Every such path in the given tree contains exactly two black nodes.

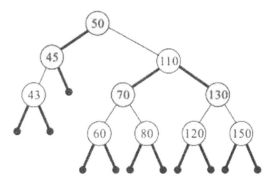

Figure 12.4. *An example red-black tree*

12.1.3. *Representation of a red-black tree*

Since a red-black tree is an extended binary search tree, the kind of node representation used for a binary search tree may be employed for the tree as well. However, since the color of a node plays a dominant role in the definition of the red-black tree, it is essential that the color is also recorded in the node structure as a field (COLOR). Another scheme could be to record the color of the two pointers emanating from the node.

The insert/delete operations quite often unbalance a red-black tree. The rebalancing of the tree may call for moving up and down the tree during the node adjustments. To facilitate this upward movement, the node structure of a red-black tree may have a provision for a PARENT field. PARENT fields of nodes are pointers to their respective parent nodes.

12.1.4. Searching a red-black tree

Searching a red-black tree for a key is in no way different from the procedure used to search for a key in a binary search tree. Algorithm 10.1 discussed in Chapter 10 and which retrieves a key ITEM from a binary search tree can be employed for the same.

12.1.5. Inserting into a red-black tree

Inserting a key K into a red-black tree follows a procedure very similar to the one employed for binary search trees. The only concern now is to determine the color to which the node must be set. If the node is set to black, then the path from the root node to the external node passing through the node would have one more black node. This results in the violation of the black condition of a red-black tree. Hence, the other alternative is to set the node to red. Now, if in doing so, it leads to the violation of the red condition, then the red-black tree is said to be **unbalanced.** To set right the imbalance, we need to undertake rotations.

Let us suppose u is the newly inserted red node and *parent-u* its consecutive red node, which is also the parent of node u. Now, u must have a grandparent, *grandparent-u* which is a black node. Based on the position of node u in relation to *parent-u* and *grandparent-u,* and the color of the other child of *grandparent-u*, the imbalances are classified as **LLb, LLr, RLb, RLr, LRb, LRr, RRb** and **RRr**. Thus, if u is inserted as the *L*eft child of *parent-u* (**L**) which in turn is the *L*eft child of *grandparent-u* (**L**) and the other child of *grandparent-u* is *b*lack (**b**) – the child may in fact be an external node which is black – then the rotation undertaken is **LLb**. Again, if u were to be inserted as the *R*ight child of *parent-u* (**R**) which in turn is the *L*eft child of *grandparent-u* (**L**) whose other child is *r*ed (**r**), then the rotation to be undertaken is **LRr** and so on.

Imbalances of the type **LLr, LRr, RRr,** and **RLr,** with "*r*" as its suffix, only call for a color change of the nodes to set right the imbalance. On the other hand, imbalances of the type **LLb, LRb, RRb** and **RLb**, with "*b*" as its suffix, call for rotations to set right the imbalance.

LLr, LRr, RRr, and RLr imbalances

Figure 12.5 illustrates a generic representation of the *LLr, LRr, RRr,* and *RLr* imbalances and the color changes that need to be undertaken to set right the imbalance. The notations **L, R** and **r** inscribed on the edges of the red-black trees illustrate the classification of the imbalance.

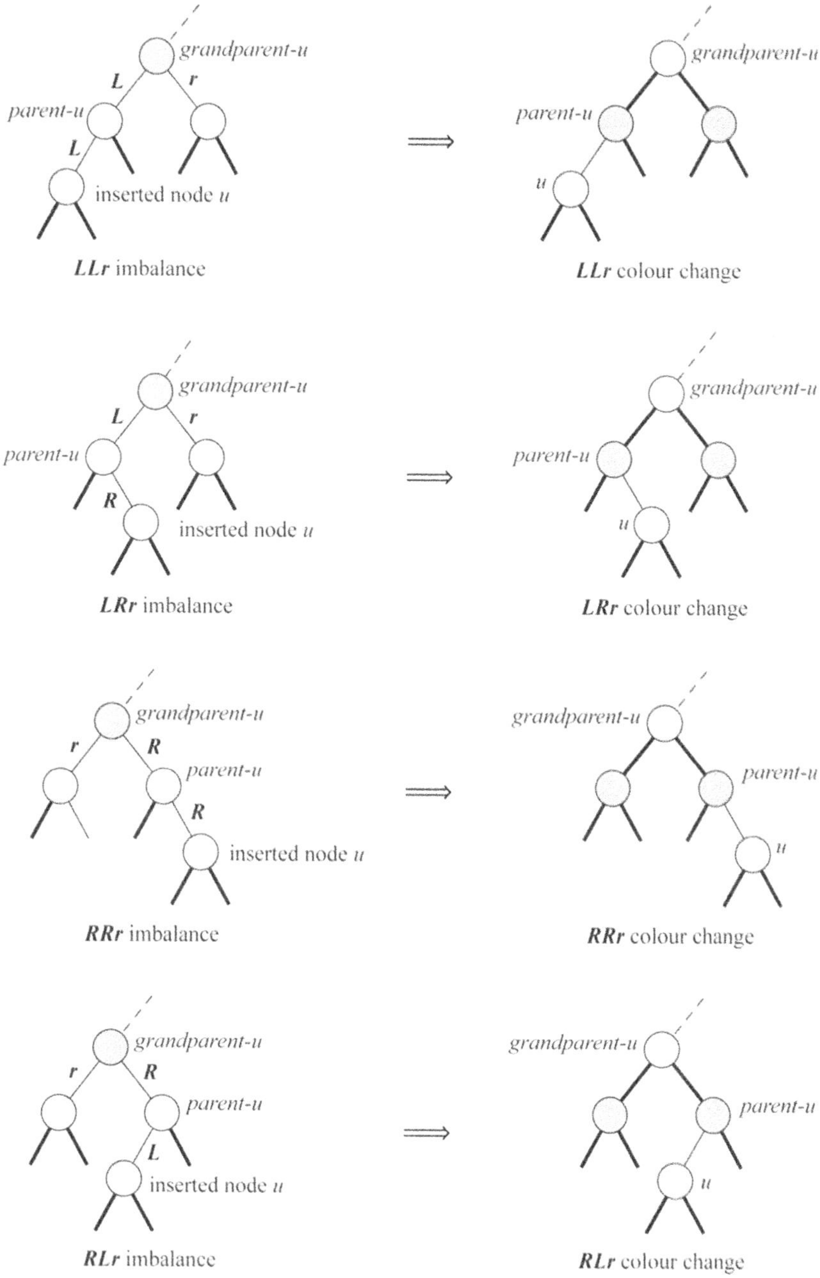

Figure 12.5. *Generic representations of LLr, LRr, RRr and RLr imbalances and their color changes*

EXAMPLE 12.2.–

Consider the red-black tree shown in Figure 12.6(a), the insertion of 60 results in an *LLr* imbalance and the tree after color change is shown in Figure 12.6(b). For the red-black tree shown in Figure 12.7(a), inserting 184 yields an *RRr* imbalance. The balanced tree after color change is shown in Figure 12.7(b).

Note how the color of the *grandparent-u* node changes from black to red in the generic representations, as shown in Figure 12.5. This is so provided that the *grandparent-u* is not the root. If *grandparent-u* turns out to be the root, then no color change on it is done. This would therefore increase the number of black nodes on all paths from the root (*grandparent-u*) to the external nodes by 1.

Also, if changing the color of *grandparent-u* to red causes further imbalance up the tree, then we identify the category of imbalance treating *grandparent-u* as *u* and so on until the whole tree gets rebalanced after undertaking the appropriate rotations or color change.

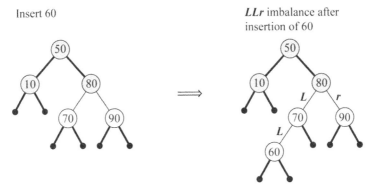

(a) *LLr* imbalance after insertion of 60

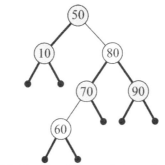

(b) *LLr* color change to balance the tree

Figure 12.6. *An example LLr imbalance and its color change*

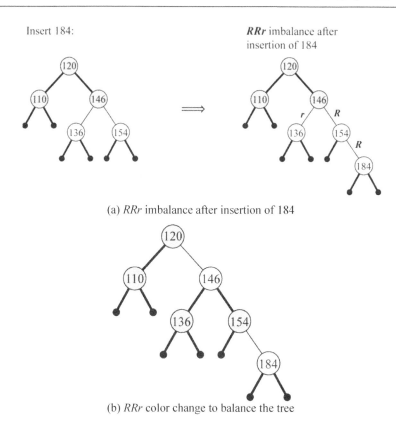

(a) *RRr* imbalance after insertion of 184

(b) *RRr* color change to balance the tree

Figure 12.7. *An example RRr imbalance and its color change*

LLb, LRb, RRb and RLb imbalances

Figure 12.8 illustrates the generic representations of the *LLb, LRb, RRb* and *RLb* imbalances and the respective rotations to rebalance the red-black tree. The notations ***L, R*** and ***b*** inscribed on the edges of the red-black trees illustrate the classification of the imbalance.

Here, *u* is the node which is inserted into the tree as the left or right child of *parent-u* which is the left or right child of *grandparent-u*. u^L, *parent-u^L* and *grandparent-u^L* indicate the left subtrees of *u, parent-u* and *grandparent-u*, respectively. u^R, *parent-u^R* and *grandparent-u^R* indicate the right subtrees of *u, parent-u* and *grandparent-u*, respectively. It may be observed that the *LLb, LRb, RRb* and *RLb* rotations resemble the *LL, LR, RR* and *RL* rotations discussed in section 10.3.3 with regard to AVL trees, apart from the color changes that are called for after the rotation.

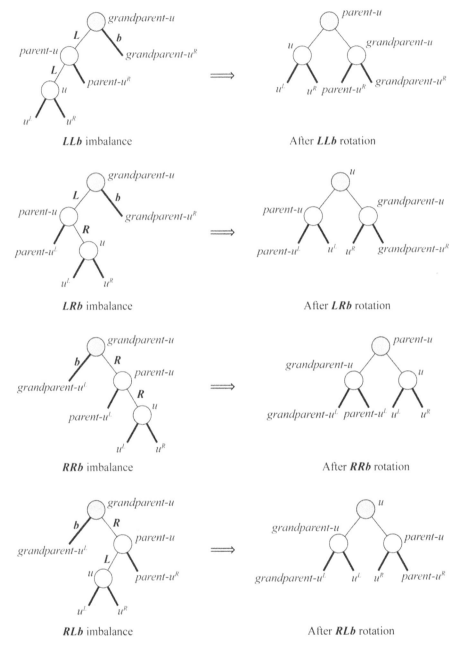

Figure 12.8. *Generic representations of LLb, LRb,*
RRb and RLb imbalances and their rotations

EXAMPLE 12.3.–

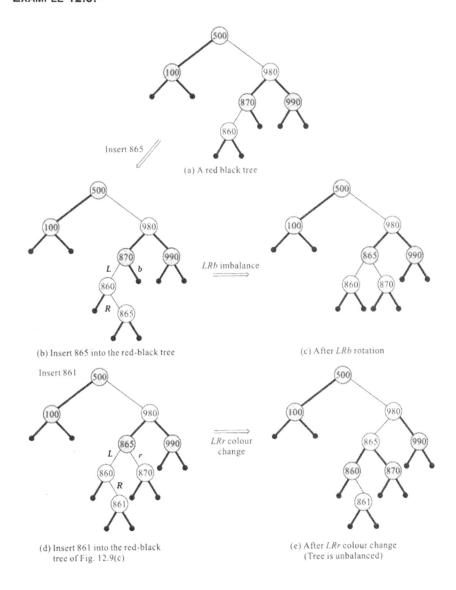

(a) A red black tree

Insert 865

(b) Insert 865 into the red-black tree

LRb imbalance

(c) After *LRb* rotation

Insert 861

LRr colour change

(d) Insert 861 into the red-black tree of Fig. 12.9(c)

(e) After *LRr* colour change (Tree is unbalanced)

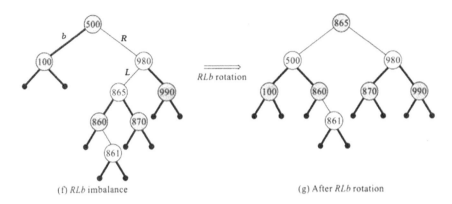

(f) *RLb* imbalance   (g) After *RLb* rotation

Figure 12.9. *An example of LRb, RLb imbalance*

Consider the red-black tree shown in Figure 12.9(a). Let us insert 865 and 861 into the tree in the order given. Figure 12.9(b) shows the *LRb* imbalance of the tree after the insertion of 865. The *LRb* rotation rebalancing the tree is shown in Figure 12.9(c). Insertion of 861 into the red-black tree shown in Figure 12.9(c) yields an *LRr* imbalance (see Figure 12.9(d)), which is set right by a color change shown in Figure 12.9(e). But lo and behold, this triggers a further imbalance of the type *RLb* with the nodes 865 and 980 turning out to be consecutive red nodes! Figure 12.9(f) shows the *RLb* imbalance in the tree. The *RLb* rotation rebalancing the tree is shown in Figure 12.9(g).

EXAMPLE 12.4.–

In the red-black tree shown in Figure 12.10(a), let us insert *I, K, L* in the order given. Insertion of *I* into the red-black tree results in an *LLr* imbalance, which only calls for a color change to rebalance the tree. Figure 12.10(b) shows the rebalanced tree after *LLr* color change. Insertion of *K* does not unbalance the tree (see Figure 12.10(c)). However, the insertion of *L* results in an *RRr* imbalance, the rebalancing of which triggers an *RLb* imbalance. Figures 12.10(d) and (e) illustrate the *RRr* color change and *RLb* rotation, respectively.

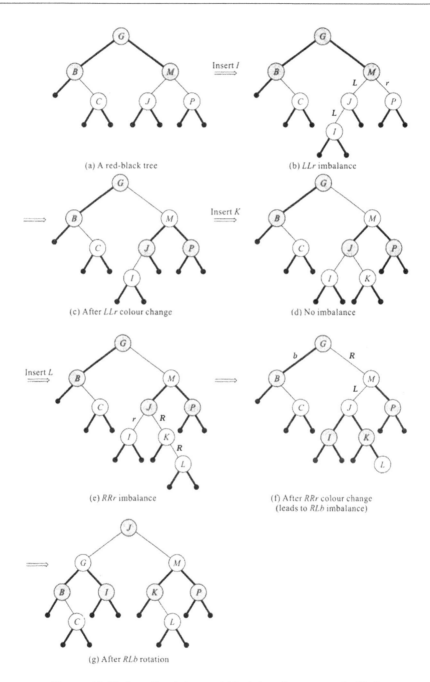

(a) A red-black tree

(b) *LLr* imbalance

(c) After *LLr* colour change

(d) No imbalance

(e) *RRr* imbalance

(f) After *RRr* colour change
(leads to *RLb* imbalance)

(g) After *RLb* rotation

Figure 12.10. *Inserting into a red-black tree (see example 12.4)*

12.1.6. *Deleting from a red-black tree*

Deleting a key K from a red-black tree proceeds as one would to delete the same from a binary search tree. In this regard, the cases discussed in section 10.2.6 in connection with the deletion of key K from a binary search tree, when K is a leaf node or K has a lone subtree (left subtree or right subtree only) or K has both left subtree and right subtree hold true here as well. However, if the deletion results in an imbalance in the tree, then this may call for a color change or a rotation if necessary.

If the deleted node were to be red, then there is no way that the black condition would be violated and hence no imbalance is possible. On the other hand, if the deleted node were to be black, then there is every possibility of the violation of the black condition due to the shortage of a black node in a specific root-to-external node path. In such a case, the tree is said to be ***unbalanced.***

The imbalance is classified as Left (***L***) or Right (***R***) based on whether the deleted node v occurs to the right or left of its parent node, *parent-v*. Again if the sibling of node v, *sibling-v* is a black node then the imbalance is further classified as ***Lb*** or ***Rb***. If *sibling-v* is a red node, then the imbalance is classified as ***Lr*** or ***Rr***. Based on whether *sibling-v* has 0 or 1 or 2 red children, the *Lb*, *Rb* imbalances are further sub-classified as ***Lb0***, ***Lb1*** and ***Lb2***, and ***Rb0***, ***Rb1*** and ***Rb2***, respectively. Similarly, the ***Lr***, ***Rr*** imbalances are also sub-classified as ***Lr0***, ***Lr1*** and ***Lr2***, and ***Rr0***, ***Rr1*** and ***Rr2***, respectively. During rebalancing, v denotes the node that was deleted but physically replaced by another node, which takes its place as called for by the delete process.

We deal with imbalances concerning ***R*** in the next section. Those pertaining to ***L*** will be demonstrated in illustrative problems 12.3 and 12.4.

Node labels superscripted with L indicate their left subtrees and those superscripted with R indicate their right subtrees. The nodes shaded gray emanating from thick lined edges indicate black nodes and those shaded white emanating from thin lined edges indicate red nodes. Nodes that are cross-hatched indicate either red or black nodes.

Rb0, Rb1 and Rb2 imbalances

Figure 12.11 illustrates the generic representations of ***Rb0***, ***Rb1*** and ***Rb2*** imbalances. The notations ***R***, ***b*** and ***0/1/2*** inscribed on the edges of the red-black trees illustrate the classification of the imbalance.

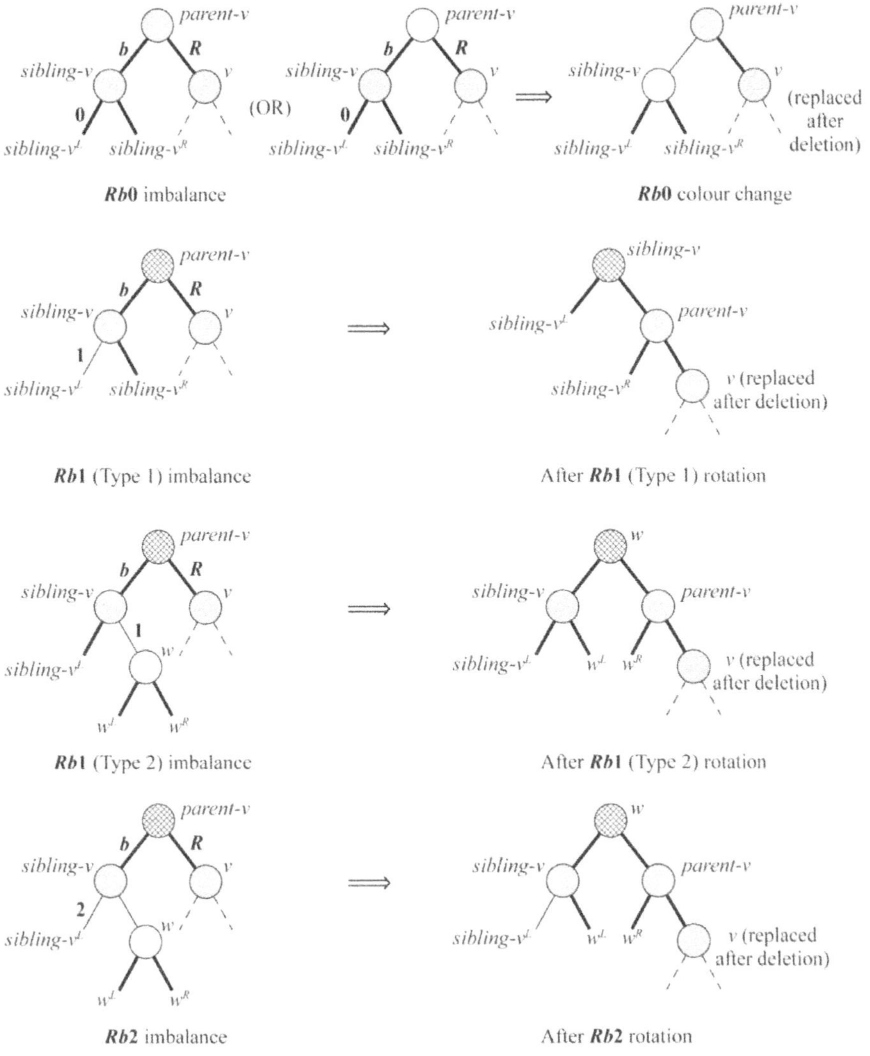

Figure 12.11. *Generic representations of Rb0, Rb1 and Rb2 imbalances and their rebalancing mechanisms*

In the case of *Rb0* imbalance, the rebalancing only calls for a color change of nodes. The two possibilities of *Rb0* imbalance are shown in the figure. *Rb1* imbalance is of two types: *Rb1(type 1)* and *Rb2 (type 2)*. In these, the node *sibling-v* has a single red child in either *sibling-v^L* or *w*, respectively. The *Rb2* imbalance has *sibling-v* holding two red children in *sibling-v^L* and *w*. Rotations as illustrated in the figure are performed for the *Rb1* and *Rb2* imbalances.

Rr0, Rr1 and Rr2 imbalances

Figure 12.12 illustrates the generic representations of *Rr0*, *Rr1* and *Rr2* imbalances. The notations **R**, **r** and *0/1/2* inscribed on the edges of the red-black tree illustrate the classification of imbalance. Rotations are undertaken in all the three cases to rebalance the trees. *Rr1* imbalance is of two types indicated as *Rr1(type 1)* and *Rr1(type 2)*.

EXAMPLE 12.5.–

A series of red-black trees, the *Rb0*, *Rb1* and *Rb2* imbalances and their rebalancing rotations, are shown in Figure 12.13. The **R**, **b**, *0/1/2* notations are inscribed on the tree to help classify the kind of imbalance.

Deleting 36 from the red-black tree shown in Figure 12.13(a) leaves the tree violating the black condition. The imbalance is classified as *Rb0*. The rebalancing calls for a mere color change with 28 set as a red node.

Deleting 32 (see Figure 12.13(b)) leads to *Rb1 (type 1)* imbalance with a violation of the black condition. The rebalancing rotation pushes 28 up as a red node and changes 26 and 30 to black nodes thereby ensuring the satisfaction of both red and black conditions.

Deleting 59 (see Figure 12.13(c)) is a case of *Rb1(type 2)* imbalance. During the rebalancing rotation, 48 moves up to become the root of the subtree. The red and black conditions are satisfied after rotation.

Deleting 99 (see Figure 12.13(d)) is a case of *Rb2 imbalance* and the rebalancing pushes 78 up as the root of the subtree. The red and black conditions hold true after rebalancing.

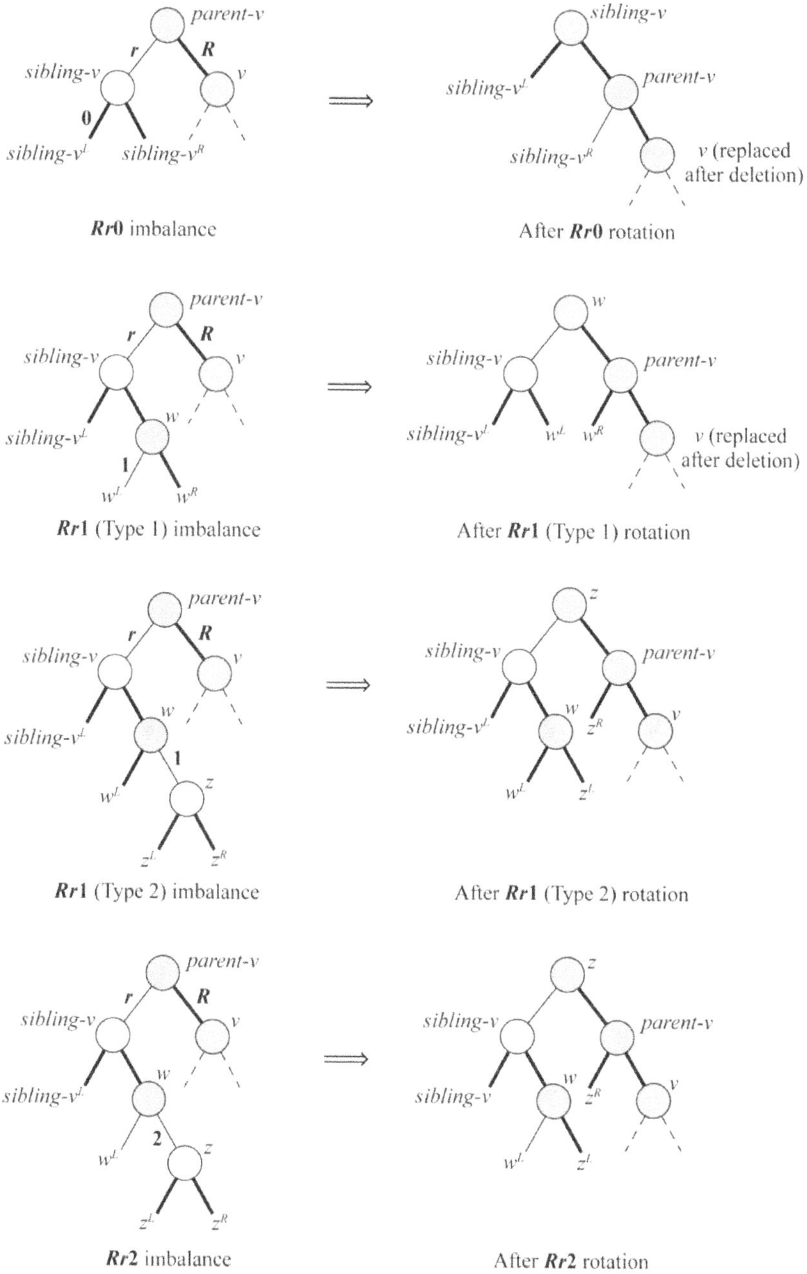

Figure 12.12. *Generic representations of Rr0, Rr1 and Rr2 imbalances and their rotations*

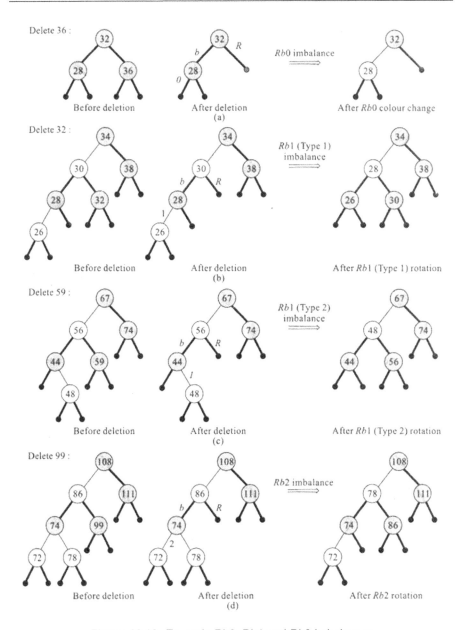

Figure 12.13. *Example Rb0, Rb1 and Rb2 imbalances*

EXAMPLE 12.6.–

Figure 12.14 shows a series of red-black trees and the respective deletions, which trigger the *Rr0, Rr1* and *Rr2* imbalances. The rotations illustrated are self explanatory.

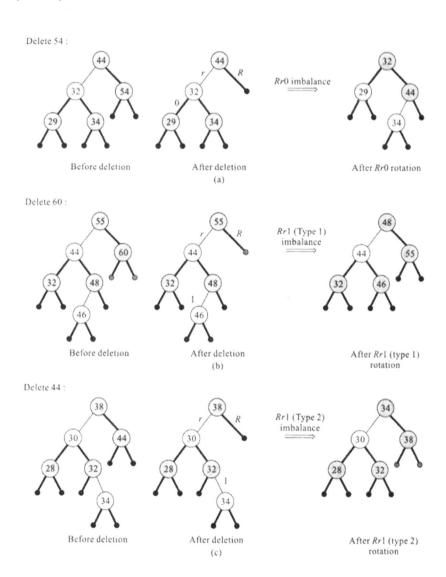

Delete 41 :

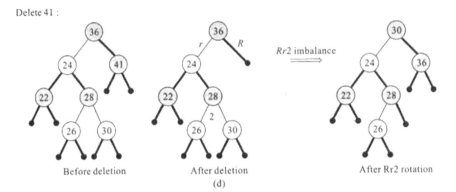

Before deletion   After deletion   After Rr2 rotation
(d)

Figure 12.14. *Example of Rr0, Rr1 and Rr2 rotations*

EXAMPLE 12.7.–

Consider the red-black tree shown in Figure 12.15(a). Let us delete the following keys from the tree:

F, S, O, L, K

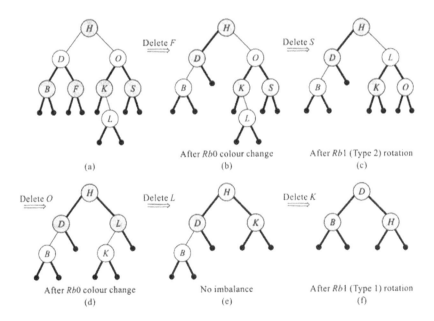

Figure 12.15. *Deletion operations on a red-black tree (see example 12.7)*

All deletions except that of L trigger a series of *Rb0/1/2* kind of imbalance. The snapshots of the tree after the respective rotations that were undertaken to rebalance the tree are shown in Figures 12.15(b–f). Note that the deletion of L only triggers the deletion of a red node, after L has been replaced by K. Therefore, this deletion does not lead to an imbalance in the tree due to the non-violation of the black condition.

EXAMPLE 12.8.–

Consider the red-black tree shown in Figure 12.16(a). Let us delete the following keys from the tree:

M, L, H

While deletion of M does not result in an imbalance since it only causes the deletion of a red node, the rest of the deletions call for an *Rr0/1/2* kind of imbalance. Figures 12.16(b–d) illustrate the snapshots of the trees after the appropriate rotations to rebalance the tree have been performed.

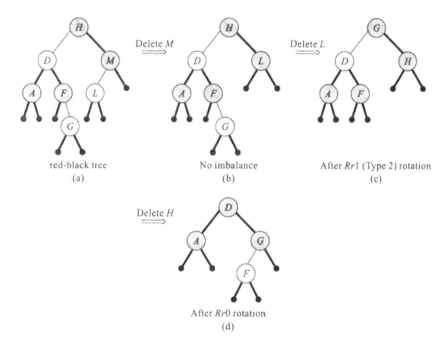

Figure 12.16. *Deletion operations on a red-black tree (see example 12.8)*

12.1.7. *Time complexity of search, insert and delete operations on a red-black tree*

Since the search operation on a red-black tree is similar to that on a binary search tree, the time complexity of the operation is $O(log\ n)$. In the case of insertion or deletion, the operation may call for a color change that can, in the worst case, propagate up to the root and may also call for a rotation to rebalance the tree. Though the color change and rotation needs only a constant time ($\Theta(1)$), the overall time for an insert/delete operation in the worst case would be $O(log\ n)$. It can be shown that the height of a red-black tree is at most $2log2(n + 1)$ and therefore all search, insert and delete operations that need $O(h)$ time would have a time complexity of $O(log\ n)$.

12.2. Splay trees

12.2.1. *Introduction to splay trees*

In the case of binary search trees (see section 10.2), it was observed that the worst case time complexity of the tree is $O(n)$. Assume a case where a group of records is stored as a binary search tree. Now, if a record were to be repeatedly accessed (m times), then the time complexity of the operation sequence would be $O(m.n)$ in the worst case scenario. In fact, studies have shown that information or a node that is accessed once are likely to get accessed more often. What if there were to be a data structure which once a node is accessed, radically changes its shape to push the accessed node as the root? This adjustment, though expensive the first time an access for a node is made, can make the repeated accesses to the node cheaper. Also, during the process of adjustment, where the nodes are moved around to make room for the new node, the other nodes which are deep down may move up making their accesses relatively cheaper as well.

Splay trees are such data structures, providing this mechanism. These are binary search trees with a self adjusting mechanism, which renders them remarkably efficient over a sequence of accesses. Nodes which are frequently accessed are moved toward the root, thereby rendering further retrievals of the same to be efficient. Thus, every time a node is accessed either for search or insertion, the newly accessed node is pushed toward the root. This would dislodge the other nodes to a position away from the root and in a course of time would have the inactive nodes moving farther and farther away from the root.

Unlike AVL search trees which are always height balanced, there is no guarantee that the splay tree would always remain balanced. In fact, if the splay tree turns out to be unbalanced, then an access may turn out to be fairly expensive. However, over a long sequence of accesses, splay trees may prove to be even cheaper than AVL trees by way of the number of operations. Such an analysis which spreads over a sequence of operations and in which the expensive operations are averaged over the less expensive ones is what is called **amortized analysis**. If the time complexity of a single access turns out to be $O(n)$, then the amortized analysis of the access in a splay tree for a sequence of m operations is $O(m.\ log\ n)$.

12.2.2. *Splay rotations*

An insert or search operation on a splay tree proceeds as one would on a binary search tree. However, after the operation is over, the tree is splayed with regard to the specific node. This would mean pushing the node upwards toward the root methodically following what are known as **splay rotations**. Splay rotations are more or less similar to AVL tree rotations (see section 10.3.3) and proceed bottom up from the node toward the root.

The splay rotations are performed with regard to the specific node u, its parent *parent-u* and grandparent *grandparent-u*, until the root node becomes the parent of u. At that stage, which is the last step, the rotation involves only u and the root node. The aim of splaying is to move the accessed node u up by two levels at every step. To do this, we track the path from the root to the accessed node u. Every time the path turns left we term it *zig* and every time it turns right we term it *zag*. Thus, in the case of a single step down the tree, the path could be either a *zig* or *zag*. If two steps were to be considered, the path could be any one of *zig-zig, zig-zag, zag-zig* or *zag-zag*. Since the splaying proceeds bottom up, if the length of the path from the root to the accessed node u is even, then the rotations appropriate to the two step series, viz., *zig-zig, zig-zag, zag-zig* or *zag-zag* are undertaken. On the other hand, if the length of the path from the root to the accessed node u is odd, then the final rotation may turn out to be the one corresponding to a single step series, either a *zig* or a *zag*. The rotations corresponding to the single step and two step series are shown in Figure 12.17.

It can be seen that while *zig* and *zag* represent single rotations corresponding to those of AVL trees, *zig-zig* and *zag-zig* represent double rotations corresponding to the same. However, *zig-zig* and *zag-zag* are not the same as performing two single rotations. Figure 12.18 demonstrates the incorrect implementation of a *zig-zig* with two single rotations.

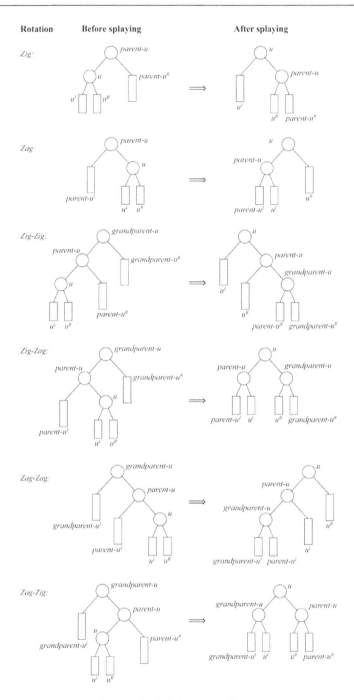

Figure 12.17. *Splay rotations*

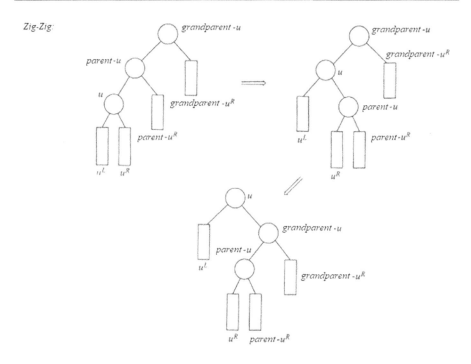

Figure 12.18. *Incorrect Zig-Zig using two single rotations*

EXAMPLE 12.9.–

Consider the binary search tree shown in Figure 12.19(a). Let us attempt splaying the tree at node 9. The path from the root to node 9 involves the path 24-12-10-9. Proceeding from bottom-up, we perform a *zig-zig* on the triad, 9 (node *u*), 10 (node *parent-u*) and 12 (node *grandparent-u*). Figure 12.19(b) shows the tree after the first step. Now the path from the root to node 9 involves only a single step, viz., zig. At the end of the *zig* rotation, the tree shown in Figure 12.19(c) is obtained.

Let us continue to splay the tree shown in Figure 12.19 (c) at 36. The path from the root to node 36 is given by 9-24-48-36. Proceeding from bottom-up, the first step involves a *zag-zig* case. The rotation yields the tree shown in Figure 12.19(d). Finally, a *zag* case shows up which results in the splay tree shown in Figure 12.19(e).

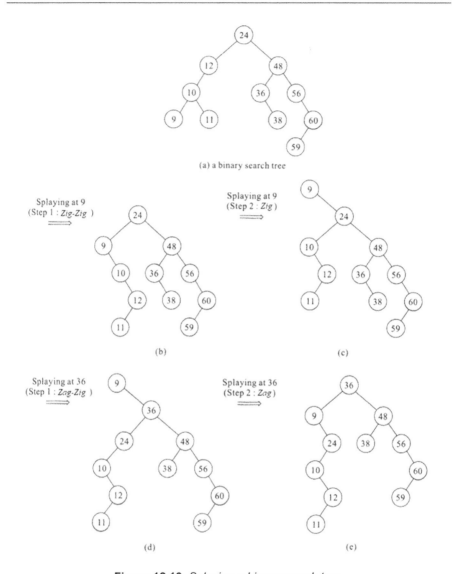

Figure 12.19. *Splaying a binary search tree*

EXAMPLE 12.10.–

We build a splay tree by inserting the following elements in the sequence:

H, Q, A, N, P, O

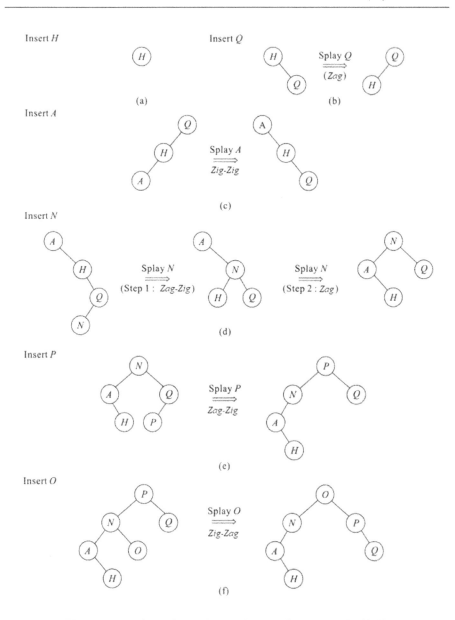

Figure 12.20. *Snapshots of the splay tree (see example 12.10)*

The snapshots of the splay tree during the insertion of each of the elements are shown in Figure 12.20. Insertion of *H* determines the root of the splay tree (see Figure 12.20(a)). Insertion of Q calls for a *zag* rotation yielding the tree shown in Figure 12.20(b). While insert A calls for a *zig-zig* case, insert N calls for two splay rotations, viz., *zag-zig* and *zag*. Insert P calls for a *zag-zig* case and insert O calls for a *zig-zag* case.

12.2.3. *Some remarks on amortized analysis of splay trees*

Analysis of algorithms involves the computation of best, worst and average case time complexities based on the input instances to the algorithm. The analysis determines the work done by the algorithm over an instance or a specific class of instances.

Amortized analysis is different from these analyses in the sense that it estimates the work done by an algorithm over a long sequence of events rather than any single or a specific class of events in isolation. It is the worst case performance of an algorithm over a long sequence of events. In fact, "to amortize" itself means to extinguish a debt over a long period of regular installments.

It can be observed some times that one operation, though expensive to perform for the first time, can lead to the same or other operations performed in a sequence thereafter to get executed at a cheaper cost. Amortized analysis involves problems of such a nature. Thus, amortized analysis is not an average case analysis. While an average case analysis deals with the work done by the algorithm over a set of independent input instances, amortized analysis deals with the same over associated or related instances.

In the case of splay trees, it is observed that an insert splay or a search splay after its operation results in the specific key moving up to become the root. Let us suppose we were searching for a key K in the splay tree. Though the time complexity of such an operation is $O(n)$ in the worst case, a subsequent execution of the same operation after splaying would only incur a time complexity that is definitely much less than $O(n)$! In fact, splay trees report an amortized time complexity of $O(\log n)$. Though an individual search operation in a splay tree may not be $O(\log n)$, the amortized time complexity of m operations on a splay tree would be $O(m. \log n)$.

During the splaying process of a binary search tree T, let $T_i(u)$ be the subtree of a node u which undergoes splaying in step i. Then the *rank* of the node u ($r_i(u)$) in step i of the splaying process is defined to be:

$$r_i(u) = log_2|\ T_i(u)\ |$$

where $|\,T_i(u)\,|$ indicates the size of the subtree $T_i(u)$. In other words, if the subtree comprises s nodes, then the rank of node u is given by $r(u) = log_2s$. The **credit** of a node u is given by its rank $r(u)$. If u is a leaf node, then $r(u) = log_2\,1 = 0$ and if u is the root of the tree T with n nodes, then $r(u) = log_2n$. As heights of trees act as potential functions for the computation of their time complexities, ranks act as equally potential functions for the computation of amortized time complexities of splay trees. In fact, while the heights of many nodes in the splay tree may get affected during a rotation operation, the ranks of the participating nodes, viz., u, *parent-u* and *grandparent-u*, alone get affected during rotations.

The total credit balance for a tree is the sum of all the individual credits of its nodes. That is $Cr_i = \sum_{u \in T_i} r_i(u)$ where Cr_i is the credit balance of the tree during the ith step of splaying the tree, $r_i(u)$ is the rank of the node u in the ith step of splaying and T_i is the splayed tree in step i.

The amortized complexity A_i of a splay step i is given by:

$$A_i = t_i + Cr_i - Cr_{i-1}$$

where t_i is the work done for the splay operation and Cr_i and Cr_{i-1} are the credit balances of the tree before and after the splay operation. t_i is computed as the number of levels the target node rises during a splay operation. In the case of *zig-zig*, *zig-zag*, *zag-zag* and *zag-zig* splay operations, t_i is counted as two units, whereas in the case of a simple *zig* or *zag* splay operation it is counted as 1 unit. $(Cr_i - Cr_{i-1})$ gives the change in the credit balance after the splay operation. Since the ranks of the participating nodes, viz., u, *parent-u* and *grandparent-u* alone change during a splay operation, it is obvious that the credit balance $(Cr_i - Cr_{i-1})$ needs to be computed only with regard to these nodes. The rest of the summation with regard to the other nodes merely gets cancelled.

The following results hold true with regard to the amortized analysis of splay trees:

i) The amortized complexity A_i of the splay tree, if step i of its splaying process initiates a *zig-zig* or a *zag-zag* step at the specific node u, satisfies the following relation:

$$A_i < 3.\,(r_i(u) - r_{i-1}(u)).$$

ii) The amortized complexity A_i of the splay tree, if step i of its splaying process initiates a *zig-zag* or a *zag-zig* step at the specific node u, satisfies the following relation:

$$A_i < 2.\,(r_i(u) - r_{i-1}(u)).$$

iii) The amortized complexity A_i of the splay tree, if step i of its splaying process initiates a *zig* or a *zag* step at the specific node u, satisfies the following relation:

$$A_i < 1 + (r_i(u) - r_{i-1}(u)).$$

iv) In a binary search tree with n nodes, the amortized cost $C(n)$ of an insertion or search of a specific node with splaying does not exceed $(1 + 3 \log_2 n)$ upward moves from the specific node.

v) In a binary search tree with not more than n nodes, the total complexity of a sequence of w insertions or search operations with splaying, does not exceed $w.(1 + 3 \log_2 n) + \log_2 n$.

12.3. Applications

Red-black trees which are derived from B trees of order 4 are only a variant of binary search trees. Hence, any application that calls for binary search trees can also call for red-black trees.

On the other hand, splay trees which are typical binary search trees undergo splaying to favor retrievals, which are efficient with regard to their amortized complexity. They are suitable for applications with the characteristic that information that is recently retrieved is highly likely to be retrieved in the near future. For example, in the case of a university information system, at the beginning of the admission season, those records pertaining to newly admitted students are highly likely to be accessed over and over again in the first few weeks of their entry. In such a case, it would be a good move to store the records as a splay tree rather than a binary search tree. A splay tree pushes the recently retrieved records to stay closer to the root and in due course those records that were remotely used to move farther and farther away from the root and occupy positions close to the fringe of the tree. Maintenance of patient records in a hospital information system and maintenance of records pertaining to seasonal items in a supermarket information system are some examples where splay trees find ideal applications.

Splay trees have also found applications in data compression, lexicographic search trees and dynamic Huffman coding.

Summary

– Red-black trees are derived from B trees of order 4 and are variants of binary search trees. Red-black trees need to satisfy the red condition, which entails no two red nodes can occur consecutively on a path in the tree, and the black condition that insists that the number of black nodes on all root-to-external node paths must be the same.

– A search operation on a red-black tree is undertaken the same way as that on a binary search tree. The insertion of a key in a red-black tree is similar to the one in a binary search tree. However, the inserted node is set to red initially to avoid violation of the black condition. If this results in a violation of the red condition as well, then the tree is said to be unbalanced. The imbalance is classified as XYr or XYb where X, Y may represent an L or R. All XYr imbalances call for a mere color change to set right the imbalance. On the other hand, all XYb imbalances call for rotations to set right the imbalance.

– The deletion of a node in a red-black tree proceeds as one would in a binary search tree. In the case of any violation of the black condition, the imbalances are classified as $Xb0$, $Xb1$ and $Xb2$ or $Xr0$, $Xr1$ and $Xr2$ where X may be L or R and the appropriate rotations are undertaken to set right the imbalance.

– Splay trees are self-adjusting trees that are variants of binary search trees. The search and insert operations proceed as they would on binary search trees. However, after the operation, the inserted key or the searched key is pushed up as the root using splay rotations.

– Splay rotations are classified as *zig, zag, zig-zig, zig-zag, zag-zag* and *zag-zig* rotations based on the position of the specific node at which the splaying is initiated.

– Though an insert or search operation on a splay tree may be expensive when undertaken for the first time, the same when considered over a long sequence of operations may prove to be efficient. Such an analysis which spreads over a sequence of operations and in which the expensive operations are averaged over the less expensive ones is what is called as *amortized analysis*. The amortized analysis of an access in a splay tree for a sequence of m operations is $O(m. \log n)$.

12.4. Illustrative problems

PROBLEM 12.1.–

Construct a red-black tree inserting the following keys into an empty tree in the given sequence:

40, 16, 36, 54, 18, 7, 48, 5

Solution:

The snap shots of the red-black tree during its construction are shown in Figure P12.1. During the insertion of 54 into the tree, an *RRr* imbalance is encountered (see Figure P12.1(d)). Rebalancing the tree calls for a color change which affects the color of the root (36) violating the property that the root of a red-black tree should be black. In such a case, the color change is made such that the number of black nodes in all the paths from the root to the external nodes increases by 1.

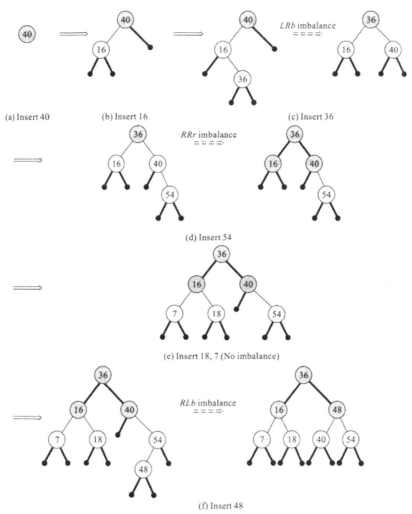

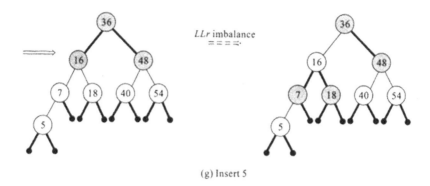

(g) Insert 5

Figure P12.1. *Construction of a red-black tree for the keys {40, 16, 36, 54, 18, 7, 48, 5}*

PROBLEM 12.2.–

Build a red-black tree using the keys given below:

PEEPUL, OLIVE, MAPLE, PINE, BANYAN, CHESTNUT.

Solution:

Figure P12.2 illustrates the snapshots of the red-black tree during its construction.

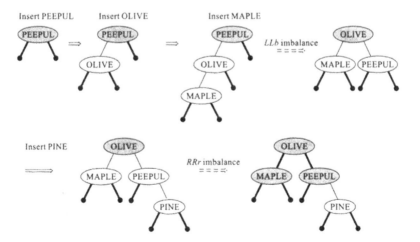

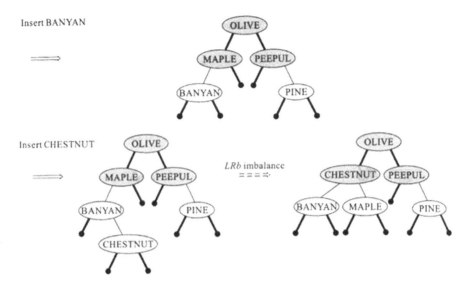

Figure P12.2. *Building a red-black tree for the keys {PEEPUL, OLIVE, MAPLE, PINE, BANYAN, CHESTNUT}*

PROBLEM 12.3.–

Obtain generic representations for the $Lb0$, $Lb1$ and $Lb2$ rotations on lines similar to that of their Rbx counterparts discussed in section 12.1.6, with regard to deletions in a red-black tree.

Solution:

The generic representations of the rotations following similar notations and style of their Rbx counterparts are shown below:

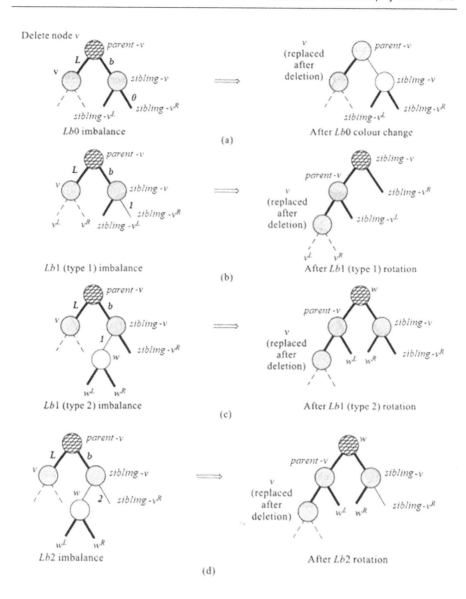

Delete node v

$Lb0$ imbalance

(a)

After $Lb0$ colour change

$Lb1$ (type 1) imbalance

(b)

After $Lb1$ (type 1) rotation

$Lb1$ (type 2) imbalance

(c)

After $Lb1$ (type 2) rotation

$Lb2$ imbalance

(d)

After $Lb2$ rotation

PROBLEM 12.4.–

Obtain generic representations for the $Lr0$, $Lr1$ and $Lr2$ rotations on lines similar to that of their Rrx counterparts discussed in section 12.1.6, with regard to deletions in a red-black tree.

Solution:

The generic representations of the rotations following similar notations and style of their *Rrx* counterparts are shown below:

Lr0 imbalance   After **Lr0** rotation

(a)

Lr1 (Type 1) imbalance   After **Lr1** (Type 1) rotation

(b)

Lr1 (Type 2) imbalance   After **Lr1** (Type 2) rotation

(c)

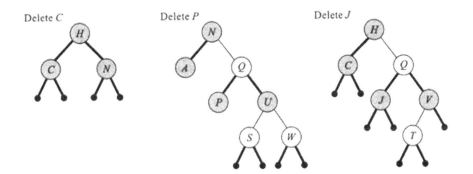

Lr2 imbalance   After *Lr2* rotation

(d)

PROBLEM 12.5.–

Perform the corresponding operations on the red-black trees shown below:

Delete *C*   Delete *P*   Delete *J*

Solution:

The snap shots of the red-black trees after the performance of the operations and after rebalancing are shown below:

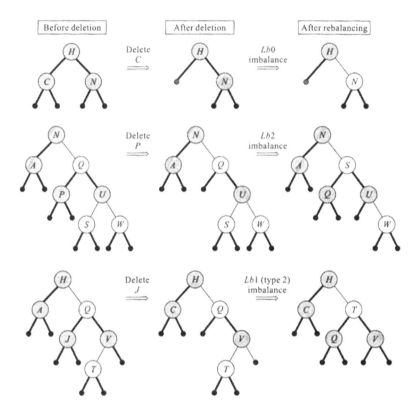

PROBLEM 12.6.–

Undertake the respective delete operations on the red-black trees shown below:

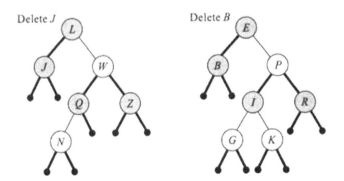

Solution:

The state of the red-black trees after the delete operations and after rebalancing are shown below:

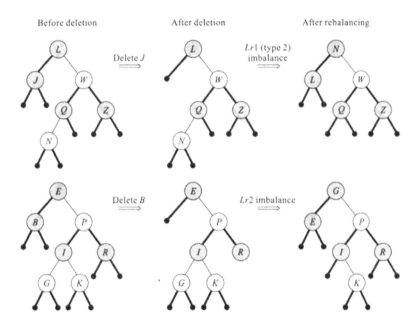

PROBLEM 12.7.–

Undertake splaying of the following binary search tree at key 81:

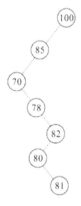

Solution:

The snap shots of the tree during the splay rotations are shown below:

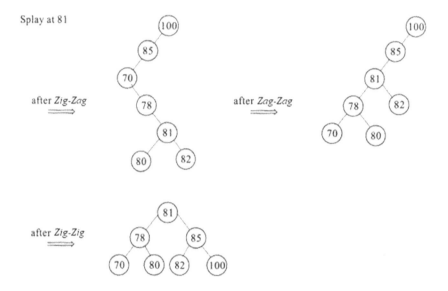

PROBLEM 12.8.–

Build a splay tree inserting the following keys in the order shown:

Fujiyama, Zao, Mt. Etna, Vesuvius, South Sister, Usu.

Solution:

The snapshots of the splay tree during its construction are shown below:

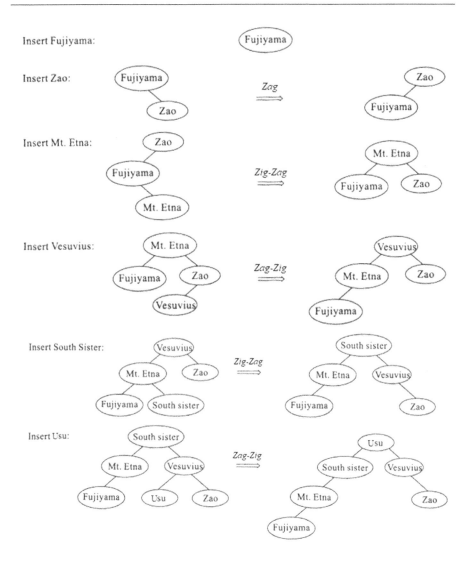

Insert Fujiyama:

Insert Zao: *Zag* ⟹

Insert Mt. Etna: *Zig-Zag* ⟹

Insert Vesuvius: *Zag-Zig* ⟹

Insert South Sister: *Zig-Zag* ⟹

Insert Usu: *Zag-Zig* ⟹

PROBLEM 12.9.–

For the splay tree shown in illustrative problem 12.7, trace the ranks of the involved nodes during the splaying steps.

Solution:

The ranks of the participating nodes, viz., $r(u)$, $r(parent\text{-}u)$ and $r(grandparent\text{-}u)$, are shown in Table P12.9. The ranks of the other nodes during the splaying steps are also shown. Note how there is no change in their ranks though the heights of some of these nodes do undergo changes during the rotations.

Operation	Other nodes in the tree				Node u	Node parent_u	Node grandparent_u
(Step 1)	100	85	78	70	81	80	82
Rank of the nodes before zig-zag operation	$\log_2(7)$	$\log_2(6)$	$\log_2(4)$	$\log_2(5)$	$\log_2(1)$	$\log_2(2)$	$\log_2(3)$
Rank of the nodes after zig-zag operation	$\log_2(7)$	$\log_2(6)$	$\log_2(4)$	$\log_2(5)$	$\log_2(3)$	$\log_2(1)$	$\log_2(1)$
Operation	Other nodes in the tree				Node u	Node parent_u	Node grandparent_u
(Step 2)	100	85	82	80	81	78	70
Rank of the nodes before zig-zag operation	$\log_2(7)$	$\log_2(6)$	$\log_2(1)$	$\log_2(1)$	$\log_2(3)$	$\log_2(4)$	$\log_2(5)$
Rank of the nodes after zig-zag operation	$\log_2(7)$	$\log_2(6)$	$\log_2(1)$	$\log_2(1)$	$\log_2(5)$	$\log_2(3)$	$\log_2(1)$
Operation	Other nodes in the tree				Node u	Node parent_u	Node grandparent_u
(Step 3)	82	80	78	70	81	85	100
Rank of the nodes before zig-zag operation	$\log_2(1)$	$\log_2(1)$	$\log_2(3)$	$\log_2(1)$	$\log_2(5)$	$\log_2(6)$	$\log_2(7)$
Rank of the nodes after zig-zag operation	$\log_2(1)$	$\log_2(1)$	$\log_2(3)$	$\log_2(1)$	$\log_2(7)$	$\log_2(3)$	$\log_2(1)$

Table P12.9. *The ranks of the participating nodes during the splaying of the tree shown in illustrative problem 12.7*

PROBLEM 12.10.–

Obtain the amortized complexity of each of the splay steps during the splaying of the tree at node 81 shown in illustrative problem 12.7. Make use of Table P12.9 for ease of computation.

Solution:

The amortized complexity of a splay step i is given by $A_i = t_i + Cr_i - Cr_{i-1}$, where t_i the work done is 1 unit for a zig or a zag operation and 2 units for all other operations. The change in the credit balance $(Cr_i - Cr_{i-1})$ is computed as the difference in sum of the ranks of the participating nodes.

The amortized complexities of the three steps involved in the splaying of 81 is given as follows:

– *Step 1: zig-zag operation*:

$$A_1 = 2 + ((\log_2(3) + 0 + 0) - (0 + \log_2(2) + \log_2(3))) = 2\text{-}\log_2 2 = 1$$

It can be observed that the amortized time complexity A_i of the zig-zag operation satisfies the relation $A_i < 2.\,(r_i(u) - r_{i-1}(u))$.

that is, $A_1 = 1$

$$< 2.\,(r_i(81) - r_{i-1}(81)) = 2.\,(log_2\,3 - log_2\,1) = 2.\,log_2\,3$$

– *Step 2: zag-zag operation*:

$$A_2 = 2 + ((\log_2 5 + \log_2 3 + 0) - (\log_2 3 + \log_2 4 + \log_2 5)) = 0$$

It can be observed that the amortized time complexity A_i of the zag-zag operation satisfies the relation $A_i < 3.\,(r_i(u) - r_{i-1}(u))$.

that is, $A_2 = 0$

$$< 3.\,(r_i(81) - r_{i-1}(81)) = 3(log_2\,5 - log_2\,3)$$

– *Step 3: zig-zig operation*:

$$A_3 = 2 + ((\log_2 7 + \log_2 3 + \log_2 1) - (\log_2 5 + \log_2 6 + \log_2 7)) = 1 - \log_2 5$$

It can be observed that the amortized time complexity A_i of the zig-zig operation satisfies the relation $A_i < 3.\,(r_i(u) - r_{i-1}(u))$.

That is, $A_3 = 1 - \log_2 5$

$$< 3.\,(r_i(81) - r_{i-1}(81)) = 3(log_2\,7 - log_2\,5)$$

Review questions

1) Which among the following properties does not hold true for a red-black tree?

i) The root node is always a black node.

ii) All external nodes are black nodes.

iii) Two red nodes can occur consecutively on the path from the root node to an external node.

iv) The number of black nodes on the path from the root node to an external node must be the same for all external nodes.

a) (i)   b) (ii)   c) (iii)   d) (iv)

2) Which among the following calls for a rotation to set right the imbalance?

(i) *LRb*   (ii) *LRr*   (iii) *RLr*   (iv) *RRr*

a) (i)   b) (ii)   c) (iii)   d) (iv)

3) In the context of deletion of a node from a red-black tree, state whether true or false.

i) If the deleted node were red, then the black condition would be violated and hence the tree is unbalanced.

ii) If the deleted node were to be black, then the black condition is violated and hence the tree is unbalanced.

a) (i) true (ii) true   b) (i) true (ii) false

c) (i) false (ii) true   d) (i) false (ii) false

4) Which among the following properties is not satisfied by a splay tree?

i) Splay trees are binary search trees.

ii) Splay trees result in efficient repeated accesses.

iii) Splay trees like AVL trees are always height balanced.

iv) Splay trees have their frequently accessed nodes moving toward the root.

a) (i)   b) (ii)   c) (iii)   d) (iv)

5) In the context of splay rotations, state whether true or false.

i) If the length of the path from the root to the accessed node *u* is even, then the rotations undertaken are associated with *zig-zig*, *zig-zag*, *zag-zig* or *zag-zag*.

ii) If the length of the path from the root to the accessed node *u* is odd, then the rotations undertaken are associated with either a *zig* or a *zag*.

a) (i) true (ii) true   b) (i) true (ii) false

c) (i) false (ii) true   d) (i) false (ii) false

6) What are the merits of red-black trees over B trees of order *m*?

7) Outline the generic representation of an *XYr* imbalance, where *X*, *Y* could be either an *L* or *R*.

8) What is the need for splay trees?

9) How are splay rotations performed?

10) What is the amortized time complexity of a search operation on a splay tree?

11) For the following list of data construct a red black tree:

LINUX, OS2, DOS, XENIX, SOLARIS, WINDOWS, VISTA,

XP, UNIX, CPM.

Undertake the following operations on the tree:

(i) Insert MAC   (ii) Delete WINDOWS   (iii) Delete UNIX

12) Represent the data list shown in review question 11 as a splay tree. Tabulate the number of comparisons undertaken for retrieving the following keys:

(i) LINUX   (ii) XENIX   (iii) LINUX   (iv) LINUX   (v) LINUX

Programming assignments

1) Implement a function RB_IMBALANCE(T), which given a red-black tree T would test for the violation of red and black conditions.

2) Execute a menu driven program to insert keys into an initially empty red-black tree. Make use of the function RB_IMBALANCE (T) developed in programming assignment 1 to test for any imbalance. Display the tree after rebalancing it.

3) Implement a program to accept a non-empty red-black tree as input and delete all its leaf nodes. Rebalance the tree after every deletion and display the rebalanced tree on the screen.

4) Execute a program with animations and graphics to demonstrate the splaying of a tree given a specific node *u* in the tree.

5) In the menu-driven program implemented in programming assignment 1 of Chapter 10 to perform the search, insert and delete operations on a binary search tree, introduce functions to splay the tree soon after every insert and search operation is executed.

References

Aragon, C.R. and Seidel, R. (1989). Randomized search trees. In *Proc. 30th Symp. Foundations of Computer Science (FOCS 1989)*. IEEE Computer Society Press, Washington, DC.

Donald, K. (1998). *Art of Computer Programming, Vol. III*. 2nd edition. Addison-Wesley Professional, Reading, MA.

Garey, M.R. and David, S.J. (1979). *Computers and Intractability: A Guide to the Theory of NP-Completeness*. W.H. Freeman, New York.

Hoare, C.A.R. (1962). Quick sort. *The Computer Journal*, 5(1), 10–16.

Knuth, D.E. (1973). *The Art of Computer Programming, Volume 1: Fundamental Algorithms*. 2nd edition. Addison-Wesley, Reading, MA.

Malik, S. and Lintao, Z. (2009). Boolean satisfiability, from theoretical hardness to practical success. *Communications of the ACM*, 52(8), 76–82.

Perlis, A.J. and Thornton, C. (1960). Symbol manipulation by threaded lists. *Communications of the ACM*, 3(4), 195–204.

Pugh, W. (1990). Skip lists: A probabilistic alternative to balanced trees. *Communications of the ACM*, 33(6), 668–676.

Shell, D.L. (1959). A high-speed sorting procedure. *Communications of the ACM*, 2(7), 30–32.

Index

Summary of Volume 1

Chapter 7. Linked Stacks and Linked Queues

References

Index

Summary of Volume 3

Chapter 14. File Organizations

Chapter 15. *k*-d Trees and Treaps

Chapter 16. Searching

Chapter 17. Internal Sorting

References

Index

Other titles from

in

Computer Engineering

2022

MEHTA Shikha, TIWARI Sanju, SIARRY Patrick, JABBAR M.A.
Tools, Languages, Methodologies for Representing Semantics on the Web of Things

SIDHOM Sahbi, KADDOUR Amira
Systems and Uses of Digital Sciences for Knowledge Organization (Digital Tools and Uses Set – Volume 9)

ZAIDOUN Ameur Salem
Computer Science Security: Concepts and Tools

2021

DELHAYE Jean-Loic
Inside the World of Computing: Technologies, Uses, Challenges

DUVAUT Patrick, DALLOZ Xavier, MENGA David, KOEHL François, CHRIQUI Vidal, BRILL Joerg
Internet of Augmented Me, I.AM: Empowering Innovation for a New Sustainable Future

PÉTROWSKI Alain, BEN-HAMIDA Sana
Evolutionary Algorithms
(Metaheuristics Set – Volume 9)

PAI G A Vijayalakshmi
Metaheuristics for Portfolio Optimization
(Metaheuristics Set – Volume 11)

2016

BLUM Christian, FESTA Paola
Metaheuristics for String Problems in Bio-informatics
(Metaheuristics Set – Volume 6)

DEROUSSI Laurent
Metaheuristics for Logistics
(Metaheuristics Set – Volume 4)

DHAENENS Clarisse and JOURDAN Laetitia
Metaheuristics for Big Data
(Metaheuristics Set – Volume 5)

LABADIE Nacima, PRINS Christian, PRODHON Caroline
Metaheuristics for Vehicle Routing Problems
(Metaheuristics Set – Volume 3)

LEROY Laure
Eyestrain Reduction in Stereoscopy

LUTTON Evelyne, PERROT Nathalie, TONDA Albert
Evolutionary Algorithms for Food Science and Technology
(Metaheuristics Set – Volume 7)

MAGOULÈS Frédéric, ZHAO Hai-Xiang
Data Mining and Machine Learning in Building Energy Analysis

RIGO Michel
Advanced Graph Theory and Combinatorics

2015

BARBIER Franck, RECOUSSINE Jean-Luc
COBOL Software Modernization: From Principles to Implementation with the BLU AGE® Method

CHEN Ken
Performance Evaluation by Simulation and Analysis with Applications to Computer Networks

CLERC Maurice
Guided Randomness in Optimization
(Metaheuristics Set – Volume 1)

DURAND Nicolas, GIANAZZA David, GOTTELAND Jean-Baptiste, ALLIOT Jean-Marc
Metaheuristics for Air Traffic Management
(Metaheuristics Set – Volume 2)

MAGOULÈS Frédéric, ROUX François-Xavier, HOUZEAUX Guillaume
Parallel Scientific Computing

MUNEESAWANG Paisarn, YAMMEN Suchart
Visual Inspection Technology in the Hard Disk Drive Industry

2014

BOULANGER Jean-Louis
Formal Methods Applied to Industrial Complex Systems

BOULANGER Jean-Louis
Formal Methods Applied to Complex Systems:Implementation of the B Method

GARDI Frédéric, BENOIST Thierry, DARLAY Julien, ESTELLON Bertrand, MEGEL Romain
Mathematical Programming Solver based on Local Search

KRICHEN Saoussen, CHAOUACHI Jouhaina
Graph-related Optimization and Decision Support Systems

SOTO Maria, SEVAUX Marc, ROSSI André, LAURENT Johann
Memory Allocation Problems in Embedded Systems: Optimization Methods

2011

BICHOT Charles-Edmond, SIARRY Patrick
Graph Partitioning

BOULANGER Jean-Louis
Static Analysis of Software: The Abstract Interpretation

CAFERRA Ricardo
Logic for Computer Science and Artificial Intelligence

HOMÈS Bernard
Fundamentals of Software Testing

KORDON Fabrice, HADDAD Serge, PAUTET Laurent, PETRUCCI Laure
Distributed Systems: Design and Algorithms

KORDON Fabrice, HADDAD Serge, PAUTET Laurent, PETRUCCI Laure
Models and Analysis in Distributed Systems

LORCA Xavier
Tree-based Graph Partitioning Constraint

TRUCHET Charlotte, ASSAYAG Gerard
Constraint Programming in Music

VICAT-BLANC PRIMET Pascale *et al.*
Computing Networks: From Cluster to Cloud Computing

2010

AUDIBERT Pierre
Mathematics for Informatics and Computer Science

BABAU Jean-Philippe *et al.*
Model Driven Engineering for Distributed Real-Time Embedded Systems

BOULANGER Jean-Louis
Safety of Computer Architectures

WALDNER Jean-Baptiste
Nanocomputers and Swarm Intelligence

2007

BENHAMOU Frédéric, JUSSIEN Narendra, O'SULLIVAN Barry
Trends in Constraint Programming

JUSSIEN Narendra
A TO Z OF SUDOKU

2006

BABAU Jean-Philippe *et al.*
From MDD Concepts to Experiments and Illustrations – DRES 2006

HABRIAS Henri, FRAPPIER Marc
Software Specification Methods

MURAT Cecile, PASCHOS Vangelis Th
Probabilistic Combinatorial Optimization on Graphs

PANETTO Hervé, BOUDJLIDA Nacer
Interoperability for Enterprise Software and Applications 2006 / IFAC-IFIP I-ESA'2006

2005

GÉRARD Sébastien *et al.*
Model Driven Engineering for Distributed Real Time Embedded Systems

PANETTO Hervé
Interoperability of Enterprise Software and Applications 2005

Printed and bound by CPI Group (UK) Ltd, Croydon, CR0 4YY

26/11/2023

08194712-0001